AF544684

Israel and Me

A Behind-the-Scenes Look
By a Longtime U.S. Zionist
Leader and Returned
Israeli Immigrant

Israel and Me

A Behind-the-Scenes Look By a Longtime U.S. Zionist Leader and Returned Israeli Immigrant

Morris Alexander

SCHENKMAN PUBLISHING COMPANY, INC.
TWO CONTINENTS PUBLISHING GROUP, LTD.
Cambridge, Massachusetts—New York

This book is dedicated to the memory of Henry Monsky, Charlie Zakon, Pierre Van Paassen and Soloman S. Levadi.

Schenkman Publishing Company, Inc.
3 Mt. Auburn Place
Cambridge, Massachusetts 02138

Library of Congress Cataloging in Publication Data

Alexander, Morris, 1909-
  Israel and me.

1. Israel—Description and travel. 2. Alexander, Morris, 1909- 3. Jews in the United States—Biography. 4. Zionists—Biography. I. Title.
[DS107.4.A32] 915.694'04'5 77-30
ISBN 0-8467-0265-7

Printed in the United States of America

Contents

Preface

From the end of World War II in Europe in 1945 until Israel declared its independence on May 14, 1948, I was deeply involved in the efforts to sustain the remnants of European Jewry and to create a home for them in Palestine in a free Jewish state of their own.

During those years I had come to the realization that the creation of a Jewish nation called for wholly new dimensions of attitude and organization within the American Jewish community — and soon. Because of my central position as president of the B'nai Brith Council of greater Chicago in 1947 and 1948 and the interest in Israel that was just beginning to generate among the organization's worldwide membership, I foresaw a real chance to focus some of the energy and resources of that large amorphous Jewish service organization toward developing beneficial connections beween American and other Jews dispersed around the world and those in the emerging Jewish nation. By the end of 1948 this exciting idea had become an all consuming passion with me. I resolved to go to Israel as soon as possible to take the first step — to see for myself what God had wrought. In January, 1950, I set out to fulfill that dream.

My feelings and attitudes about Israel to this day (though drastically altered) are irrevocably related to those first two weeks in that nascent land. I witnessed the frenzied ingathering of the exiles and was caught up in the maelstrom created by the war — in Europe and in Palestine. Seeing the swirl of refugees in the reception camps along the Mediterranean shores from Haifa to Tel Aviv and inland from the Galilee to B'er Sheva, I dimly sensed glimmerings of the clash to come between the new and the established settlers. I convinced myself that the success or failure of the fragile experiment of Israel reborn lay in the hands of the millions of diaspora Jews who at that time had only the foggiest notion of what was going on in Palestine.

On my return home, the luxury of the flight to London and subsequent voyage to New York on the magnificent Queen Mary sharply contrasted with the mud and squalor in which Jewish refugees existed in the tents of the *ma'abarot* (temporary Israeli immigrant encampments) and etched in my mind a sense of mission that permeated my life for the next two decades. My own eyes had persuaded me that the efforts of the previous years had been eminently worthwhile, and I felt that I must find a role for myself in the myriad tasks necessary to create a viable nation for the Jews already in Israel and the hundreds of thousands who would go there in the years ahead.

This chronicle is a record of my continuous connection with Israel over the ensuing years — as an American and as an immigrant myself. It is written not with the objectivity of a reporter, but the passion of a paramour.

Some years ago, talking to a group of first-time Jewish tourists in Haifa, I said, "I have had a love affair with Israel for a long time. I hope you too, will experience the joy of falling in love with this little land."

My good sabra friend, Ovadia Rasiel, sitting next to me exclaimed spontaneously, "Yoffee!" which roughly translated means "beautiful" or "right on". He wasn't, I am sure, expressing admiration for a felicitous remark. Rather, he had discovered in my words, I think, a clue to the fascination for Israel I had manifested for a generation. It seemed to make clear to him what attracted this non-religious, not overtly Jewish American to Ovadia's homeland.

In these pages I have tried to explain this love of mine which is shared with many thousands of Jews in all the diasporas of the world. It is altogether Jewishly appropriate to talk about Israel in terms of connubial love. I need cite only one of the many examples of the lover approach. In the Jewish ethos, the quiet loveliness of the Sabbath has been likened for centuries by Jewish poets to an exquisitely beautiful bride as she approaches the wedding canopy.

The love of Israel is a love of people, a love of sandy shores and mystical hills, of shimmering white lights and dancing shadows on tetons of scattered tels, of sun-baked wadis in beige southern deserts. It is the love of a father for a son, of a little girl for her rag doll. More than anything else, it is a love for life itself.

If any one word can describe the reborn country it is the word "alive". Everyone who visits Israel, whether he is turned on or off, feels the incessant unrelenting and rhythmic beat of the tempo of life. It is an inescapable precious phenomenon in a world where human aliveness is daily denigrated by automata.

Forgive me if I have in these pages been harsh or inaccurate or obtuse or superficial with people, places, or events. I plead the extenuation of a lover who so wants the beauty and goodness of his beloved to remain pristine.

When I left Israel in 1972 with the young family of my sere years, after living there for four years, to return to my native land, my friend Ovadia sorrowfully accused me of a lover's desertion. The charge is unfair. I plead not guilty. There is not even the semblance of a lover's quarrel involved.

In these pages I have sought to discover through my experiences with and in Israel what my Jewishness is and how it related to the Zionist dream of yesterday — and what my connection is with the Israel of today. If I succeed to some small extent in blowing away some of the more cloying myths to reveal a glimpse of the genuine mystique of Israel, I will be overjoyed. If haters of Israel find any corroboration or comfort in these pages for their misology, I will have been, as the French Canucks say, "unbuttoned". In all events my love for Israel remains deep and deathless.

Acknowledgements

A number of people encouraged me to write this book (and not a few discouraged me!).

Janet Williams edited the first drafts, organized and excised them and unremittingly played devil's advocate. My daughter, Professor Lynn Margulis, generously proferred consistent encouragement and supported me when I faltered. Beth Fishman, of Ann Arbor and Jerusalem, miraculously was able to decipher my scrawls and render them into neat typewriting. Philip Katz helped me to find and verify factual material and statistics. I am deeply grateful to all of them.

The author and Abba Eban, Israeli ambassador to the United States and the United Nations, with Governor Adlai Stevenson.

I

Immigrants and Israel

1. "They Shoot Horses, Don't They?"

One summer night in 1968 a few months after I had immigrated to Israel with my family, I had a bad dream. I awoke out of a nightmare, wet with sweat, gasping and dazed. A horde of horses, all colors, shapes and sizes were rushing, plunging, staggering, falling, dying in a swirl of pink dust. It was like an old Western movie — except that these animals all had ageless, timeless Jewish faces of men and women and children. In their misery, they were being shot at from some place by somebody or something; I awoke before I could identify their persecutors.

Somehow I knew that three seemingly unconnected activities of that day had combined to create the nightmare. What did I do that day? In the morning I went to the offices of the Jewish Agency in Tel Aviv. I mentioned to a cheerful English-speaking young lady clerk that I was a neighbor of and acquainted with her boss. Our similar American accents required no further comment. I was not surprised that my business was handled with dispatch.

A young man wearing a skull cap, trailed by a buxom young blonde peasant wife and three children, the eldest no more than five and the woman big-bellied with (at least) a fourth child, literally barged into the small overcrowded office and started to shout in surprisingly good Hebrew. At the husband's demand, he and a secretary left the room to seek out an official — someone who could not only explain to him why he could not be provided a flat in Petach Tikvah, but who would also arrange it for him. "It won't do them any good," my cheerful young lady informed me.

I asked the wife in my bad Hebrew where they were from. She shook her head, uncomprehendingly. I tried again in Yiddish. She smiled broadly. "Groozia", she answered. "How long in Israel?" (in Yiddish again). "Three months". I asked my cheerful young lady, "Where the hell is Groozia?" "Georgia", she replied. "Not Georgia, U.S.A. — Georgia, Russia".

I walked through the crowded corridors and down the stairways depressed, despite the success of my own mission. I sensed anger and frustration and deep doubt just below the surface of the seeming purposefulness of the people I saw, new immigrants all. They looked at each other defensively. Even with hostility. There seemed to be an almost conscious taking on of the protective coloration of the Israelis' studied brusqueness. Callousness. I had the impression they didn't seem to consider a knowledge of Hebrew as important (my cheerful young lady had asked me, of all people, how to spell a word in Hebrew) as to act like the Israelis — competent, self-sufficient, complacent, indifferent. An island each to himself. Not necesarily proud. But certainly not a stranger in a strange land — as all of these immigrants certainly were — me too — and being told so in no uncertain terms by the natives — in the unspoken language of glances and shrugs that the human animal learned long before spoken words were invented.

That afternoon I went to the Tel-Aviv Museum. The majestic galleries were too good to be true. I somehow felt guilty in this Biblical Balm of Gilead atmosphere. What right did I have to be here while those anguished immigrants were milling around a few blocks away?

Chaim Soutine has always been to me an inspiration as a painter, a symbol of Jewish doubt, suffering and restlessness translated into the art form of painting. I knew that there were a dozen of his best canvasses hanging in the gallery. They were all old friends that I had seen in exhibitions or in art books.

The scenes of the immigrants at the Jewish Agency building impelled me directly to the Soutine paintings. I had last seen his portrait of himself, so poignantly entitled "Grotesque" at Expo '67 in Montreal. I stood there looking at it for an hour. Modigliani dying had said, "Mourn me not. I leave you Chaim Soutine." I wondered how this inarticulate, ugly Jewish boy would have felt and would have been treated in 1970 if he had come directly from his native Vilna to Israel instead of going to France in 1917, there to sicken and die in 1943 during the Nazi's occupation, unknown and unsung until a generation later.

It was a comfort to see Soutine properly ensconced in that beautiful art gallery in the most elegant section of Tel-Aviv. He might have felt proud, even though uncomfortable in his dirty old sweater and slippers. And smelling of cheap wine and herring. His twisted old "Lady in Red" with the big floppy hat winked at me as I left. "The Waiter" in his sharp uniform bowed and winked too.

That night, I went to an American movie in the neighboring bourgeois suburb of Herzylia. The bad sound system made the English raucous, almost unintelligible. Somehow it fit the story. In the depth of the economic depression of the 1930's young dancers, actors, vaudevillians, carnival workers, drifters, came to a big hall to compete in a marathon dance. The winning couple would be the last ones on their feet after many days and nights of staggering in each other's arms as the music blared on and the people came at all hours of the day and night to watch their agony. A clever master of ceremonies, straight out of the centuries old carnival circus tradition, cheered them on, urged the audience to throw pennies at them for specialty numbers and made patriotic speeches about these "brave young people, showing their courage and sportsmanship in the American Way."

The whole picture was a progression of unmitigated horror. A graphic tour de force of the universal inhumanity of man to man; the peeling off of all indicia of human dignity, until the surviving contestants lurched like wounded animals to the final *denouement* — the disclosure to the young heroine that there would be no winners; the promoters would not even pay the prize. She and her partner left the hall. She handed him a gun and begged him to shoot her. He did. The police came and took him away. They asked him why he did it. "They shoot horses, don't they?" he replied.

The word "community" in the singular is not accurate as applied to Israel. The Israelis are not one community. Israel is a nation consisting of a large number of ethnic groupings, wildly disparate in some cases, very similar in others. All are bound together by a commonality of goals, hopes, aspirations, fears, frustrations, rivalries, aggressions, and greeds. The common religion, Judaism, upon close examination, is not doctrinaire creed but part of the ethnic subcultures of the groups, despite the mystique of shared sources, the Book, the Talmud, and the ancient history.

The fact is that Israel is a lively, disorderly, frenzied little country engaged in creating a modern industrial nation. Its model is the United

States, good and bad. More bad than good. It is a country that, in miniature, is developing a formidable military-industrial complex that influences its economy much like it does in the United States today.

It is not a developing nation emerging from primitive feudalism like those of Africa, Asia, and South America. It is not throwing off colonialism like former outposts of the British, French, Portuguese, Dutch and American empires. Israel came into being almost fullblown from the pressure cooker forces released after the Second World War. Like the very survival of Jews, it's a phenomenon unique in history. Israel was created by millions of Jews who survived in the human family as a recognizable entity for two thousand years without a land of their own, survived through some kind of weird mystical accident of history, a clinging to a religio-ethnic way of life as inexplicable as the mystery of the lemmings. It is a conglomerate of incompatibilities. Any similarity between Israel today and the Palestine of the early Zionist settlers is minor and incidental.

For one thing, Israel is not any longer a country eager to bring in and welcome its so-called fellow Jews throughout the world, whether they are called coreligionist, brethren, oppressed relatives, or anything else. The spirit of the Law of Return is a dead letter, though it is on the statute books and will remain as the technical law of the land for generations.

The Israelis — in government or out, religious or not — don't want to admit this, even to themselves. And the circumstantial evidence is altogether to the contrary. The cumbersome and costly superstructure of the Jewish Agency known as *aliyah* (immigration) is going full blast. Millions of dollars are marshalled in the United States and other Jewish communities throughout the Diaspora and within Israel to stimulate and aid emigration of Jews, especially from the Soviet Union. Efforts to bring out the remnants of Jews in Syria, Iraq, Egypt, Yemen, Morocco, and Algeria, are unremitting and earnest, though not very successful.

* * *

The furor about the Russian Jews in recent years, which continues with undiminished force, is a little understood and much misinterpreted and propagandized phenomenon. Wholesale immigration of the almost three million Soviet Jews is completely unlikely. Many of them do not want to leave their country. They consider themselves, as they are, citizens of their native land. They do suffer discrimination as Jews but if they are not religiously oriented, as most of them are not, the discrimination is not unbearable and no worse than the oppression to which Solzhenitsyn and other artistic and intellectual Soviets have been and are subjected.

The position of the Jews in the Soviet Union is not dissimilar to the general unease of Jews in every country ruled by a monolithic dictatorial political system, where individual freedom is generally minimal and freedom of enterprise is limited or nonexistent. It is becoming known that Jews in Russia who are well-informed and sophisticated about the facts of life in Israel, Europe and the United States — and there are hundreds of thousands of them — express no desire to emigrate (even if they want to), unless they can go to any country they wish — including Israel. Those desiring to emigrate will, for the most part, be young people whose life styles, skills, and professions have not completely been established.

What has this to do with the "Let My People Go" campaigns? These campaigns are not particularly Israeli inspired or led. They are essentially an American and English and French agitation. They derive from guilt felt by Jews in these communities, an inheritance of their general silence at the time of the Nazi and Stalin pogroms. Well-meaning these efforts are, but there is more than a little hysteria and religious fanaticism involved. And the echoes reverberate from the Wailing Wall and are heard in street parades in Tel-Aviv and New York.

Despite the lip service given to the hope that the majority of Soviet Jews will be allowed to come to Israel, the administration in Israel does not want it and neither do the Israelis. A joke current in Israel for years has it that the Russians can sink Israel easily, not by giving the Arabs military aid, but by sending all the Russian Jews to Israel.

In fact, the substantial numbers who arrived in the early seventies, coming at the rate of more than 30,000 a year, presented substantial problems and are causing serious friction within the Israeli population. On the one hand, the Russian immigrants found that Israel is not quite paradise on earth. They were received with less than open arms. Furthermore, they are unreasonably demanding about housing, jobs, schools, and even less basic amenities. The atmosphere was not the same as during the great immigration years of 1946-1953. It was not an ingathering of the exiles. The enthusiasm for Russian immigration exists abroad, not in Israel. The Israeli agrees intellectually that it is his duty to make the newcomers welcome — that it is even the Russian Jew's legal and moral right to return to the homeland. But, most of the population has no stomach for them, except possibly their relatives.

The newcomers from Georgia are particularly obstreperous. Least-skilled and educated, mostly Orthodox Jewish, they make excessive and wild demands and try to implement them with sit-downs in the airports, invasions of government offices, and other disruptive tactics. Many of them have been well coached by friends and relatives already in Israel. They want to stay together to maintain the continuity of their religious and communal lives. This is a wholly natural and understandable aspiration, but difficult and often impossible to implement. Unfortunately, this tumult and shouting is sauce for the religious political ganders who, as usual, are long in supporting immigrants' demands and complaints, but short on real help. Promise them anything, but give them rhetoric.

* * *

Immigration from areas other than the U.S.S.R. varies from country to country, but the total number of immigrants from all countries has been considerably less since 1970 than before, and it is likely to continue to diminish. There was until the Yom Kippur War a significant reimmigration of former Israelis who are returning home, several thousand a year. Up until 1972, they had been encouraged to return by laws that offered expatriate Israelis the same incentives as other immigrants, such as the right to bring in automobiles, refrigerators, tools and other durable goods duty-free, or to pay only nominal fees and receive income tax abatements and so on. With the expiration, in 1972, of these advantages to Israeli citizens this re-immigration grimly diminished. In 1976 the Jewish agency and the government immigration department revived some of the "goodies" in an effort to lure them back.

The total number of returnees, perhaps 25,000 since 1967, is a mere trickle compared to the number of Israelis who have emigrated since 1948. The government in 1973 released the statistic — 250,000. It is estimated that of these, several hundred thousand are former Israelis living in the U.S.A. This population includes students, who may or may not return to Israel. Many of them do not return, especially engineers, scientists, technologists, and doctors who have found in the United States lucrative and challenging employment upon graduation. The situation will probably change as the ranks of unemployed American engineers and other technicians swell. The Israelis in the United States also include many who came to Israel in the 50's and 60's because it was the only country they could enter at the time of their emigration. They had resided in Israel sitting on their packed suitcases waiting for the chance to go to the United States, Canada, England or Australia, France, South America. Some of these immigrants stayed in Israel only a year or two and can hardly be classified as Israelis. Certainly they do not regard themselves as Israelis. Most of the Israelis in the United States, however, are sabras (native born Israelis) or residents of Israel from childhood, including many born in Palestine before 1948. Many of them are now American citizens. With the United States Supreme Court decision recognizing the validity of dual citizenship, it can be expected that almost all of them will become *de jure* Americans.

The Israelis in the United States and Canada not only hold dual citizenship, they also suffer from dual personality complexes. They are on a double track, to borrow Tom Wolfe's expression. To a man (and woman), they passionately are Israeli patriots. Their ties with their native land are close and real. They are bombastic in their praise of the beauty of Israel, the intelligence of her residents, the valor and might of her armed forces, the skills of her scientists, engineers, and craftsmen, the sophistication of her art and music, the high achievements of her technology, the safety of her streets at night, and (until October 1973) the certain glory of her future. These paeans of praise are usually sung in unfavorable comparison (unfortunately) with American counterpoint. Disdain for things American, except the American dollar, is not unusual among former Israelis in the United States.

When the obvious question is asked, "Why don't you go back, then?", the patriots answer, "Why, of course we will. We're just building a stake so we can go back to live and work in comfort. Our lives were so hard there, and the opportunities so limited."

The fact that few of them return to Israel contradicts the set speech. Israeli emigres feel guilty — that's all. They feel a bit like traitors but don't want to be regarded as such, especially by native Americans. These feelings of guilt are much like those felt by American Jews who lived safely and comfortably in the United States through the Hitler period.

If you were to say to a former Israeli living in the United States, "Oh come now, you know you don't intend to go back to live in Israel. You like it here in the United States. Not only are you more prosperous and physically more comfortable, but you feel freer and less constricted than you did there. Your children are growing up better educated and with a wider scope for their energies and talents. Why do you have to be ashamed of being an American and liking it? Don't you owe a degree of loyalty and respect to the country that has given you these opportunities? Must you run down the United States to build up Israel?," the questions would be considered insulting in the extreme. If you were a friend, you would have lost a friend. Moreover, you would be classified as anti-Israeli — perhaps even anti-Semitic.

Top: Leo Pevsner, Israel Bond leader, Senator Estes Kefauver, and the author, 1952.

Bottom: The author and Theodore Roosevelt McKeldin, governor of Maryland, on the eve of McKeldin's nomination of Dwight Eisenhower for president, Chicago, 1952.

2. The Anglos and the Americans

In Israel immigrants from Morocco, Algeria, Iran, Iraq, India, Syria, Lebanon, Libya, Egypt, Yemen, Bucharina, Cirkassia, Greece, Turkey, Italy, Spain, Bulgaria are all conveniently, if not accurately, designated as *Sephardi* or *Franks*, to distinguish them from Jews from Romania, Hungary, Czechoslovakia, Yugoslavia, Poland, Russia and all the Soviet satellites, Germany, Scandinavia, Holland, France, Belgium, Canada, the United States, Mexico, the South American countries, the British Isles, Australia, South Africa, Rhodesia, all of whom are conveniently, if not accurately, designated as *Ashkenazi*.

There is a world of difference however between Sephardic Jews from Turkey and Greece and those for example, from the Arab countries. These two groups are as culturally and ethnically different as say an American Jew born and raised in a small midwestern town and a Polish Jew who arrived in Israel as an adult from a DP camp in 1950. There are differences in physical appearance as well . European Sephardim are taller and heavier and their features have a continental cast not unlike other natives of their countries of origin. True, most of them have dark eyes and black hair, but their skin is several shades lighter than their Jewish brethren from Arabia and North Africa. Actually, all the Jews of Israel look very much like the people of the countries from which they came. Most Israelis cannot distinguish an American Jew from any other American. And most American Jews can't tell the difference between a Jewish Moroccan and a Moroccan Moroccan; the Yemenite Jews in Israel look exactly like the Yemenites of Yemen. Some of the Oriental Israeli young people wear a *Magen David* (Shield of David) necklace to avoid being mistaken for an Arab, not unlike some of the young women in the United States with "Jewish" features who prominently display crosses so that they will not be mistaken (heaven forbid) for a Jewess.

A further popular differentiation of peoples is the lumping together of all the immigrants from English speaking nations (United States, Canada, British Isles, Australia, New Zealand, South Africa and Rhodesia) as "Anglos." This subdivision of Ashkenazi is convenient for the Israelis, if manifestly inaccurate. Although most Israelis don't know it, there is also a world of difference among the Anglos.

After June, 1967, for the first time since the arrival of the early Zionist pioneers of the 1910's and 1920's, Jews began to emigrate to Israel from the Anglo countries and Western Europe and Latin America in significant numbers. This immigration was based upon personal conviction and freedom of choice as contrasted with the necessity that motivated most of the immigration between 1945 and 1967. A small but steady Anglo immigration from South Africa also has continued apace after June 1967. The earlier South African immigration, of course, is not entirely comparable to other post-1948 Anglo immigration. Materially secure and prosperous though they are, the ruling White South Africans' nagging guilt feelings of apartheid and their stuffy parochialism and religious fundamentalism are never far from the daily routines of South African Jews. The clannishness of the South African Jews in Israel and their general seeming lack of patriotic fervor for Israel would seem to bear out the proposition that, for most of them immigration to Israel was more pragmatic than romantic. Having come with considerable money and skills and being nonreligious and hedonistic by nature, they have adjusted much better than most Anglos. They tend to regard Israel as a kind of a South African Jewish Miami Beach.

What of the other Anglo, Western European, and South American immigration? The Jews who emirated from Rhodesia, New Zealand, and Australia are only a few hundred altogether. Their style and attitudes in Israel, relating as they do to their backgrounds in their native lands, are similar to the style of immigrants from England, the principal difference, perhaps is that many of the British immigrants are religiously observant Jews, in the Jewish high church style similar to the aristocratic synagogues of New York, Paris, and Berlin. Reunion with their religious brethren has hardly been an important factor in their immigration. About 12,000 Jews from the British Isles came to live in Israel since 1948, the majority after 1967. The number decreases each year, and there is no reason to believe that there will be an increase in the future. Many Britishers have left Israel, and most likely the number of returnees will soon equal the number of newcomers.

The English have tended to adjust better than most of the other Anglos, except perhaps the South Africans. Why? Probably because they brought with them the pragmatic *sang froid* of their English brethren. Their religiosity is also a factor. Furthermore, the period of the Mandate created circumstances that help British Jews to be comfortable in Israel. The Jews of England were much better informed about and had closer ties with Palestine than any other group during all the years after World War I. After all, Palestine had been a part of the British Empire. English Jews had business connections with Palestinian Jews and some of the earlier settlers came from England, though few as labor *chalutzim* (pioneers). Consequently, many of them had family and friendship ties in Israel before they immigrated. Despite this history, very few young English Jews go to Israel to live. The loosening of the formal religious ties together with the youth revolt stance (in England as throughout the world) largely account for this.

A common theme in the motivation to immigrate to Israel (and in some cases, the overriding motive) is the "grass is greener" syndrome — an altogether human desire to get away, to make a change. This impulse is non-religious, non-ethnic, non-economic, non-social, though overtones of all are involved, based upon feelings of unhappiness and unfulfillment. It is a *malaise d'esprit,* a dissatisfaction with one's present life, profession, job, business. In some cases, the decision involves a critical rejection of the current scene in one's own land, or more parochially in one's city, town, village, neighborhood, house. Sometimes it is triggered by a failure of personal relationships between husband and wife, children and parents, colleagues, fellow workers. The phenomenon is very human and motivates migration to anywhere as surely as it does to Israel. It serves to explain the movement of non-persecuted individuals from one country to another in any historical period and especially now, when air travel and air freighting make such movement quick and easy.

The "grass is greener" syndrome perhaps stimulated more young American non-Zionist immigration in Israel during the post-1967 War period than any of the other groups. Why? On the one hand, Americans were the least knowledgeable about Israel as it really is and therefore the more readily did they romanticize that land as an escape hatch down which to slide into the land of the forefathers; to fly to the *AlteNeuland* of Herzl, where modern Davids slew Goliaths and created a society into which they, their brothers not only were welcome, but where the very law of the land was a "Law of Return." The scenario was superficial and cinematic, but it had a strong influence on students and young adults whose predilections conditioned them to buy the script. A second reason for the impact of the "greener syndrome" in America is the phenomenon of relocation within the U.S. Millions of Americans are moving all the time to a new town, to a different state, to a new business. In recent years, many Americans have moved to other countries just to get away — to get away from home, to get away from it all. So why not to Israel?

The numbers of Americans who went to Palestine as Zionist pioneers in the early years were only a few hundred and constituted a miniscule though important fraction of the total until the establishment of the State in 1948. Some few hundred came to Jewish Palestine-Israel in 1948 as military volunteers, with no intention of remaining (and very few did stay). From 1948 to 1967, some ten thousand came as new immigrants, *olim hadashim,* less than one percent of the total of newcomers during those years. This small number was a disappointing achievement for the immigration department of the Jewish Agency and other organizations that worked assiduously (if not very successfully) and spent millions of dollars to proselytize the American Jews.

During those years, it was the ardent hope of the Israel government, the political parties, and of most of the Israeli people as well, that from the largest Jewish community in the world, some six million souls, at least several hundreds of thousands would come to Israel.

The American Jews were unceasing in helping to re-enforce a pro-Israel climate in a nation whose government and people already were sympathetic to the notion of protecting and developing the gallant little land. Their material support is legendary. A new nation was being created. A two-thousand year-old dream was unfolding. Why then shouldn't these Jewish brethren, and co-religionists, return to the homeland? It seemed logical enough, but they didn't go.

The impetus of the Six-Day War gave an adrenalinic boost to these campaigns, though the organized effort to promote immigration was a minor reason for the great increase in the number of Jews from the United States and Canada who went to Israel to live. Starting in 1967, immigration from the United States and Canada began to assume some numerical importance. From 1967 through 1972 some 26,000 Jews emigrated from the U.S. and 3,000 from Canada.

Who were they, these American neo-Zionists? Mostly young people, a new breed. These youngsters, student age if not students, were native-born Americans of first, second, and third generation American parents. Some were college and university drop-outs. A few were thrill-seekers, hitting the road with their packs and their pot, sleeping on the beaches and in the forests. They might just as well have been in Tahiti as in Israel. The great majority however, were young idealists, imbued with a humanist spirit, not necessarily Jewish religious, or otherwise oriented.

At the beginning, in 1967-68, they were well-received in the kibbutzim and even in the cities, and some adjusted and became permanent kibbutz members, especially in the kibbutzim and agricultural settlements established since the Six-Day War. But in recent years the gloss has come off the pumpkin, both for the hosts and their "guests." The wholly disparate way of Israeli life clashed with their own mores and customs, which they sought to introduce. There was a not unfounded fear on the part of the older members in the settlements of the "bad" influence on their own youngsters these American "hippies" might exercise. The natural taciturnity and downright bad manners of many of the kibbutzniks (they are not called "sabra" — fruit of the cactus, prickly on the outside, soft on the inside — for nothing) and petty irritations and misunderstandings impeded assimilation.

As a result, the Americans largely kept to themselves and few of them became integral members of the communities. Ultimately they became a sort of unpaid, unskilled, hired-help pool, not too different from the Arabs who were employed as day laborers. The result, of course, has been that most of the young Americans who were not primary members of the new settlements left for the cities, and from there left the country.

Many of the youngsters who came to Israel in the post-1967 period had been brought up in Zionist households and accepted attachment to Israel as natural and desirable. However, most of the older immigrants from America during this period were not Zionists. They were second and third generation native-born Americans, ethnically more American than Jewish, though they were members of Jewish communities and belonged to temples, synagogues, Jewish social and fraternal organizations. It was a well-known fact (old-line Israeli Zionists considered it a scandal) that American Zionists did not emigrate to Israel. Some wags defined an American Zionist as one who works assiduously to persuade other Jews to go on *aliyah*. In 1971 a resolution requiring delegates to World Zionist Congresses to emigrate to Israel or forfeit their eligibility to become delegates in the future was narrowly defeated.

The post-1967 middle-aged American immigrant was not persuaded to go to Israel by Zionists. His *aliyah* was based on romantic mysticism — the "grass is greener" syndrome. His profile is that of an affluent Jew planning to retire or to involve himself in a business or philanthropy or hobby that will not occupy all of his time. He is politically liberal but not left-wing, and he tends to support the nationalistic hard line of the Israeli right-wing parties. He has transferred to Israel his strong American patriotism, intense and unadulterated from birth through his salad years, tarnished and diffused since the end of World War II, recycled and once again unsophisticated and uncritical. He believes that what's good for Israel is good for the Jews, and what's good for the Jews is good for the world! Golda's alleged crack when asked if she wanted some American generals — "yes, General Electric, General Dynamics, General Motors" — somehow works for him.

Here are some vignettes of earlier migrants to Jewish Palestine and later immigrants to Israel that is.

Soloman Schoenberg Levadi

Sol Levadi was born in Poland in 1897 on the border of Lithuania in the very Jewish city of Slonim, the scion of a wealthy timber merchant family and the descendant of a long line of *misnagid* rabbis. The Jews of Eastern Europe, Poland and Russia in the 18th and 19th Centuries, who did not succumb to the hassidic hysteria that swept the ghettos of those times were designated *Misnagdim* "Aginners" — the term derived from the Hebrew word for opposition.

He was brought up in comparative luxury in the relaxed atmosphere of a deeply religious milieu not constrained by poverty nor problems of survival or fear. His family had cordial economic and social connections with the Polish pans of the area. They belonged to an elite rich cadre that enjoyed an intensely Jewish and pleasant life style.

Young Shlomo was sent to a famous private Yeshiva, a seminary where secular learning was interspersed with religious Jewish teaching. During the three years he lived there, he was exposed to the dilemma that every sensitive young Jew had to face in those halcyon days just before World War I — to be a committed religious Jew or a secular man of the world. Events made the decision for him. He returned to Slonim for a vacation, and while at home a pogrom occurred. His lively little city was invaded by Russian and Polish goons, officially part of the Czar's army. Jewish homes and businesses were looted, pillaged, burned, their synagogues desecrated. Their Polish friends were horrified, but their efforts to prevent the pogrom were ineffectual. Levadi's grandfather, the patriarch of the family, was murdered.

Apologies and commiseration followed soon enough. The Polish neighbors were genuinely concerned and made some effort to right the havoc wreaked by the Russian Cossacks. Most of the Schoenberg family resignedly accepted the overtures to reestablish the ante-bellum relationships. Not Levadi.

Young Shlomo rejected the prospect of being a Jew living in a country that was not his own, hoping to be accepted and tolerated by sufferance, not by right. He became an instant Zionist, and a warrior. Soon thereafter, he took off for Palestine at the age of 15. He arrived in Jerusalem in 1913 just before the beginning of World War I and quickly became immersed in the intellectual romantic turmoil of idealistic Zionism. He sought out relatives, made friends, somehow managed to exist, just above survival level. His knowledge of Polish, Russian, Yiddish and Hebrew stood him in good stead.

Levadi immediately upon arrival in Palestine changed his name from Solomon Schoenberg to a prophetic Hebrew name, Solomon Levadi — "a soul alone, a lonely soul; one who is private" — the name he carried throughout his life. In a couple of years he was proficient enough in Hebrew to become a disciple of the founder of modern Hebrew, Ben Yehuda, and an instructor at the first Hebrew teacher's seminary in Jerusalem. He shed all vestiges of religious Judaism, but continued to remain a devout ethnic nationalistic Jew.

Well before the Balfour Declaration of 1917, when World War I was militarily in the balance, Levadi joined a group of young ardent Zionists who were convinced that the Ottoman colonial administration of which Palestine was then a part would fulfill the promise of the Shah to grant independence to Jews in Palestine after the war — a pledge that had the support of the principal ally of the Central Powers, Kaiser Wilhelm of Germany. At the turn of the century the Kaiser had visited Jerusalem and there had granted an audience to Theodor Herzl and a committee of Zionists. He told them he would encourage the return of Jews to the Holy Land.

Levadi joined the Turkish army and was sent to Constantinople to train as a teacher of Turkish Army conscripts — Arabs, Jews, nondescript mercenaries. In Turkey he also received military training and quickly improved his knowledge of the language. He developed a taste for the military, which he retained all of his life. Soon after his return to Palestine in early 1918, he was captured by a British expeditionary force, led by the famous General Allenby, and was interned for a year in a British military prison camp in the desert. His prison life was shared not too oppressively with a number of young fellow Palestinian Zionists, including Moshe Shertok, afterwards known as Moshe Sharett, the second prime minister of Israel, and later until his death the international chief of the Jewish Agency. In prison they polished their Turkish, in which Levadi was more fluent by virtue of his sojourn in Turkey, and Levadi learned some English from the erudite Shertok.

The rather more pure Zionism of Levadi and Shertok and their fellows in opting for the Turkish-German promise of Jewish statehood instead of the politically motivated, ambiguous Balfour Declaration is a footnote of modern Jewish history that has been buried. The perverse British resistance to the United Nations Partition in 1947-48 and the mean way in which their forces left Israel in April and May 1948 (expecting to return when the Arabs, with the armaments left for them by the withdrawing British forces, would overcome the Jews), is evidence of Levadi's and Sharett's early prescience in giving more credence to the Turkish promises of Jewish independence than to the British double talk.

Levadi was released from the British prison and returned to Jerusalem for a few months. He was disaffected by the atmosphere there. Some 20,000 of the 88,000 Jews in Palestine in 1914, at the beginning of World War I had left the country, returned to Europe or emigrated to the United States.

He was then all of 21 years old and already had lived in two different worlds. He left for the United States to try a third. Somehow he wound up in Chicago, and there he enrolled at the University of Illinois to study dentistry. He became an oral surgeon and an American. He involved himself in the Yiddish intellectual life in that big-shouldered city, performed in the Jewish theater, married, fathered two sons, joined the Medical Corps of the United States Army, and learned the English language perfectly, although he spoke it in an accented Russian-Polish brogue. He eventually became the chief of the oral surgery department of one of Chicago's largest hospitals.

In the 1930's he journeyed to Poland to visit his aging parents. His father while forgiving him for deserting the religion, extracted a promise from his "Amerikane" son. Levadi had mentioned to his father that he was contemplating writing a chronicle of his experiences as a boy in Poland, as a young man in Palestine, and now as a mature doctor in America. He confessed to the old man that he had not mastered the language sufficiently to write in English and was planning to write the book in Hebrew. His father insisted that he should write it in Yiddish, *Momme Loshin,* the mother tongue he knew so well. Levadi agreed readily enough.

The casual assent became a sacred promise several years later when Levadi learned that his mother and father, brothers and sisters, and the rest of his family had been murdered by the Poles and Nazis. He activated his reserve status in the medical corps and when America entered the war in 1942, despite his 44 years, he entered the army, spending the next four years in Australia and the South Pacific. He became well-acquainted with General Douglas MacArthur, serving as his personal dentist when he was not setting up dental stations in the Islands. He returned to the United States sick from an improperly diagnosed heart ailment for which he was never compensated by the army medical board, despite protracted litigation. The report in which the army rejected his claim was prefaced by the gratuitous insult, "Dr. Solomon S. Levadi was born in Russia in 1897..." Rally around the flag boys, and sing it once again.

In 1963 he traveled to Israel to see what miracles God had wrought there. He spent three ecstatic and strange months revisting places — many of which he could not recognize they had changed so much — and looking up old companions he could not recognize, they had changed so much. One solace was the large group of people from his hometown of Slonim who were in Israel in such numbers that they had organized an active society of *Slonimer.*

Sol journeyed to Israel again in 1972, this time with his wife, Hanna, a Virginia Jewess from a quasi-assimilated family. They lived in our apartment in northern Tel Aviv near the sea. At first the tongue-tied barrier of her monolingual English was agony for her. Hanna had never been away from the American scene. She was afraid to cross the street. Shopping in the stores, even in supermarkets not unlike those in her native Evanston, was a nightmare chore. However, after a few weeks, while her husband scurried about looking up old friends, his wife quietly became adjusted. Finally, she began to enjoy the lively tumultuous city, the bright sunshine, the seaside where they lived, the beautiful children. Quite weirdly, as Dr. Levadi became more and more vexed with an Israel he never had known, his wife became enamored of this Collins Avenue on the Mediterranean. When they were ready to return home, Hanna candidly admitted she wouldn't at all mind returning to Israel to live. Dr. Levadi was not at all sure he wanted to live in Israel. He had discovered that he was a bit too much Amerian to spend his remaining days in a land so different from the Palestine he had left 50 years ago.

Dr. Levadi's greatest disappointment on his last visit to Israel was the frustration of not being able to arrange for a Hebrew edition of his Yiddish trilogy, *Shvelin* (Thresholds), acclaimed for years by Yiddishists as a classic fictional history of the Jews of Eastern Europe before World War I and of the Jews of Turkish Palestine before the British mandate. The late President of Israel, Zalman Shazar, a distinguished Yiddish scholar who had known Dr. Levadi in the early days, told him that it was a "must" for his opus to be published in Hebrew so that the younger generations in Israel could know of the chapter of Jewish history that Levadi had brilliantly depicted. President Shazar urged Levadi to undertake the task of translation. Levadi could not convince the gentle old man that his 1920 Hebrew and his failing health were hardly up to such an assignment.

Levadi lived out the final chapter of his life trilogy quietly in his Evanston home. He died in March 1973, still flirting with the idea of returning to bask in the warm sun shining on the sand and hills and waters of the beloved little land in which his Jewish heart has always been, despite all his disappointments and the long estrangement. His very American wife of 50 years would have gone with him in a shot if he had chosen to return. Hanna had never realized the grip that Israel had on her man until she saw him bloom in the presence of his old comades and his *Slonimir landsleit* (home town friends).

The Rosenbergs

Rosenberg was drafted into the United States Army at the beginning of the Korean War and remained in the service as an officer in the quartermaster's corps. He was a Jew and a New Yorker and therefore something of an anomaly as a professional soldier.

In the middle fifties he met and married a pretty little New York Jewish girl. During the next ten years Julia was happy enough to accompany him on army assignments throughout the country — bearing four children on the way. In 1965 he became eligible for early retirement. He had advanced no higher than captain and felt aggrieved about his lack of progress in the service.

He attributed his lack of success to anti-Semitism — which may exist in the professional armed services — but in his case had little relationship to his indolence, to his acerbic posture of unmerited superiority. He resigned from the army and decided to take his family to Israel "where a Jew could be a Jew."

His wife's mother, an Amerian immigrant from Russia, was an elderly widow who had received a small inheritance from her late husband, a shopkeeper in New York. This happy circumstance had more than a little to do with the captain's sudden discovery of his Jewish heritage. The captain and wife Julia, the mother-in-law, and the children came to Israel and moved into a rented house in Nof Yam, a village near the sea north of Tel Aviv. Rosenberg had made connections in New York and several other cities to distribute Israeli-made gift items and souvenirs. He rented a warehouse in New York and set up an office there. Within a couple of years he demonstrated thoroughly the inadequacy of his quartermaster training in the U.S. Army, his own ineptitude for private business, and his small but exquisite genius for squandering other people's money.

During these years he traveled back and forth between Israel and the United States while his bewildered wife and frightened children floundered miserably in Israel. His wife became a fat hysterical slattern. His handsome bright children became sullen juvenile delinquents. My wife, Kitty, met Julia in a grocery store, and befriended the forlorn lady and her children. They were frequent visitors at our home in nearby Kfar Shmaryahu during the year before they returned to the States in 1970.

The captain had maneuvered to transport a stupid but pretty Israeli secretary to New York as his mistress and manager there. She barely could speak English and could not, of course, read or write a word of it.

He had convinced her that he was an American millionaire, which all Americans in Israel can do easily enough. There still exists a built-in predisposition in Israel to identify American Jewish male with American millionaire.

When the money was all gone — the mother-in-law's, his wife's and his own savings — the family moved back to the United States. Rosenberg had been in the U.S. for almost a year. Only after his disillusioned mistress returned to Israel did he proceed to make sporadic arrangements to send for his wrecked family and his prematurely senile mother-in-law. The sojourn in Israel for his wife and scarred children had been an unmitigated nightmare. The setting of the tragedy was incidental, given the brutishness of the chief protagonist. Captain Rosenberg could have stayed in New York or Tuskegee or Timbuctu with the same inevitable results, except that Israel had a mythic lure for him and his wife and her old Jewish mother. It also had scapegoat value.

* * *

Rabbi Morton Berman

When my friend Rabbi Morton Berman retired from his pulpit at Temple Isaiah Israel in Chicago he was only 60 years old, and restless to emigrate to Israel to put into practice the Zionism he had advocated all his life. His wife of many years had died. A couple years after her death, he married a young woman completely uninvolved in the Jewish scene. His new wife was dubious about the move. She was a chemist and was deeply immersed in her research and university teaching and questioned her ability to adjust to Israel or to find a place in her discipline; but she realized the depth of the Rabbi's commitment and they moved to Jerusalem in the early 1960's.

There Rabbi Berman, as an important American Zionist leader for years, quickly found a position with the Jewish Agency and Elaine Berman became a member of the Hebrew University science faculty. The Rabbi is retired now from his job with the Agency. He never quite succeeded in contributing the service he had longed for. He found more enjoyment in looking after his apartment and his two young children, a welcome bonus of his ripe years. He remains, however, an American in a world that is not quite his. It had been easier for him to be a Zionist in Chicago. Wife Elaine, on the other hand, is perfectly at home in the academic milieu of Jerusalem amongst colleagues hardly different than the professors and researchers with whom she worked and associated in America. She is immersed in her work and she finds Jerusalem comfortable. She is something of an Israelite.

Ann Medalie

Ann Medalie has been in love with painting all of her long spinster life. Brought to the United States from Lithuania as a child, she early decided on a career as an artist and achieved some success, particularly after a long sojourn in Mexico during the 40's. I met her in Chicago upon her return there, through her nephew, Bernard Howard, a friend and business associate of mine. I treasure the painting of gardenias I bought from her at that time. She had always been intrigued with the idea of visiting Israel because of the opportunities to paint landscapes, flowers, and cityscapes in that shining land. She also was eager to meet Israeli relatives who had emigrated from Europe and South Africa.

Opportunely, she came to Israel when the ancient city of Safed, high on the hills of Galilee was creating an art colony. Painters, sculptors, and craftsmen were buying old Arab houses perched near the summit of the Canaan Mountains on which Safed is built and reconverting them into charming studios and homes. Ann bought one of these and has lived there ever since. I visit her each time I travel to Safed. She has become a veteran Israeli artist. Her canvasses today bring high prices and her work is exhibited in the most prestigious galleries of the country. She has scores of friends among the artists of Safed and throughout the country and lives a happy and fulfilled life. She rarely uses the smattering of Hebrew at her command. Not being able to master Hebrew has never bothered her in the least. She truly loves Israel, which has been very good for her and to her. She is not an Israeli. She is an artist contentedly living and working in Israel.

* * *

Eva

Eva, a grade school teacher in Boston, retired at age 65 and came to Israel to live. She enrolled at Ulpan Akiva to learn Hebrew, in which pursuit she had no success. She remained at the ulpan as a permanent occasional student, and soon was deeply involved with the town's neglected welfare youngsters. She became a permanent paying guest who had found a new life for herself conducting a private juvenile welfare crusade for her neglected little kids, most of them Sephardic, Afro-Asians. All of her fellow students were happy to contribute. Originally appalled that such conditions could exist in the new Jewish land, the valiant little lady ruefully recalled that even in America the poor kids get the dirty end of the stick. She had no desire to return to the United States. She had found her mission.

The Baskins

Sol Baskin was born and raised in Chicago. His family were deeply observant Jews and when he was a young boy he decided to become a rabbi. As a student at the University of Chicago in the early 1940's he was still toying with the idea. World War II service in the United States infantry decided for him. He returned from Europe after the War and entered the advertising business, a congenial environment for his talent as an artist and a writer. We were close associates and friends in Chicago. Not only did his firm handle advertising for my company, but our mutual interests in Israel and in painting brought us together frequently. A few years before our immigration we had a two man showing of our paintings at a Chicago gallery.

His intense Jewish nationalism and Zionist fervor brought him to Israel in 1948 and again to the Sinai campaign as a volunteer infantry officer. Before he returned to Chicago in 1956, he met and married a good-looking daughter of a devout family from Mea Shearim.

In Chicago he prospered in his profession. His shy religious wife Rachel easily adjusted to the secular life of the bustling big city. Their three children, two boys and a girl, were typical American youngsters. But Sol did not abandon his consuming desire to emigrate to Israel. His wife, trained in the obedient docility required of an Orthodox girl, acquiesced. The family emigrated and Sol launched a career as a representative of American and Israeli firms. His experience in business and his connections with American manufacturers interested in buying and selling Israeli and American products seemed to assure a good life for Sol and his family.

Despite Sol's proficiency in Hebrew and the fact that his wife is a Jerusalem sabra, adjustment has been difficult. Sol encountered two distressing facts. One, with all his skills, Hebrew proficiency, American know-how, and experience in a profession that is peculiarly American, he found the going rocky. He had every logical reason to believe that it would be easy enough to progress, given his undoubted credentials, Israel-side and State-side. Like most Americans who have emigrated to Israel with similar reasonable beliefs, he was not aware of the pervasiveness of the Israeli arrogance — "Don't tell us, we'll tell you!"

Secondly, despite his religion, his good Hebrew, his sabra wife, his love of the country, his army service and valiant war record, his intense nationalist Jewishness — he is an Amerian and not an Israeli. How could he accept this? To believe it would be repudiation of all that he has considered sacred truth. Sol left the United States because he considered himself more Israeli than American. He was a Jew and a Jew should live in the only Jewish country in the world — Israel. Like me, he found out in Israel that for an American it is easy to be a Jew in the U.S. and difficult to be a Jew in Israel — at least to be accepted as a Jew there. In Israel, you are an American and not an Israeli. Israel is not a Jewish country, it is an Israeli nation. To this day I think Sol refuses to buy this. I suspect his wise sabra wife always knew this truism.

Sol's wife was happy to go to America to get out of the Mea Shearim atmosphere, to avoid shaving her head and wearing a wig like her mother does. How could she suggest to her husband that for all of their sakes, hers, the children's, and his most of all, they should pack up and go home — to America?

Perhaps, as Sol saw some of his American friends and associates, who like us emigrated to Israel to become Israelis, weaken on the idea of living in Israel, he too might have decided to return to his native land. But it wasn't likely. Undoubtedly, the Yom Kippur War strengthened his resolution to remain with his people in their adversity.

Christian Immigrants

Christian Americans often find Israel a pleasant place to live, and some of them have become long-time residents in genuine contentment. They did not come to Israel seeking the impossible dream and have no hang-ups of disappointment or guilt as do so many of their Jewish fellow American immigrants. Moreover, most of them come to Israel on a specific mission or to fill a job. They take up their work and when it is done they leave for home. Generally their assignments are long-term, even life-time, and if they are successful in their jobs they carry on with equanimity. If they are not successful in their work, or if their mission proves unrewarding to them,they pack up and leave. Other Christians in the Holy Land are motivated by religious romanticism and just plain curiosity. But unlike so many of their Jewish brethren, the pilgrimage is not a matter of do or die. They experience no feelings of inadequacy if they become bored or if they find Israel is something less than they expected or hoped for.

They have the ineffable advantage over the Jewish immigrants in knowing that Israel is a Jewish country — and that they are not Jewish, and therefore, must accept it as it is. They are the *goyim*, the gentiles, the strangers. only those who come as the husband or the wife of a Jew hoping their conversion to Judaism will stick, feel otherwise, and even most of these do not get too hung up. In many instances, it is the Jewish mate who finds it more difficult to become an Israeli than the Christian convert to Judaism.

Andy and *Linda* were art students in Chicago, who married, and decided to try Israel. My wife, Kitty, had known them as fellow students at the Chicago Art Institute and was delighted to run into them again in Kfar Shmaryahu. Neither of them was religious, but Linda decided seriously to convert to Judaism for the sake of her future children. Andy's Jewish parents came to Chicago shortly before the Nazi take-over of Hungary. Andy was then five years old and has no conscious memory of his European babyhood. He is midwestern big city, pleased with his capacity to enjoy his life and his work. He has a kind of tziganer (gypsy) irresponsibility that doesn't impinge on others. He is lithe and graceful, with blue eyes deep set in an aquiline face accentuated by a luxurious magyar moustache. Wife Linda came came from a small town in central Pennsylvania. She is a statuesque blond woman, seductively a lioness in appearance and movement, altogether even-tempered and a fine calm mate for her volatile gypsy. Both of them are members of a generation of American young people who make their own judgments without revolt against their parents or the establishment, nor were they impressed by the material and cosmetic values of Nixon's silent majority. Both have found Israel the right place for them to be and for their two lusty babies born there. Andy teaches art at the American school in Kfar Shmaryahu and paints. Linda also paints, makes jewelry and leather belts, and looks after the children in their comfortable flat in Herzylia. They are Israelis.

* * *

The Smith's were unlikely immigrants. They came to Israel on a tour after Jim Smith retired as a minor executive of the Ford Motor Company in Detroit. They came to Israel as casual Christian visitors to see the holy places. After they completed their tour, they decided it might be a pleasant idea to stay a bit longer in that warm climate, and they enrolled as students to study Hebrew at Ulpan Akiva. They had no success in learning Hebrew, but they did become enchanted by the dynamism of Shulamit, the principal of the school, and the many interesting people they met there. When the institution moved from Netanya to a new site farther north, Shulamit invited them to join the staff and help organize the new headquarters. They have been there for years now — busy, involved, happy. At Akiva they have no problems getting along with their (only language) English, interspersed with an occasional Hebrew word. They are living in Israel. They remain hard-shell Baptists, midwesterners from rural Michigan. Yet, they too are Israelis.

* * *

The Campbell Family decided to emigrate to Israel from Philadelphia where their families had lived since revolutionary times. Bruce was a prosperous engineer and building contractor, his wife a medical social service worker. Bruce gave up his partnership in the family building business, with his wife and four sons, aged seven to twelve, decided to seek a new life in a new land. They are deeply fundamentalist Christians, though they belong to no sect. They knew something of the agricultural communes of Israel and decided quite simply that it might be interesting for them to become workers of the soil in the land of the Ineffable Shepherd. I knew them at Ulpan Akiva where the family were the darlings of the school. Handsome all of them, good-natured, alive. The sons took to Hebrew like sabras, and the young parents, too, absorbed more Hebrew than the average student. The whole family participated in all of the activities, the music and drama programs, the folk dancing, the bull-sessions, even in the religious services.

During the five months they lived at Akiva, father Bruce applied to a number of cooperative settlements seeking to become a member. Particularly, he hoped to become a member of Moledet B'nai Brith, a settlement in the lower Galilee, because it represented to him the most intriguing kind of life for the Campbells — a cooperative colony in a setting of private family living. Moledet had never had a Christian family apply for membership, and *Yekkes* (German Jews) that they are, they had to take their time to decide on this novel application despite the impeccable credentials and obvious strengths this stalwart family had to offer. Though Moledet is not a religious community, the fact that the Campbells were Christians was a concern. The Moledet admissions committee had never been confronted by a religious problem. There are no religious members in Moledet, and the committee failed to recognize that the religion of the Campbells was a matter of private commitment, not sectarian attachment. In that sense, the members of Moledet are quite as religious as the Campbells.

Understandably, the Campbells were discomfited to discover that they were not acceptable to a non-religious agricultural settlement because they were Christians. They were not embittered however. The sojourn in the ulpan was more than satisfying for them, and they were fully aware of their half-way house status. When an offer to become a building engineer with the municipality of Arad arose, Bruce and his family accepted it. Though they had hoped to join a farming community, the idea of Arad, a new development city carefully planned on a rise in the Negev desert, appealed to their pioneer spirit and sense of adventure. They could see the southern end of the Dead Sea from their new home. The air is thin and fresh, the nights are cold and bracing. Everything was new abuilding. Only the ancient Bible history of the area was old. All the people in Arad were newcomers like the Campbells. No problem of acceptance was involved. The Campbells believed they had found in

Arad what they sought. If not, in their equanimity and high good humor, and the certainty of their close familial relationships, they could look elsewhere — in Israel, hopefully. More than likely. They had the feel of Israelis.

The author, Golda Meir, and Dov Joseph, minister of commerce, in Jerusalem, 1953.

Top: The author and Bartley Crum, member of the United States Commission on Palestine and first chairman of Americans for Haganah, 1948.
Bottom: Max Swiren, Chicago leader of Americans for Haganah, Max Bressler, Chicago Jewish community leader, Moshe Sharett, second prime minister of Israel, Judge Harry Fisher, Chicago Jewish community leader, and the author, 1950.

3. Other Aliyahs

Hungarians and Romanians

Since 1948, in addition to the hundreds of thousands of DP's brought to Israel after World War II, many Jews emigrated from Eastern Europe especially from Hungary and Romania, during the early 1950's and again in the 1960's. Those who came before 1967 were motivated more by necessity than choice. They were refugees, despite the growing liberalism of the Romanian and Hungarian Communist regimes as compared to the Soviets. Beween 1949 and 1952, 118,000 Romanian Jews came to Israel. Today they are Israeli and their integration is well nigh complete, even if their happiness is not. Since 1967, a few thousand more came, more or less on a voluntary basis. Their enthusiasm for Israel was enhanced by the great victory of the 6-Day War and their absorption of course was greatly ameliorated by the post-1967 improved economic conditions and opportunities, plus the fact that most of them had relatives in Israel to help them become established. Their lot in their native lands was not too onerous and restriction of individual freedoms of thought and movement, including religious worship, was much less severe than in the Soviet Union.

It is unlikely that of the some tens of thousands of Jews still living in Hungary and Romania many more will come to Israel. Any further migration will depend largely on economic conditions in those countries and in Israel. If the Jews of Hungary and Romania prosper, if there is a measure of "free enterprise," if a benign climate for small craftsmen and tradesmen will obtain, Jews will stay. If not, they will emigrate, some to

Israel if they have relatives there, others to countries where they are welcome and can join friends and relatives.

Latin Americans

An interesting *aliyah* consists of Jews who have come to Israel from South America, Mexico, and other Central American countries. Most of the Latin American Jews moved to Israel and still do because they wanted to, not because they were oppressed. Particularly is this true of the Jews from Mexico, Venezuela, the Isthmus nations, and Brazil.

Most Mexican and Venezuelan Jews have been prosperous for years. Why then do some of them emigrate? The reasons are religious and ethnic. The majority of the Jews in those countries are relative newcomers there — most of the "oldtimers" came to Latin America as immigrants after World War I, the others as refugees after World War II, many of them because they couldn't get into the United States. The Latin-Indian mestizo and his cultures and mores were strange and alien to them. Being free to establish their own cultural and religious life the Jews have done so. Steady uninterrupted prosperity made this possible to accomplish on a lavish scale in Mexico and Venezuela. There the Jews live in a sort of technicolor ghetto of their own choice and making. But they also continue to live in some uneasiness and doubt. Life may not always continue to be so good! Romanticism about Israel after 1967 and their uneasiness at home combined to lure some of them to Israel (and often disenchantment sent them back).

In Latin America most Jews did not try to assimilate with the general population, to become Mexicans or Venezuelans. They were clever and skillful in adjusting as business people and middle-class merchants, manufacturers, bankers, financiers, importers, and exporters. Their contributions to the development of the Latin-American countries have been substantial and positive. But most of them have remained apart. Few of them became involved with politics except as financial contributors. They have established their own schools and their own community centers, in most cases connected with their synagogues. They created their own private social life, though they are frequent patrons of good cafes, theater, ballet, concerts. Being prosperous and peripatetic, they are highly visible and sometimes resented. They are aware of this and perhaps tend to exaggerate the extent of the resentment. The Hitler days are not far behind, at least for the parents, if not for their children. In any event, they are somewhat ill at ease. It can be assumed that with the years these attitudes will evaporate. The succeeding generations are native-born. Many are university-trained and have found friends among non-Jewish peers. They also have developed sincere patriotism and love for the countries of their birth. Like the Israeli sabras, they are not uneasy. Some of them too, like students the world over, became caught up in left-wing youth movements. Traditional Jewish and religious ties and family relationships do not attract them to Israel.

What is true of Mexico and Venezuela applies to some extent to all the Jewish communities of South America. The similarities between the Jewish minorities in Brazil, Argentina, Columbia, Peru, Chile, Uruguay, and Paraguay are great and the differences are minimal. They all largely consist of first generation immigrants and their second and third generation children. They too have become prosperous as they have helped to create a middle class in countries where a middle class barely existed and still remains very small. Except for Mexico and Venezuela the Jews are different in three distinct ways: 1) they live under much less stable regimes, either more right-wing or neo-communist; 2) they include a higher percentage of Sephardic and Oriental Jews from the Arab countries, indeed, there is even a significant number of former residents of Palestine and Israel living in Latin America; 3) their countries contain an influential German population including former Nazis, which manifestly deepens their uneasiness. What can be said about the native-born Jewish youth of Mexico and Venezuela cannot be said with equal validity about the young Jews of other South American countries. The chance of their immigration to Israel will depend on the future political climate in these countries.

In Cuba, as in Mexico and Venezuela, there were several thousand middle-class Jewish immigrants from Europe. With the advent of the Castro revolution, they found themselves in the front showcase as middle-class exhibits "A". Most of them left post-haste, with or without their possessions and wealth. Those who remained found it difficult to adjust, though there has been no discrimination against them that can be termed anti-Semitic. Castro may be a dictator but he is no Hitler or Stalin. The Jews have suffered because of their class, not because of their religious or ethnic background.

By the beginning of the 1970's, the Cuban Jewish community had pretty much emigrated, but only a few to Israel. Most of them are in Miami and Miami Beach where many of them have successfully reestablished themselves. They make no pretense about going back to Cuba, nor forward to Israel.

Scandinavia and the Low Countries

There has been some immigration from the small Jewish communities of Denmark, Norway, Sweden, Holland, and Belgium. This immigration is very recent, mostly since the war of 1967, and it has consisted mostly of young people. The thrust of it has been romantic to the extreme, motivated much like the youthful American immigration during the same years. It is doubtful if from those countries more Jews will come to live in Israel in the years ahead than will leave Israel.

The French

"French" Jews as Israeli immigrants, fall into four groups: 1) the Algerians who emigrated to France during the last years of the revolt against France and the years immediately after independence, that is, the decade from 1955 to 1965; 2) the Jews who went to France from Morocco during the same period; 3) the Jews who came to France as refugees from Germany and Eastern Europe during the Hitler period; and 4) the Jewish citizens of France whose history goes back several centuries before World War I and II.

Algerian and Moroccan Jews who spent some years in France cannot ethnically be considered French Jewish immigrants, even though they came to Israel from France instead of from their native lands. True, they speak French, and many choose to consider themselves former Frenchmen rather than former Algerians or Moroccans. But their generations in North Africa as Jews were hardly affected by the few years they spent in France. In France, they were refugees from North Africa and were so regarded by both the French and Jewish communities. In Israel, they look like, act like, and are considered by Israelis to be Moroccans and Algerians, not French Jews. Also, most of them have come to Israel to rejoin friends and relatives and they tend to enter directly and permanently into the Moroccan and Algerian communities in Israel.

On the other hand, the few French Jewish immigrants from old line French families who have come to Israel integrate with the cosmopolitan sophisticated French Israeli community — who are generally non-religious and prosperous — and they continue to maintain close fraternal ties with their French compatriots, Jewish and non-Jewish. The Israelis who were refugees in France between the wars, and especially those who came to France as exiles during World War II, assimilate in Israel with relatives and friends from their former homes in Germany and Eastern Europe. The euphoria engendered by the Six-Day War was a compelling stimulus for emigration from France, which totalled some 18,000 between 1967 and 1972 as compared to approximately 10,000 for all the years from 1948 to 1967. In contrast, 45,000 Jews came to Israel directly from Morocco between 1949 and 1952.

Another factor, of course, was the *volte-face* of Charles De Gaulle, continued with undiminished enthusiasm by the late Georges Pompidou and his colleagues. Many French Jews have had difficulty swallowing the new pro-Arab anti-Israel line of a government that for years before 1967 was Israel's best friend in Europe. Particularly galling to them was the fact that some of the chief architects of the inimical new stance of Le Grand Charles and Pompidou were Frenchmen of Jewish ancestry, like Maurice Schumann and Marcel Debré. A number of French Jews whose remembrance of their sojourn in Germany and in Eastern Europe was a nightmare, decided to go to Israel, albeit reluctantly. When France sold fighter planes to Gadaffi's Libya to be used by Libya and Egypt against Israel while the embargo to Israel continued in the name of "strict neutrality," the future to some of the Jews in France appeared bleak. Even after the Yom Kippur War, the French government continued to deliver Mystere fighter planes to Libya, blithely asserting that the Israelis had not proved that any of the French planes were engaged in that war and Libyan oil continued to flow to France. However, most Jews of France have been Frenchmen long enough to acquire the Gallic characteristic of pragmatic cynicism and are not much affected by the current realpolitik. As Jews and Frenchmen they say, "This too, will pass." Hopefully it will as did the Dreyfus period. The attitude of the French government toward Israel is not shared by the great majority of the French people, whose admiration for Israel and the Israelis is unbounded. Anti-Semitism in France has always been endemic, but today it affects only a small minority of the population as a serious disease.

Few French university students have emigrated to Israel. Some of them went to Israel at the time of the Six-Day War as volunteers and returned soon afterwards. Many young French Jews, university students and their age peers, were rebels and leaned towards the "new left," much as their counterparts did in the United States. In fact, a significant number of the leadership of the New Left in France (as in the United States) were Jews, or their parents were at any rate. In all events, they did not leave the Jewish fold to become good Frenchmen like the politicians and industrialists, but to become revolutionaries. (They'll probably be the French politicians and industrialists of the future. *Plus ça change plus la meme chose).*

The Turks

The Turkish Jewish community was never very large but during the 18th and 19th Centuries and the first quarter of the 20th Century, the communities of Istanbul (Constantinople), Ismir (Smyrna), Bursa, and other larger cities were affluent and enjoyed a large measure of religious and cultural freedom and economic prosperity. The Jews of Ismir had lived in that pleasant Mediterranean port for generations. Their Jewish traditions, religious practices and customs had remained intact, but much like the Sephardim of Greece, Italy, and France, affluence brought secular education and the gracious living styles of all well-off Europeans. The Turkish Jews sent their children off to school in Paris and London. In their homes they spoke French, Turkish, Spanish, Ladino. After World War I the Jewish communities declined in size and wealth, and by the end of the Second World War, many of the Turkish Jews had emigrated to Europe or the Americas. Some of them went to Palestine.

Many Jews remained in Turkey. Turkey on the decline for centuries never recovered from a series of major calamities beginning with the defeat of the Central Powers and the breakup of the degenerate Ottoman Empire after World War I. Kemal Ataturk Pasha (himself part Jewish, I was informed by Jewish Turks in Israel) had made a good start in bringing Turkey out of the Levantine of the middle ages, but after his death in 1938 no leadership developed to carry on the impetus he initiated. The position of the Jews had always been somewhat delicate in a nation that was almost entirely Moslem and always divided psychologically as well as geographically between Asia and Europe. The rise of Arab political nationalism inevitably had some effect on the attitudes of Turks towards Jews; although nothing comparable to the wretched discrimination and oppression that occurred in Egypt, Iraq, and Syria developed in Turkey after the creation of Israel. Today many former Turkish Jews live in Israel, more than 40,000 of them.

The Turkish Jews move with ease in all circles, although the first generation parents feel much more at home with their fellow Turkish Jews and with French-speaking Israelis. They learn to speak Hebrew, of course, but like most adult immigrants, they rarely completely master the language.

The Indians

Most of the Israeli immigrants from India were members of a wealthy elite who had become established in the India of the British Raj during the hundreds of years of British rule. Many of these merchant, banking, industrial brahmins came from Mesopotamia, now Iraq, where for centuries Jews had been a prominent segment of the small middle-class in that Levantine land. The Sassoons, the international banking family of India, China and England, whose position and power rivaled the Rothschilds', originated from Iraq.

The long period of British colonial tradition in India (including what is now Pakistan) created many opportunities for Jews who settled there in the larger cities (and in all the Far East for that matter) and many established themselves as exporters and traders, shippers and bankers, under the benevolent patronage of the Union Jack. Since India gained independence the picture has changed, and there has been a steady emigration from its formerly well established Jewish community. The migration of Jews from Pakistan has been even greater and swifter; the Moslem atmosphere there after the Indian partition was hardly congenial for Jews.

The pro-Arab bias of Indira Ghandi and her servile government has in recent years even more heated up anti-Israel attitudes in India, further accelerating the Jewish migration.

Not all the Indian Jews migrate to Israel. Those who have and do adjust well into the upper strata of Israeli society. Though the majority of them derive from Iraqi backgrounds and look like Indians they are considered Anglos in Israel.

From left: Irving Kupcinet, Chicago columnist and TV talk show star, the author, Adlai Stevenson, and George Jessel, Chicago Stadium, 1952.

4. Strangers in a Strange Land

Some Jewish tourists who visit Israel for a few weeks and experience rudeness and ill-concealed contempt on the part of some of the Israelis put it down to bad manners and the understandable nervousness of a people under constant siege and stress. They generally laugh it off or forgive it. Most Jewish tourists aren't even aware of the fact that to some Israelis they are not welcome. Their eyes are so filled with the stardust of the preconceived miracle of Israel reborn that they translate every encounter into a joyous experience or a whimsical incident. Understandably, this kind of reaction serves to infuriate many Israelis. "How dumb can these *Americanim* be?" they ask. The apparent obtuseness of the tourist in the face of studied rudeness tends to confirm the notion on the part of some Israelis that American Jews are like their Christian counterparts, the caricature of which is the American tourist the world over. After a quarter of a century, Israel like all tourist countries in the world, has come to accept the prototype of the tourist with his flashy clothes, guide book in hand, and camera strapped over the shoulder. Acceptable when they are Germans, Swedes or Japanese. But Jews? My God! And the Jews, as the late David Ben-Gurion once said, "are exactly like all other people, only more so."

Jewish tourists frequently try out their half-forgotten or never-known Yiddish on Israeli Sephardi and are amazed that they aren't understood. "You mean you don't understand Yiddish?" asks the American matron of the Yemenite or North African emigré. "What kind of Jew are you?" Some of the young Sephardim have picked up a few Jewish words from their mothers and sisters who work as maids in Ashkenazi homes or from fathers employed in Ashkenazi establishments — although only a small number of Ashkenazis know the language themselves. These efforts at communication in *Momme Loshen* (mother tongue) are even assayed by Jewish tourists with Arab employees in establishments visited by tourists. The tourist industry in Israel has progressed so far that the Arabs, often more polite and courteous than their Jewish fellow workers, don't bother to enlighten their American cousins by telling them that they are Arabs, not Jews.

The tourist experience is merely suggestive. It is superficial and not serious. There is little danger that the tourist industry, which until the Yom Kippur War was rapidly becoming the biggest hard currency earner for Israel, will seriously be affected by the rudeness encountered by Jewish tourists. These same tourists have had similar experiences and bad service in other countries they have visited. They scarcely are aware and are not prepared to believe that in Israel it is a Jewish thing. But sometimes it is!

The experiences of Jews, especially since 1967, who have come to Israel to visit for long periods, or hav come as prospective immigrants (officially designated as temporary residents) are on occasion rough and sometimes shattering. Many of these innocents had completely cut their ties with their native countries, entering Israel on permanent *aliyah.* The jarring that many of them undergo is not always transitory. Often, the new immigrant's malaise deepens as the years go on and he fails to merge into the Israel scene. The depth of his disappointment is in direct proportion to the romantic never-never land misconceptions he brought with him. Many had conjured up the most absurd and erroneous preconceptions of Israel as a land to live in, and of the Israelis as a people with whom they could join on a basis of equality, welcomed as returning brethren. They had believed they were coming to a sort of heaven on earth, only to discover very soon that they had come to a sort of hell — that the majority of Israelis were strangers, not brethren. In short Jewish emigrés in Israel often find themselves strangers in a strange land.

They rationalize their discovery of the reality of their situation. Often their pride will not permit them to admit that they have made a mistake, so they stick it out for a time, or even permanently. Many of them, however, return home after a year or two or three. Those who remain finally settle down and adjust to their situations by consorting mainly with their fellow ethnics, Anglos, or French or South Americans or Eastern Europeans. Few of them ever really become Israelis, though they think they are because of their insistence on the cultural plurality of Israel. After all, they argue, Israel is made up of Jews and even non-Jews from scores of countries, speaking many different languages, displaying a kaleidoscopic collection of ethnic and cultural backgrounds and religious persuasions (and prejudices). "They're all Jews though, aren't they?" they ask hopefully. "There is room for all under the big Jewish Israeli umbrella, isn't there?," they insist, inveighing a myopic myth. The answer, I think, is no!

Moishe the Teamster

"I fuck your shvester!" It wasn't a casual offer of exotic sexual activity. It came from a teamster driving a horse and wagon in the center of a busy Tel-Aviv street, on a steaming summer day at high noon. The heat of the day didn't match the pure venom in his blazing eyes and choleric face. He had hurled the ultimate of insults he could muster from his ten-word English vocabulary, when I had the temerity to drive narrowly past his overloaded wagon. His curse was a direct translation from the Arabic. One of the newfound blessings the Israeli have acquired in the promised land is a choice collection of Arabic curses.

"Up yours!" I replied inelegantly and uncertain about his comprehension demonstrated the point with a closed fist and middle finger rising straight heavenward. I was almost as angry as he and didn't intend my retort as a pleasantry. We would gladly have killed each other at that moment.

He wasn't an Oriental Jew from an Arab country. He was a blue-eyed, blond-haired, broad-faced immigrant from Poland or the Balkans. I easily recognized his ancestry. My people had derived from the same Eastern Europe; if they hadn't come out of Poland to the United States by way of England some 75 years before, he could have been my brother. He was probably a distant cousin, anyway.

The reason for his anger had little to do with me or the inconvenience he fancied I had caused him. Walking in the street he might have bumped into me or I into him with only the slightest annoyance. If this had happened I would have apologized. He wouldn't have. And my apology would be acknowledged by him with a sullen silence or perhaps a slight grin, or sneer. That's all. He was angry because I was an Anglo, probably an American he would guess. But an Anglo for sure — English, South African, Canadian, Australian, Rhodesian, New Zealander.

How would he know? Definitely by the white background on the license of my comparatively new German Ford. Even without this certain clue he could identify my background as surely as I had his. He need only look at me, to see how I was dressed, the cast of my face, my haircut. He also could guess that I might have been his cousin.

I had an automobile, I looked prosperous, and he resented me completely. It was that simple. He had lived in misery in Europe, probably in a wretched German DP camp. He had come to Israel in the late forties, shortly after the creation of the State. He had lived in an equally wretched temporary *ma'abara* (immigrant's settlement) for a year or more. His expectations and dreams of coming home finally to a Jewish country had been battered by the incomprehensible Hebrew language, the lack of decent food, the lack of education, the lack of a skill or trade. He had touched the depths of misery and hopelessness living in a tent or a ramshackle temporary hut with no decent furniture, no modern plumbing, nothing. He had been a number in Europe and he was once again just a number in his new country.

He finally left the *ma'abara* and got a job as a teamster, and after a few years he owned his own horse and wagon and was his own boss. He was able to rent a flat for his family, and to bring up his children in some decent fashion. But he didn't prosper. He had wanted to go to America instead of Israel, but hadn't been able to manage it.

He cannot understand why American Jews come to Israel as immigrants, voluntarily, especially if they had been prosperous in the United States. It is an insult to his thwarted desire. Believing (fallaciously) that they are all prosperous, he sees Anglos setting an example of ease and mobility, of having possessions that shame him in the eyes of his children. They offer a constant intolerable rebuke.

He dosn't mind tourists too much. American Jewish tourists to him are somewhat ridiculous. They see everything through rose-colored glasses. Everything impresses them as heroic, historic, religious, holy, unreal. Every Israeli they encounter is a dear one. An Israeli teamster is picturesque. It all reminds American Jewish tourists of the stories their parents told of the *shtetl* (hometown) in Europe, or even in the United States a couple of generations ago. Tourists seem silly to Moishe in their flashy well-made clothes, crowned by *Koveh tembils* (peaked hats worn in the kibbutz) or *yarmelkes* (skull caps). Their women wear too much makeup, are heavily perfumed, and speak in high flat tones; they remind him of *Goyim.* It is hard to believe that they really are Jews. When they patronize him, he can likewise kid them and play at being picturesque.

But when they come to Israel as immigrants, they are something else again. They represent a threat. They are a constant reminder of his failure, of his inability to escape from the ghetto, from the *Goyim*. They create a bitter taste in his mouth, with their clean expensive clothing, their overt affluence, their glib speech, they represent a rebuke — unacceptable. They remind him somehow of his German captors and the *kapos* (Jewish informers) in the camps where he was a slave laborer. The fact that he knows quite well they are nothing of the kind is the more galling. He probably rebukes himself for his feelings. And does not realize that his attitude towards these newcomers is quite normal, quite natural, and can be summed up in a word or two — envy and frustration.

Perhaps behind the curse is an unconscious tribal memory. Perhaps he is saying, "you know who I am. I'm Moishe, the son of your father's brother. Don't you remember me?, your cousin whose father was left behind in the Hell of Poland when your father escaped to your heaven in America!"

The Aliyah Experience

Manifestly, the *aliyah* experience varies in many ways. The success or failure of a new immigrant to adjust can be predicted in a measurable degree by categoric variables, not excluding old lady luck herself.

A variable affecting the success or failure of immigration is the occupation of the immigrant. Those who come to Israel to take on a position in their own professions or trades have a big head start. The nature of the job or profession is of the utmost significance. Some medical doctors do not adjust too well, because of the differences in the way medicine is practiced in the United States and in Israel. American physicians have an appalling time trying to fit into the public medicine structure of Israel. Almost everyone in Israel belongs to a *kupat holim* (sick fund), most of them to the *Histadrut Kupat Holim,* which includes the majority of the workers in the country — about half of all the people. The rest of the population belongs to insurance health funds that are comparatively inexpensive and include hospitalization, surgery, drugs — in fact everything but dental service. This health setup functions well for the average Israeli. It is, however, impersonal and the income of doctors is far below that enjoyed by American practitioners who, in the United States and in other Anglo countries and Western Europe, are members of the economic elite.

The Israeli scale of medical know-how and scientific sophistication is measurably lower than in the Anglo countries and seriously frustrates the immigrant doctor whose motivation usually is not economic aggrandizement, but medical service. He also encounters the same arrogance of ignorance and the "Don't tell us how to do it, we know better" syndrome endemic throughout Israel. It is generally accepted that the overall performance and administration at Hadassah Hospital in Jerusalem, lavishly equipped and supported by the Jewish Zionist ladies of America,is below the standard of comparable hospitals in the United States, including those not nearly as well financed and supported as the Hadassah Hospital.

Lawyers do not fare much better than doctors. The language problem is more serious for lawyers than for doctors, because their function is based on verbal communication. Furthermore, in Israel as in all nations, lawyers occupy political and governmental positions that immigrant lawyers cannot easily enter. In the free-wheeling days at the beginning of the state, immigrant lawyers were able to find a spot with no difficulty. The Chief Justice of the Supreme Court, Simon Agranot, came from Chicago to Palestine as a young man with his immigrant parents and rose to a prominent position in the legal profession before 1948. The late chairman of the Jewish Agency, Louis Pincus, came to Palestine as a lawyer from South Africa. Few other Anglo lawyers, however, have succeeded in becoming part of the hierarchy after the Mandate Period. In fact, very few immigrants in recent years who were lawyers in their native lands have attempted to practice their profession in Israel, including me.

Professionals who have found it relatively easy to move into their metiér are pharmacists, engineers and others in fields where knowledge and skills are dominated by American and Western know-how, and the reference base is to a body of knowledge in English or French. In electronics, television, computer technology, the sciences, transplanted Western immigrants enjoy prestige and position and find their lives as Israelis pleasant and fruitful. They have been able for the most part to cope with the "I know as much or more than you" posture of some of their colleagues without much difficulty. It is to be expected that in fields of solid and esoteric knowledge, give and take is the order of the day, and chauvinistic bullshit doesn't get very far.

The story is quite different in manufacturing, business, and commerce. The history of the failure of American and Western European Jews who have come to Israel and established business enterprises or who have entered into partnerships with Israelis is depressing. Most of them have failed or have sold out at a loss, or have simply given up the effort. A wry joke so oft repeated as to become a cliché is, "Do you know how to make a small fortune in Israel?" "No. How?" "Come with a big one." One would think that the experience would have been just the opposite. The success of Jewish businessmen in the Western world is legendary; certainly this is true in the middle ground where large amounts of capital are not basic to success. Success has been achieved in the most diverse fields, especially where entrepreneurial boldness is of major importance and in new businesses and industries where no precedents exist. Adroitness and improvisation, cunning, daring, ambition, and hard work carried the Jewish immigrants in the Americas, England, and Western Europe from junkman to tycoon, from sweatshop worker to textile magnate, from pack peddler to department store owner, from green grocer to supermarket executive. Illiteracy was no big obstacle. "How come you're the rich merchant president of the synagogue, you can't even read?" "If I had known how to read, I would have been the *shamis* (sexton-janitor)." So the worn joke goes.

In recent generations the Jews in America, England, France, Italy, have moved into the formerly all gentile fields of finance, insurance, banking, construction, heavy industry, plastics — everything. And now their children and grandchildren are a significant segment of the elite in science, engineering, electronics, all the arts, and they occupy prominent positions in the judiciary, government, university faculties.

How is it possible that so many Jews coming from such a heritage have been unsuccessful businessmen in Israel? Largely because they came to Israel under the spell of a myth. At home their caution, adroitness, and alert business sense were always honed, but they came to Israel completely disarmed. Very few Jews have come to Israel from the Anglo countries for the purpose of increasing their fortunes, to become rich or richer. They come idealistically to apply their skills and invest their capital to help build up the Fatherland. The most sophisticated Jewish businessmen from America, South Africa, England, France, Italy, Greece, Turkey turn into naive pigeons in Israel. By the time they brush the stardust out of their eyes, they find they have been taken — not necessarily by knavery (although that too) but by Levantine obscurantism, indolence, ignorance, and stiffnecked refusal to acknowledge experience and expertise, and by resentment of strangers.

Age is an important factor. Generally, the younger the immigrant is, the more likely he will adjust to Israel favorably and "make it." Young people are more flexible and more open. They are more pliable and receptive to new experience. It is especially true that they can make friends more quickly among their age peers. Their young Israeli acquaintances are more ready than their elders to accept them, to receive them into their social and cultural millieu. In short, a successful age group in adjusting is that between the ages of 18 and 22. This is the age of college and university years. Those who enter the universities soon after coming to Israel, if they come on *aliyah* with their families, often succeed.

Teen-age children have greater difficulty adjusting to Israeli life. The very young ones under the age of ten quickly learn Hebrew and in a year or two they are indistinguishable from other Israelis. But the teen-agers, especially those between the ages of 12 and 16 have a tough time. This is the age at which youngsters are most clannish and intolerant towards strangers. They have developed friendships and mutuality of interests and concerns since their early school days, and newcomers seeking to enter into their closed circles are not welcome. The difficulty of communicating in Hebrew is a further and almost insurmountable barrier. Adolescence also seems to be the most difficult period to learn Hebrew, not an easy language to learn at best. Many immigrant families have returned to the United States after a year or two because their teen-age children became miserably unhappy and dispirited, even seriously emotionally disturbed.

Most of the Americans and Anglos who have emigrated to Israel comprise family groups consisting of husband, wife and children. The age span of the children is wide, encompassing infants, twenty-year olds, and all the ages in between. Individual experiences in the adjustment (or maladjustment) of the children to the new environment vary greatly because of the different factors involved — religion; knowledge of the language; place of residence; number of Israeli relatives and friends; affluence and education of the parents; and many others. The degree of success of the children in the effort to assimilate is often decisive to the family's determination to remain in Israel or go back to America.

The problems of Anglo immigrant housewifes are difficult in Israel. The male spouse is more frequently the one who wanted to move to Israel. The wives usually acceded with reluctance and resignation or with mixed enthusiasm and trepidation. They were less ready to leave family and friends, the neighborhood, the familiar shops. They were less romantic, more conservative, and more realistic. Women are more aware of the potential loneliness and frustrations the children will face. They often anticipate the boredom ahead. The husband knows or thinks he knows what he is going to do in his business, job, or profession. Even if he doesn't succeed, or if he encounters unanticipated and unexpected problems, he keeps occupied. The "little woman" stays at home surrounded by neighbors with whom she can scarcely talk beyond pidgin Hebrew. Even the routines of shopping and taking care of simple household matters, which ordinarily would have been welcome chores, turn into minor nightmares because of the language barrier. Second only to the unhappiness of children, the unhappiness of wives lures immigrant Anglo families back to their native lands.

In Israel there are several thousands of older immigrants from the United States, most of whom live in nursing homes. Several hundred of them come each year, and they will continue to come in the years ahead. This is an immigration that started before the turn of the century and has continued uninterrupted through the years. The earlier ones were religious. They didn't come to live in Palestine or in Israel, they came to die in the Holy Land and settled mainly in Jerusalem, Safed, or B'nei Brak. Many of those who come now are not religious and they fondly hope to develop an interesting life for themselves in a Jewish country. If they have some funds and can afford the more expensive establishments, their material existence is very satisfactory. But they are not assimilated into the land. They live much as they would in similar institutions in America. They are lonely of course, but no more so than they would be back home. The Jewish tradition of the grandparents living with their married children has disappeared in America as in many other countries. The intrigue of living in Israel for these old folks is a plus, but it is diminished by not seeing their children or grandchilren except on rare occasions when they come to Israel as tourists.

Israelis do not normally confine their "senior citizens" (what an abominable phrase!) in institutional type hotels or hostels. This form of "enlightenment" exists only minimally in Israel. Cost, of course, is a factor, but the Jewish tradition of the grandparents living with their children still is strong among the Israelis and one would like to believe the practice will continue even when they can afford to place their parents in nursing homes. Love, affection, and respect for parents obtain among all Israelis. The family as a unit is a real foundation of Israeli society and the unchallenged position of parents as the heads of the family is de rigueur. Although the Yom Kippur War shook all Israeli institutions, the family unit became stronger than ever.

The Israelis, therefore, look somewhat askance at these old folks from America, dully living out their years in modern, sterile buildings. They pity them compassionately, recognizing them for what they are, strangers in a strange land.

My own Aliyah started with more than an average dose of innocent idealism. To appreciate how this old Israeli hand was himself blinded by the stardust, I'll have to take you back to the beginning of my life, my Jewish consciousness, and my long involvement in the history and development of the Jewish state.

Top: Late Prime Minister Levi Eshkol and the author, circa 1955. The author was then national chairman of B'nai Brith Israel activities and Israel bonds as well as Midwest Israel bond chairman.

Bottom: Late President of Israel Itzhak Ben-Zvi, head of the Jewish National Fund (former Israeli ambassador to Brazil and France), the author, then international chairman of the B'nai Brith Israel Commission, and Samuel Levitsky, the author's successor as B'nai Brith chairman, Jerusalem, 1962.

II

Turning Out Jewish

When did it start with me? To be a Jew? To be Jewish? Probably hundreds and hundreds of years before I was born. Thousands more likely. Somewhere in the mob chasing around in the Sinai desert waiting for Moses to come down from the mountain, and when he did he screamed at them, my forebears, for dancing around the golden calf. Or years later in some crooked little lane in Jerusalem trying to avoid the heavy-footed drunken Roman soldiers, and hating them. I became Jewish? Or, maybe in Baghdad trying to make social sense out of the harsh chapters of the *Tanach* (Old Testament). Or maybe in Alexandria fashioning leather saddles and camel harnesses; and later in Madrid, maybe still working the leather and then, perhaps in Italy on the Adriatic Sea and later trudging eastward to Prussia and on into the ghetto of Plotsk on the Dnieper River, 100 versts from Warsaw; and all the time swaying and poring over the Talmudic obscurities, the multi-colored robe of Joseph sobered into a black caftan and the gay-colored turban into a round fur *stremele* (hat worn by religious Jews in Eastern Europe). The same costume much like this for hundreds of years among the unfriendly uncircumcised Poles.

But I was always with my people, my wives and children, my grandparents and my grandchildren, uncles and cousins; always restless, dissatisfied, possessed and dispossessed, I always knew who I was and where I had come from and who my people were. I was a Jew; a man of the Book and no question about it. The Book was the beginning and end whether I believed it or not. Even when I disobeyed it, defiled it, I didn't dare ignore it. I didn't deny the fact that I was emboweled in it, or dare to question why. Ever it encircled me like the *tallis* (prayer shawl) wrapped around my people's heads in the synagogue all those centuries. And the synagogue was my home; to live in or to run away from. But my home nevertheless.

It had been ever so, all of those years since we plunged through the raging waters of the Red Sea grasping Moses' skirts while Pharoah's soldiers were drowning behind us; Hittites and Assyrians, the Roman soldiers, the Moslems and the Spaniards, and the Moors and Polacks and Russians harried us, chased us, robbed us, and yea, often befriended us. But even as they befriended us, they huddled us into dirty casbahs and ghettos in little villages and market towns and into the great cities of North Africa, Spain, Italy, the Netherlands, the German principalities, Balkan kingdoms, Turkey and Greece, Russia and Poland, Latvia, Lithuania, Galicia, Bessarabia, Minsk, Pinsk, Plonsk, Munich, Czernowisz, and hundreds of other consonated towns in Hungary and Serbia, Yemen and Abyssinia, Germany and Morocco, whose names they tacked onto us as *shem mishpochah* (family name). But my first name remained a talisman that I was a son of the fathers, the patriarchs, the judges, and the kings — Abraham, Isaac, Jacob, Moses, Aaron, Samuel, Noah, Isaiah, Jeremiah, however strange the spelling or pronunciation — even until me, Moses Ben Solomon Alexander.

The unbroken thread unwound on and on and on unto my very own father, revolted by the cant and hypocrisy and poverty, my own father emancipated, running away from the ghetto in Poland straight into the ghettos of London and Birmingham, seeking and finding his own people, whether consciously or not. Finding his little *Plotzker* bride from a Polish *shtetl* (village) in his province and sailing across the sea to the *Goldeneh Medinah* (the golden land) and back into a midwest small town ghetto in Grand Rapids, Michigan — this time, however, no walls, no caftan, no restrictions, legal or illegal of church or state, not even a particular neighborhood, and half shunning the synagogue, even scoffing at it; rationalizing its obvious absurdity. But not escaping it. Escaping it only much later — or at least avoiding it — in the musty cells of the backs of delicatessen stores, and finally assaying futilely one last escape to California there to die in a city park in the ghetto under the pleasant Los Angeles sun.

But with me, this was all Jewish history. Real, but remote. It didn't burn me. It was not my bag, not my scene. Not much more real than George Washington and the cherry tree. Abraham Lincoln studying in the candlelight and walking in the winter to return a borrowed book was more my father Abraham than that other bearded one who, they say, was ready to cut his son up to prove his faith in his demanding unlovable Jehovah.

My God was not that Jehovah — my God was an ephemeral do-gooder, pleasant, beneficent and merciful. A red, white and blue flag-waver who freed the slaves so that George Washington Carver could invent peanut butter in Iowa. My God was the one who in his all-knowing wisdom helped the valiant American pioneers and Civil War generals, the Custers and Sheridans and Shermans and their cowboy scouts to kill the savage Indians and settle their survivors in nice reservations and teach them to be farmers so that the noble white American pioneers could steal their land and possess the continent from sea to shining sea. The Lord who blessed America was my God and often as not he wore a turned around collar and his hair was cut in a crew-cut, and he had pink, clean-shaven cheeks. And he sure didn't look like a rabbi.

The *cheder* (Hebrew school) and synagogue I attended in Grand Rapids as a small boy were not oppressive to me but also not important. Mostly it was a rather annoying inconvenience and imposition on my playtime after school. The smatterings of Bible stories — Hebrew and Yiddish — gleaned there were remote and unreal to me and I made no effort to relate them to my existence. My real life was in Union Public School and in the streets and backyards of Grand Rapids and the fields and forests and the banks of the Grand River that flowed past my house.

My concern with God was a concern with the all-seeing guide and censor to whom I wrote my own prayer at the age of six.

> "Father, I thank thee for the day
> And now I am going to pray.
> Forgive me the sins I did in the day,
> and tomorrow I will try to do the right.
> Father, good night.
> (And please, Father, wake me up
> early in the morning!)"

So in my early years at least I was not tied by the historical Jewish string. The hundreds and thousands of years of differentness, ghetto living, religious observance, anti-Semitism, and simply pure Christian snobbery did not shape me to be set and baked in Jewish concrete. All of this had existed, had been real for Jews throughout the years and ineluctably made them who they were. As long as they remained observant and in the ghetto — tallis Jews — they were, of course, total Jews — constrained, parochial, myopic, filled with myths concerning the goyim and the strange world outside the walls.

It seems to me that as a child I didn't have any conscious or even subconscious awareness of Jewishness as a special circumstance that set me apart or molded me to live in a style substantially different from the other children in my community. True I went to synagogue on occasion. More often not. So also did my companions in school and in the neighborhood go to church or did not. True there were some other Jewish kids in school, a few even in my classes. I knew them all, and of course I knew that they too were Jewish. But they weren't necessarily my friends, or chums, and some of them I didn't like at all. We had something in common, to be sure. Most of us went to *cheder* after regular school two or three times a week. But we weren't united against a common enemy — the goyim, the others. Nor did I and the other Jewish youngsters feel like traitors if our chums were non-Jewish kids.*

When I was ten years old, my family moved from Grand Rapids to Newark and shortly thereafter to Ridgewood, New Jersey. There for the first time in my short life I became aware of the fact that some Jews lived entirely as Jews in America, and that this Jewish community culture was current, present, and real, not musty ancient history. I was introduced to the startling fact of the great ghetto of the lower east side of New York City.

I met for the first time my grandfather, my mother's father, a venerable old gentleman with an awesome white beard. He had lived in England and the United States for 30 years and still spoke only Yiddish. I couldn't communicate with him and though I respected and liked him, he was a strange foreign being to me. I had to tell myself that he was related to me. Although he wore an immaculate Prince Albert coat, fine shirts, and a derby hat that fit him, he lived with his wife and two grown sons in a two-room flat on the fifth floor of a walk-up tenement on Lewis Street in the heart of the ghetto. They had no bathroom but shared a toilet in the hallway with all four families living on their floor. The poorest families in Grand Rapids lived in better quarters.

My grandfather's wife, my mother's step-mother, was a handsome woman not much older than my mother. She spoke good English and I became well-acquainted with her during the next few years. But I didn't regard her as my grandmother, but rather as my grandfather's wife. Her two sons were of course Americans. But they had always lived in the Jewish milieu of New York and they were products of that intensely Jewish atmosphere. It was a lively, colorful, culturally rich and pulsating environment, but very foreign to me. And so were my uncles.

There did not develop in me any trauma or uneasiness in becoming acquainted with my new found relatives and their life style. My mother's full brother, seven years younger than she, had been brought to England as a baby, and at 15 came to the United States with his father and step-mother. A few years later, he left the New York City ghetto and went to work as a tailor in East Orange, New Jersey. He had learned the tailoring

*My closest and oldest Jewish friend, Abe Drasin, was elected Democratic Mayor of Grand Rapids in November, 1975 — to the discomfiture of Jerry Ford.

trade from his father who had been a master tailor in Poland and England. At the time I first met him, some fifteen years after he came to America, he had become well-established as a respected businessman in a non-Jewish community. But he remained all of his life ethnically Jewish, the stamp of the ghetto indelibly on him.

My family remained in Newark only a year and a half. The neighborhood in which we lived and the school that I attended were not very much different from my school and home in Grand Rapids. However, I did become aware for the first time of the existence of big-city ethnic groups. Not just the Jewish quarter of Newark, which at that time was a considerable area, but the Italian neighborhoods whose first and second generation residents were then becoming the dominant minority group of Newark. At least half the children in my classes were of Italian extraction, as were most of my friends. The only result of this brief encounter was a facility to swear rather fluently in Italian. Even that didn't remain with me.

There was no Jewish greening for me in Newark. There was the same few Jewish kids in my classes as in Grand Rapids. I knew them all and became friendly with them or not, as personal compatibility indicated.

Even the smattering of exposure to the cheder I had attended in Grand Rapids ceased. As long as we lived in Grand Rapids, my family quite naturally established a close relationship with many of the some hundred or so families that constituted the Grand Rapids Jewish community in the early years of the twentieth century. This was pleasant and desirable for my mother, who was a gregarious and outgoing personality. My antisocial father tenuously fraternized with the other Jewish families only to please my mother. My mother even maintained a kosher kitchen, and we observed the major Jewish holidays in the traditional way. Through my child's eyes, however, I was aware of the growing restiveness of my father concerning what he considered medieval and outmoded traditions imported from the ghettos of Europe. His private attitudes and his personal ethical stance, I learned much later, were reinforced by a powerful and complete revulsion for the Orthodox Judaism he had left behind in Plotsk. An unhappy and disastrous childhood life had goaded him into running away from home and saying good-bye to all that at the age of twelve.

His father, Yossel, a prosperous leather merchant, died when my father, the last of 24 children, was five years old. After his death, those of the grown children of Yossel's first wife who remained in Plotsk, took over the business and the household and began to treat my father's mother and her brood like domestic servants. My father explained to me that this treatment was under the guise and framework of a traditional

Jewish religious atmosphere. Little wonder, then, that the certainty that Orthodox Judaism was all fraud and hypocrisy pulsated through my father's veins.

My father didn't dislike his fellow Jews *per se*. He just didn't automatically like them because they were Jews and, therefore, perforce his brethren. He was an instinctual socialist, a humanist, an ethicalist. He probably never realized (and wouldn't have cared if he had) that his attitudes concerning the equality of all men were a part of his Jewish ethos.

In Grand Rapids he had few friends or intimates. Those he had were of the same stripe and inclination as he — self-taught, independent thinking men who had cast off the shibboleths of cant and superstition. They considered the "Chosen People" concept of the Bible to be arrant nonsense. They, like my father, were first-generation Jews from Eastern Europe, mainly Russia and Poland. Most of them were craftsmen — metal workers, tailors, junkmen, workers all. My father and his brother-in-law, Aaron Wiseman, were master cabinet makers having been trained as apprentices in England. They were the only Jewish cabinet makers in Grand Rapids, which was then the capital of American furniture making.

Though their small circle of intimates were Jews, my father and Aaron and their friends had little in common with or little liking for the majority of their fellow Jewish immigrants in Grand Rapids. They had as little to do with them as possible, except in the *Arbeiter Ring,* the Jewish Workmen's Circle, a fraternal organization through which they channeled their populist aspirations in common with most Jewish workers of their generation.

By the time we moved to Newark, in November 1920, my father had become a small tradesman, a businessman. Never again did he become a part of any community. He became a loner and remained one for the rest of his life.

Despite my mother's half-hearted pleading, my father resolutely refused to let me continue to go to *cheder.* There was to be no question of my being *bar-mitzvahed,* perfunctorily or otherwise. Secretly I was greatly relieved because I could then devote my time to school and play and reading, and have more time to cultivate my new friends and acquaintances and explore the big strange city in which we lived.

The pretense of a kosher home was also quietly dropped. My father pointed out that to maintain *kashrut* at home was ridiculous while running a delicatessen store in which the principal items sold were pork products. However I became acquainted with ham, bacon, and sausages only at our store. My mother's traditional upbringing would not permit of such forbidden food in our home. My father understood this prejudice and respected it.

In the summer of 1922 my father sold his delicatessen store in Newark and bought a bigger one in Ridgewood. The regrets I had about leaving Grand Rapids, which had never completely disappeared in Newark, finally vanished in Ridgewood. It was a community, I discovered to my delight, very much like Grand Rapids, only smaller. I soon settled into a pleasant high school routine making new friends. There were only three or four Jewish families in the town and there was no Jewish community whatsoever. None of my close friends in the five years we lived there was Jewish. I never saw any of my classmates again until our 50th Anniversary Reunion in June 1976.

On Christmas Eve of 1922 my grandfather showed up at our store. He had been driven over to Ridgewood from East Orange by his son, my uncle Morris, for whom my grandfather worked as a tailor. *Zayde* (grandfather) wasted no time in announcing the purpose of his visit.

In Yiddish he admonished my father and mother. "He's a Jewish boy and he is today 13 years old." How he knew my exact birthday I never learned. "He must be bar-mitzvahed. I know you were not," he told my father accusingly, "and that you do not care about *Yiddishkeit* (Jewishness). But he must know he is a Jew. It is not fair to him otherwise." My mother was pleased and said so. My father was not at all angry, only somewhat bemused. He knew how un-Jewish I was, probably even more so than my older brother, Joe, who had been casually bar-mitzvahed at the synagogue in Grand Rapids.

So it was agreed and then and there in the back room of our store, I was wrapped in my grandfather's tallis and he and my father showed me how to wrap the *tvillin* (phylacteries) around my arm and forehead. I was amazed at how fluent my father was in reading the prayers .I read several prayers and a short passage from the Bible in very imperfect and halting Hebrew, prompted kindly by my father and grandfather. My mother and uncle stood by and beamed. I enjoyed the whole thing.

After the ceremony, which lasted about five minutes, my grandfather handed me a new silver dollar, and my uncle gave me a ten-dollar bill, the most money I had ever had. My father announced that he had bought a bicycle for me — almost new and in good condition.

I knew that this was his way of making no concession to the bar-mitzvah idea, as he had previously told me about the bike. Not only was it a birthday present, but it was a needed vehicle in our business. I was the store's delivery boy.

The bar-mitzvah was the total of my Jewish religious experience in Ridgewood, and for that matter for the next dozen years. But my mother insisted all through my high school years that I should not go to school on the Jewish New Year and on *Yom Kippur* (the day of atonement), and my father did not demur. Nor did I. I took it for granted that I was Jewish. I quite agreed that it would be a studied insult to my group and could be construed as a desire to conceal my MOT (membership in the tribe) if I attended classes on the holidays. At the time, I had very little knowledge of the American Jewish community and its complexities. I did not realize that assimilation was coveted by many American Jews who found their Jewishness a burden and hindrance and wished to cast it off.

I was not at all aware of the polite, subtle social discrimination manifested toward me in school because I was Jewish. If anyone had suggested that to me, I would have laughed. But in looking back now, I must confess that some discrimination must have been there on occasion. Slights, and they did occur, I easily explained away on other perfectly valid grounds, such as, the kid who slighted me was a jerk and I didn't like him/her anyway.

I now realize in recalling some of my schoolmates and teachers, remembering their names and their appearance, that they probably were Jewish and that their families had become assimilated to the point that they did not consider themselves Jewish. I recall particularly a favorite teacher of mine, Miss Greenwald, who was director of music and the conductor of the school orchestra. Though Miss Greenwald and I became good friends, there was no "Jewish" bond between us. In my third year at school, Miss Greenwald was married and I and several other of her students were invited to her wedding. I vaguely remember that a reform rabbi officiated at the ceremony but I cannot be sure. He may have been a Justice of the Peace or a Unitarian minister. The religious part of the ceremony obviously made no impact on me. What I do remember is how beautiful Miss Greenwald looked in her wedding gown, and the piece of wedding cake she gave me to put under my pillow for good luck.

Being a small, underdeveloped boy in my high school years and younger than most of my classmates, I had very few "girlfriends." The only girl I had any success with was a beautiful blonde schoolmate named Frances Strezeski. We both lived in the same neighborhood, so far from Ridgewood High School that we had to take a school bus every morning. Through this daily contact, and because she was the art editor of the school magazine and I was a reporter, we became good friends and constant companions. She even let me kiss her on occasion, although I'm sure her interest in me was purely platonic, even though mine in her was not. My friendship with Frances triggered the only racial prejudice ever manifested by my father.

Frances' father was a prosperous florist, a first generation Pole who had lived in the Ridgewood area for many years. My father had met him several times. They had even spoken a bit of Polish to each other. One day I happened to mention that Frances and I were friends. My father bristled. "She's that Polack's daughter, isn't she?" "Yes, what of it?" "I don't like him." "Why not?" "Because he's a Polack. All Polacks are lousy. Let me tell you something. When I was a boy in Poland most Polacks treated Jews like dirt, just because they were Jews." "That doesn't make Mr. Strezeski a bad man." "I'll tell you something else. If there is a God, he's not a just God. Poland is one of the most beautiful countries in the world. I've never seen such a land, even Germany or this country or England." "How could God create such a beautiful country and give it to the Polacks?" He was being facetious, but he more than half meant what he said. He didn't convince me at all. I was offended. "You don't have to like Mr. Strezeski. I like Frances. She's my friend. And she knows I'm Jewish, too." "Ok, ok", my father said. The subject was never again mentioned between us.

The expression "Anti-Semitism" is inaccurate and ugly. Whoever coined the phrase was presumptuously ignorant in encompassing all the sons of Shem. If the term had developed in popular usage as discrimination and racial snobbery towards all the descendants of Shem, Jews and Arabs, Palestinians, Israelis, American Jews, German Jews, Egyptians, Iraqis, Syrians, Lebanese, Yemenites, and even Iranis, Moroccans and Libyans, perhaps the Arabs and the Jews might have developed some sense of kinship in common oppression.

But unfortunately, it has always meant hatred, contempt, suspicion, and even envy of Jews alone wherever they might be. Only in Israel where it is impossible to be an anti-Semite per se, the expression is manifestly absurd. You have to call your shots much more accurately there. Nor is there a corollary of the expression. No one talks of "Semitophiles." There are Judophiles, Lovers of Zion, Nasserites, Admirers of Arabs.

I was fifteen years old when I first heard the expression. The absurdity of calling anyone an anti-Semite struck me so forcibly that I can remember the actual place where I first heard it and the man who uttered it. I was walking with my older sister and a man named Paul Stone, a Jewish emigrant from Warsaw who had been in the United States about ten years. He referred to someone about whom they were talking as "an anti-Semite." He pronounced it in the Jewish fashion, the "a" broad, and the accent on the "it". The expression was meaningless to me, but sounded menacing. "You don't know? You don't know what is an anti-Semite?" he asked. "Well , it's time you knew. It's someone who hates Jews and does bad to them. The world is full of them." "That's foolish. Why should anyone hate Jews? And besides Jews aren't the only Semites.

Most all the people in the Near East are Semites." I was displaying my erudition. "So an anti-Semite must be someone against Mesapotamians and Lebanese and all the Semitic people. And you can't be just against people that way." "No, it's only against Jews, the anti-Semites, the bastards," he said. I appealed to my sister. "Is he right?" "I guess so." "I don't believe it," I said flatly. "It's nuts."

In the years ahead I was to learn only too well how wrong I was, not only at the hands of Gentiles. I have encountered prejudice from "uppity" Jews because I was derived from Jews of Polish ancestry. In fact, I have probably experienced more prejudice from Jews than non-Jews in my own personal life.

Prejudice against Jews in Czarist Russia, Poland, and Austro-Hungarian Empire, the Balkan States and Hitler's Germany since the second half of the nineteenth century is as ugly a manifestation of man's bestiality and ignorance and incapacity for decency as any group injustice in the history of mankind. An anomaly in my own experience is that this virus has had more than considerable effect on my activities, thoughts, and concern, despite the almost total lack of personal exposure to it.

From Ridgewood High School I went to Ann Arbor, back to my native Michigan. For the next six years, from the end of the roaring twenties through the beginning years of the great economic depression of the thirties, I was a college student and, in 1933, graduated from the University of Michigan Law School. When I arrived in the fall of 1927 the physical appearance of Ann Arbor was very familiar to me; the wooden houses and brick porches, the crisp, beautiful autumns and the green, balmy springs, and the sunny cold snow-covered winters were the same as I remembered from my childhood. But soon enough I was made to realize that I had not come back to the Grand Rapids of my childhood. I had left there an innocent young child and remained innocent enough while in the New Jersey environment which was comparatively idyllic and sheltered. Even the maturation of the puberty period did not disturb me very much. I came to Ann Arbor virginal.

At college I stumbled over the threshold of the adult world rather abruptly and not too well-prepared. This lack of preparation, however, was a boon in a way. Despite the fact that my brother, brother-in-law, cousins, and acquaintances in Grand Rapids were or had been students at the university in Ann Arbor, I had not been realistically briefed about college life. From my earliest years it was taken for granted that my brother and I would go to school there and become lawyers. (This was certainly a Jewish bit.) So my preconceptions of the University and of life there were romantic dreams that in no way resembled the realities I found.

The disillusionment was complete but not profound. I was able to compare the life I found with what I had expected with a cold and judgmental eye. I discovered that some Jewish students lived in ghettos, whether of their making or not. To me their rationalizations and snobbish inventions were silly and false. At least so I quickly came to believe, and to decide that they were not for me.

The more affluent Jewish students lived in Jewish fraternity houses and their environment was secularly Jewish. I found the atmosphere artificial and stifling and after one semester was bounced out because I refused to accept the childish rigidity that required freshmen to serve the upperclassmen as batmen. I was pledged to the fraternity only because my older brother Joseph was a member. In any event, I could not afford the tariff and was relieved to live in rooming houses and to work in the kitchens of other fraternity houses.

The greater freedom of living as an independent "barb" (barbarian) made it possible for me to make friends of my own choosing, although the majority of my companions were Jewish students. I became interested in the Hillel Foundation, the Jewish student organization supported by B'nai Brith and for the first time learned about Zionism from the late Maurice Pekarsky, a young man from Grand Rapids whose father had been my *melamed* (teacher) when I was a boy in *cheder.* Pekarsky was a gentle, knowledgeable pixie of a man who became a rabbi and director of the Hillel Foundation at the University of Chicago and later in Jerusalem.

Despite my exposure to Zionism and Jewish history and my activities as an officer of the Hillel Foundation and the editor of the Hillel News Weekly, the college years affected my Jewish consciousness only superficially and mostly negatively. I had no real interest in religious Judaism and neither did most of my fellow Jewish students. I did learn, however, that the Jewish scene in America socially, at least, was deeply ethnic. Jewish students roomed with other Jewish students and associated with Jews for the most part, as a natural extension of their home environment and because most of the gentile students associated with gentiles. I too drifted quite casually into associations with Jews, that is, with students who incidentally happened to be Jewish, but not from a conscious deliberate seeking out of Jews, qua Jews, or because of an antipathy to non-Jews. In fact, my associations were most catholic. Through contacts in and out of the classroom I developed many close friendships with non-Jews. In fact, in my law school years most of my companions were non-Jewish, again for the casual reason that the majority of students were gentile.

These were the years of my American Jewish greening. I became consciously aware for the first time of anti-Semitism, polite, subtle, unspoken, but very real. Jewish students joined Jewish fraternities because they were not admitted to gentile fraternities. There were unwritten *numeri clausi* in all student activities, athletic and cerebral; and also in the faculty. Gentile coeds didn't date Jewish boys, and Jewish boys were not invited to gentile sorority parties. In my first semester, while still living in the fraternity house, I invited a classmate to a fraternity dance. She accepted only to inform me a few days later that she couldn't keep the date. Why? Because, she said, her sorority sisters had told her she could not go to a Jewish fraternity house. She was from a small town in upper Michigan and had never met a "Jew." The poor girl was more shocked and humiliated than I. But she didn't go to the dance.

Though I did get to know a number of Jewish girls during my college years, most of my girl-boy friendships in those days were with non-Jewish girls. This wasn't accidental. The Jewish girls were daughters of "Jewish Mothers", conditioned to size up every Jewish boy they met as a prospective husband. My interests were simply fun and games.

At the beginning of my junior year at Michigan I fell in love. Vivien Jean was beautiful, charming, talented — and Catholic. I met her in Grand Rapids just before classes started and spent five glorious days and nights with her. When I left for Ann Arbor we were sweethearts.

On New Year's Eve 1929 at a party in Grand Rapids we decided to elope during the February semester break, though I had no money and faced almost 4 more years of schooling. I had just turned 20. But Vivien had a job as a travelling commercial artist and we were desperately in love. The differences in religion and background were of no significance to either of us. The matter of my parents' approval or disapproval never crossed my mind, and Vivien was certain that her mother and architect father, though casual Catholics, would "adore" me.

I was amused and flattered when Vivien confessed to me that she had for months been studying with a Reform Rabbi in Rochester, New York, to convert to Judaism. She had decided that she must become a Jewess to insure the success of our marriage, even though I had insisted that I was Jewish ethnically, not religiously. I am certain that her desire to convert was a wholly romantic impulse reflecting her urge completely to identify with me. To my beloved I was very much a Jew and that to her was something exotic.

Fate decreed that our marriage was not to be. Vivien Jean smashed up her car and broke a couple of ribs while driving to Ann Arbor to fetch me to the altar. By the time she recovered, the school semester had started and Vivien had gone back to Grand Rapids. I never saw her again. Later in life, I married three Jewish girls. Not all at the same time.

By the time I arrived in Chicago to look for a job in a law office, I was quite fully aware that I would be subjected to some restrictions, however slight, by the mere fact of being Jewish, whatever that nebulous fact meant. It was 1933, the nadir of the great depression. Jobs in law offices were hard to find, and paid less for the first year or so than I had been making as a waiter in college. I was made to understand by the secretary of the law faculty, without being told outright that I should seek a job in a "Jewish firm" because my chances in the non-Jewish firms were nil, even though I was a graduate of a prestigious school whose alumni headed many of the most powerful Chicago law firms.

I was not convinced that this was true until after a few dispiriting weeks of seeking a job in a score of offices, either predominately gentile or Jewish. I didn't get a job, but I was kindly given several leads in gentile offices. It turned out that all of these possibilities were in Jewish firms. I finally got the message. After a stint as a waiter at the Chicago World Fair in 1933 (where my closest waiter friends were Syrian Arabs) I did find a job working for a lawyer. Interestingly enough, he was not Jewish.

During those years, Hitler and the Nazis surfaced in Germany and I became aware of the obscene anti-Semitism he had unleashed to propel himself to power. During the decade of the thirties, however, the horror of the impending holocaust was not obvious to me. The fascism in Germany did not seem too much unlike the ongoing Mussolini fascism in Italy and Franco's counter-socialism in Spain and the added dimension of anti-Semitism was almost unreal, remote and difficult to believe.

I was busily engaged in the practice of law and in caring for a young family and had little thought or concern or heightened awareness despite the Jewish community into which I had been catapulted as an adult in Chicago. I joined a Reform Temple because it was the thing to do, certainly not from any strong conviction of religious Judaism. I joined the B'nai Brith in 1938 and became active in a local lodge because friends and relatives asked me to, and because it provided a social outlet, and appeased a sense of uneasiness that I ought to "do something" Jewish. During this period, I even joined the Zionist Organization of Chicago, dutifully paid the nominal dues, but never once attended a meeting.

Only after Pearl Harbor and America's entry into the war did I really accept the fact that the whole of Europe was in flames, and that the Nazis had set out to conquer the world, that the theater of the absurd practices of American native two-bit Hitlers and anti-Semitic organizations was not *kindershpiel* (child's play).

I and all Jews in America discovered to our horror — and to be candid, to our deep shame and sense of guilt — that our fellow Jews in Europe were being systematically decimated and enslaved. We were faced with the stark fact that all of the three million Jews in Poland faced extermination and that millions of others in the Balkans, in Holland, Belgium, Italy, France, Scandinavia, might suffer the same fate. We could no longer rationalize away the fact that we had been warned by men like Rabbi Stephen Wise and others that the German Jewish community was being destroyed. We could no longer pooh-pooh and resignedly say, "What can we do about it?"

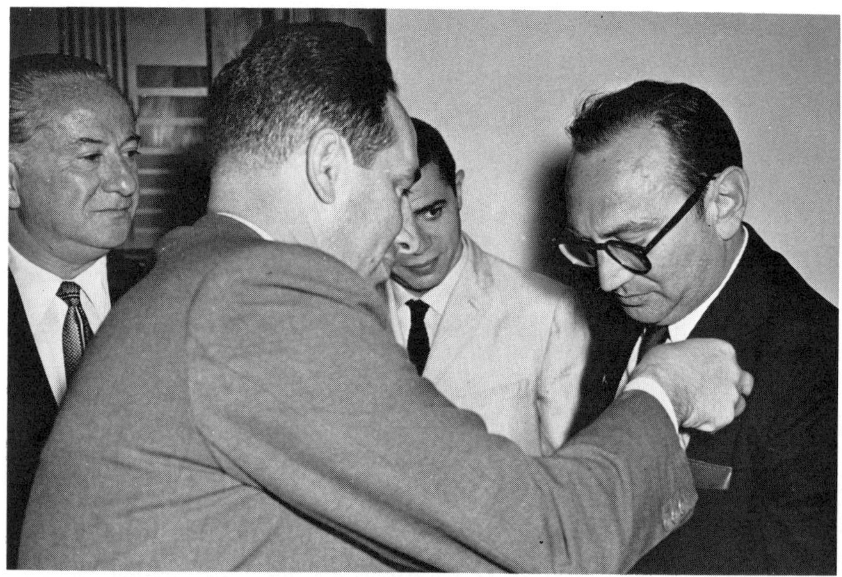

Shimon Peres, now Israel defense minister, then director general of the Israel Defense Ministry under Ben-Gurion, presents an award to the author for his B'nai Brith work for Israel U.S.O. Behind them, from left, Meyer Halperin, N.Y. Israel chairman for B'nai Brith, and Philip Katz, then director of B'nai Brith Israel Commission, now public relations director of Ben-Gurion U. Be'er Sheva.

III

Becoming Involved

1. American Federation of Polish Jews

One day in early 1942 my secretary announced that a Mr. Zaleg Tygel was in my office and wished to see me. He had been sent to me by a mutual friend, Charles Zakin. Charlie was a delightful vagabond of a Yiddishist whom I had known for years and who had introduced me to Yiddish literature and poetry. He had had little success in teaching me Yiddish but had enchanted me with his knowledge of the contemporary Jewish literary and intellectual scene in the United States and Europe. Through Charlie I had become acquainted with a fascinating world of writers, actors, playwrights, poets, of whose very existence I had never been aware.

I had not the slightest idea who Z. Tygel was. I did know that anyone who was sent to me by Charlie Zakin would be someone I would want to see. Tygel was short, slight, a dark dynamo of a man with piercing black eyes that twinkled nevertheless. In a quiet polite manner he wasted no time explaining his mission. "Mr. Alexander," he said, "are you aware of what is happening to our people in Poland?" Without giving me an opportunity to ask him who "our people" were, he went on, "I happen to know that you are a Polish Jew. Your parents came from Plotsk near

Warsaw, where I came from four years ago. You are an American-born Jew, but you are not as far away from Polish Jewry as you may think. You have many relatives in Poland, whether you know them or not." All of this was said in a calm, portentous tone that didn't allow for any possible contradiction. He spoke good English, meticulous and mellifluous, with a marked Eastern European accent — the English of a cultured intellectual European.

Having made his point and reduced me to speechlessness, he proceeded to relate the history of the Jews in Poland and then told me about the Polish Jewish communities of Europe and America. He was by profession a writer and journalist. He had emigrated from Warsaw in the middle thirties leaving a successful career as a writer, newspaper man, and reporter for several Polish newspapers, and a columnist for a leading Jewish newspaper. In New York he became a Yiddish journalist and launched a career as an encyclopedist in Yiddish and English. This is how he earned his bread. He made it clear that his sole mission in life now was to help rescue the Jews who were trapped in Poland by the Nazi invasion. During the next four hours I learned more about the people from whom I derived than I had known all of my life.

Tygel told me about an organization called "The American Federation of Polish Jews," which had been in existence since 1895. For two decades it had thrived as a philanthropic and cultural institution, but had dwindled into desuetude by the 1930's. Tygel and a group of colleagues in New York had revived the Federation as a medium for organizing efforts on behalf of their fellows in Poland. Tygel had come to Chicago to reorganize the Chicago branch. He pointed out to me that most all of those active in the work were first-generation immigrants from Poland and there was a desperate need to involve Americans of Polish Jewish ancestry.

The Federation's raison d'etre was to help Jews get out of Poland to Western Europe, to the U.S.S.R. to anywhere they could evade the Nazis. The Federation's fund raising was becoming substantial, but the money they were raising was miniscule compared to the needs. More vital than the money it raised, the Federation was furnishing contacts and leads to institutions and individuals, especially in Eastern Europe that were invaluable to the agencies involved in Jewish rescue efforts.

Most important of all, the Federation acted as an unremitting goad to the Joint Distribution Committee, the largest organization engaged in international Jewish rescue activities — reminding "The Joint" that the Polish Jews constituted by far the largest and most exposed Jewish community that needed help.

The Federation was a voice in America for the helpless victims being murdered daily in the tens of thousands. Its leaders and its members were working day and night to bring the plight of their brethren to the attention of the press and all the media, to Congress and State legislatures, to government officials from President Roosevelt down — to preachers, influential Americans, to any individual and institution that might help.

They importuned, pleaded, exhorted, begged, prayed. Their numbers were small but they made up for that in their single-minded selfless devotion to their cause. Especially did they seek to bring pressure on the governments of Western Europe. All this I learned from Tygel.

He brushed aside all of my protestations of lack of background and knowledge, my sparse Jewish education, the demands of my law practice, my activities in other public works. "You surely cannot refuse," he said. He was right, of course, I could not refuse. I had never met a man so knowledgeable and dedicated, so certain of what he was doing. I was embarrassingly ashamed of my ignorance of the slaughter of the Jews taking place in Europe. We continued our discussion through dinner, and we parted only after he elicited a promise from me to stand for nomination as a national vice-president of the Federation at a convention to be held the following week in New York. He assured me that I would be unanimously elected as he happened to be the chairman of the nominating committee. And, of course, I was elected. Thus commenced a new chapter in my life.

Tygel died before the war was over. Tragically, he died in total despair, at the height of the holocaust, died without the consolation of knowing that a pitifully small remnant of his beloved Polish Jews were able to come to a free Jewish nation in Palestine. It would have been a consolation to which this noble man was entitled. Albert Brown, who was the unquestioned leader of the Polish Jewish Federation in Chicago, also died before Israel came into being, but Albert lived long enough to participate in the post-war activities and to know that his fondest dream, the creation of Israel, might be realized.

My personal education in the meaning of a real Jewish commitment in the years after Tygel's visit was effected by my intimate contact with the men and women I met in the Federation of Polish Jews. Despite the grim horror underlying the work in which we were engaged, we shared an esprit of hope and dedication and a sense of humor and balance that was lacking in many other groups with which I later worked, despite their genuine sincerity of purpose. I was enchanted by these wise Polish Jews. Some of them were religious, most of them were not; in fact many of them were left wing socialists, former anti-Zionist Bundists, not a few of them former ideological communists. These sterile distinctions became blurred and lost during those several years at the end of World War II in our total commitment to save the remnants of the Jews in Europe.

At the height of our activity during and after the war years, we had some lively meetings in Chicago to raise money and get publicity for our cause. I chaired a dinner at which the principal speaker was none other than the "Veep" himself, Alben W. Barkley, a gracious, amusing, perspicacious man, who downed two double martinis during a briefing before the main event and later delivered a knowledgeable, sincere analysis of the situation of the remnants of European Jewry. His plea that it was an essential duty of the decent people of the world to help them, coming from this Southern WASP, was widely quoted in the press.

Very early in my involvement with the Federation of Polish Jews an event occurred that made a lasting impact on me. I had become involved in the B'nai Brith in 1939. By 1942 I was president of a local lodge and thereafter became active in the Chicago B'nai Brith Council, the governing body for all of the lodges in the area. The Federation leaders asked me to organize support for their activities from B'nai Brith and I introduced the subject at a meeting of the B'nai Brith Council. A resolution was overwhelmingly approved to create a liaison committee with the Federation and to undertake a fund-raising campaign within B'nai Brith to aid the Federation's work. Officials of B'nai Brith in Washington were appalled. Such a precedent, in their view, would open a pandoric box of involvement with "outside" organizations and would lead "God knows where." We received a peremptory letter from the late national secretary of B'nai Brith, Maurice Bisgyer, forbidding any activity in cooperation with the Polish Federation, stating categorically that "B'nai Brith law forbade it."

I was furious at this parochial rejection at a time when the Jews in Europe were being destroyed. Believing that Bisgyer had sent his ukase without the knowledge of the B'nai Brith president, Henry Monsky, I called Monsky in Omaha to find out if he had authorized Bisgyer's action. He had not and was incensed. He asked me how much I thought could be raised for the Federation through the Chicago B'nai Brith. I suggested $5,000. He said he would at once authorize transferring $5,000 from the Supreme Lodge Treasury to the Chicago B'nai Brith as a donation to the Chicago Chapter of the Polish Federation. "Carry on your work," he told me, "and don't be intimidated by Washington. They don't know what's going on in the Jewish world. You know we have an isolationist inheritance in B'nai Brith that we must overcome. Remember, I'm a Polish Jew, too, and a Zionist." During my subsequent long and often stormy tenure as chairman of the Israel Program in B'nai Brith, I never forgot those warm words of encouragement.

Most of the meetings and proceedings of the Polish Federation were conducted in Yiddish, a language all of the members were proficient in except me. When I was participating directly in the business at hand, English was spoken in deference to my ignorance. I often brought my friend Charlie Zakon to these meetings to act as interpreter and to provide a light touch, so much needed in those grim days. Charlie was neither a member of the Federation or a Polish Jew, but he was known by everyone and was very welcome.

Once at a meeting of the entire membership, I tried to speak in Yiddish. Despite Charlie's promptings on one side and Albert Brown's on the other, I floundered pitifully through five minutes of agony. It was a mistake I never repeated again. The audience was genuinely sympathetic and graciously applauded the effort. Continuing in English, I explained that only in my native tongue could I say what I wanted to. I confesed that until that moment I had never realized what an opportunity I had muffed in not learning Yiddish as a child and told the audience to quote me to their children and grandchildren on this subject.

Several years after the end of World War II, I attended a national convention of the Federation in New York City. By that time, I was convinced that the Federation should disband and urged its members to join with the general Jewish community in the task that lay ahead — to bring all the remnants of Jews out of the DP camps and to work for the upbuilding of Israel. My convictions on this subject were shared by many of the Federation leaders and members, but a strong segment of the membership wanted to continue an independent course. Most of these were former Bundists whose anti-Zionist convictions had become muted during the years of the war but by no means extinguished. They still believed in the universality of the Soviet socialist dream, and their admiration for our former Russian allies was strong. The cold war was just at its beginning.

I made a plea that having fought the good fight the Federation should disband, that in the future we should be simply Americans of Jewish ancestry, working with all other Americans of Jewish ancestry to aid our less fortunate brethren, no matter where they had come from, to achieve a hopeful future in any land where they might be free, particularly in a reborn Jewish homeland. My speech was received politely, but not enthusiastically. The fact that I spoke in English instead of Yiddish weighed against me. I was obviously considered something of a stranger, only a surrogate Polish Jew at best.

The vote on the resolution for dissolution was close but the Bundist sentiment prevailed and the Federation continued on. I resigned within a few months, as did many others, and several years later the Federation fell apart completely when it became obvious that it was being manipulated by sympathizers of the American Communist Party. It was a sorry ending for a noble and inspired effort by a decent group of American citizens. Our successes had been meagre indeed. Most of the Jews of Poland had been wiped out. But we did help to save hundreds, perhaps thousands of survivors.

The late Fred Monosson, the late President of Israel, Ben-Zvi, and the author in the president's office, Jerusalem, 1953.

2. American Support of the Newborn State

For several years after World War II, I participated in the fund raising efforts of the United Jewish Appeal (UJA) which in Chicago was called the Combined Jewish Appeal (CJA). My law practice had increased and I had prospered sufficiently to join a Jewish country club, and a city club in the Chicago Loop. Both of these clubs were dominated by old line German Jewish families. I must have been the only member of the Federation of Polish Jews ever to belong to either of them. I became acquainted with many of the men who had run the Jewish charity institutions for generations. Some of the younger sons and daughters of the old line families as well as many younger members of Polish and Russian heritage were alive to the refugee problem and were interested in raising funds for the Jews of Europe.

By 1950 I had become a chairman of the trades and professions division of the CJA and seriously considered concentrating my interest in the new state of Israel through this organization, but many leaders of the CJA were more interested in local Jewish institutions than in Israel. Though they recognized the need to help the survivors of the DP camps and raised huge sums of money for that purpose, few felt any kinship with the refugees, and many of the older members were openly opposed to the idea of a Jewish state in Palestine. The idea of Israel made them uncomfortable and I, in turn, was uncomfortable with them. I heard much blatant anti-Zionism expressed, but in the interest of the cause, I tried to hold my tongue. Often I didn't succeed.

Though I continued to work for the CJA, knowing that the big money for Jewish emigration to Israel came from that source, my major interests were focused elsewhere. As the political effort to create Israel through the United Nations accelerated and I moved up into the hierarchy of B'nai Brith, I came to realize that the circumstances of the times and my own inclinations set me up for a most fortuitous protagonist role.

In June, 1947 I became the president of the Chicago B'nai Brith Council and this position proved to be a springboard for the most intense and fulfilling activities of my life. The Zionist leadership was anxious to preserve and intensify B'nai Brith cooperation, which Monsky had initiated through the American Jewish Conference. With the death of Monsky in 1947 the Conference had collapsed, but the thrust of his effort to bring B'nai Brith into the mainstream of rescue and rehabilitation work for the survivors of the European Jewish communities continued among many of his followers.

As head of the B'nai Brith in Chicago in the fateful twelve months from June, 1947, to the Declaration of Independence of the State of Israel in May, 1948, I had a unique opportunity to project Monsky's vision. Most of the Chicago B'nai Brith leadership encouraged me and the 25,000 rank and file members — constituting almost a fourth of the adult Jewish population of the city — wanted to help European refugees and to support the Jews in Palestine struggling to create a new nation. Also, Frank Goldman, a Massachusetts lawyer who succeeded Monsky as international B'nai Brith president, was a life long Zionist.

At the national level, all of the Zionist organizations had united to form a Zionist Emergency Council (ZEC), with counterpart ad hoc committees in major cities. Rabbi Morton Berman, recently returned from active duty in the Pacific as a chaplain in the Marine Corps, became the chairman of the Chicago unit. This curly haired, black-eyed, imperious man was an activist, as much a fighting Marine as a rabbi. When he learned that I was prepared to extend the resources of B'nai Brith to our mutual cause, he invited me to sit with the Emergency Council as an observer. In truth, he invited me to become a member, but such membership would have precipitated a legal battle by anti-Zionists in the B'nai Brith council.

The effort of the Jews in America in those twelve months was directed toward mobilizing political support for the ongoing campaign at the United Nations for the partition resolution that had been introduced in September 1947. This resolution to create two independent nations in Palestine — one Arab, one Jewish — came as the result of recommendations of a United Nations committee officially called United Nations Special Committee on Palestine (UNSCOP). The resolution was debated for three months in the U.N. Assembly where a two-thirds majority was required to implement it.

The ZEC developed campaign techniques to mobilize the support of congressmen, governors, industrialists, clergymen, and others influential in the governments of U.N. member nations. In fact, every avenue of possible influence, especially the news media, was used to tell the U.N. delegates that the overwhelming majority of the Jews — and most Americans as well — wanted the resolution to pass.

Letter, telegram, and telephone campaigns were organized. Resolutions of support were solicited from organizations, labor unions, public officials. Speakers were sent to women's clubs, lodge meetings, political picnics — any place where people gathered. Their message was, "The U.N. Resolution must pass.."

As the largest mass organization of Jews in Chicago, the B'nai Brith Council took a major part in all of these activities. No one within the organization dared to challenge our activity though a small segment of the membership considered the campaign an undesirable partisan political stance on the part of a non-political non-Zionist service organization. The prestige of the B'nai Brith in Chicago had never been higher. Many nonaffiliated Jews joined the B'nai Brith for the first time, many former members returned to the fold. A large number of new lodges were organized.

On November 29, 1947 the U.N. General Assembly passed the Resolution by a vote of 33 to 13. The months of untiring work had paid off. The nations of the world had at last made a positive gesture of atonement for the sea of genocide from which Europe had so recently emerged. The rejoicing was universal.

But soon an ominous cloud gathered on the horizon. In March 1948 a cabal of diehards in the U.S. State Department, led by Under-secretary Loy Henderson, a notorious Arab partisan, came up with a scheme to postpone the implementation of the U.N. Resolution. They proposed formation of a "Trusteeship plan under the control of the U.N. to cool the tempers of the Arab states and thus avoid a shooting war.

A confused President Truman was partially persuaded to consider the idea, since a Middle East war might reignite a world just emerging from six weary years of bloodshed. Henderson and his group had the behind-the-scenes support of the British who were reluctant to give up their Palestine mandate which they considered a part of their fast disintegrating Empire. Influential French pro-Arab interests also were lending support. The Soviet Union did not oppose the trusteeship idea, though in an unexpected burst of magnanimity, the Soviets had voted for the Partition Plan.

"Ploy" Henderson had maneuvered to have the Trusteeship Plan introduced at the United Nations by the American U.N. representative,

Warren Austin, while it was still under consideration by President Truman — without Truman's consent. The President was placed in a difficult position. He could not repudiate Austin, his representative, who it is believed was innocently manipulated by Henderson. Furthermore, Truman half believed that a delay in the implementation might be desirable.

The American Jewish community was appalled to hear of the trusteeship plan introduced at the U.N. They could not believe that Mr. Truman could have been a party to what was obviously a complete about face from his November position. But the President remained silent and it became apparent that once again a public campaign had to be launched to block the State Department move.

The campaign to quash trusteeship was initiated on two fronts. In Palestine, the Jewish community immediately made it clear that the partition plan would in all events be put into effect by their continuing armed resistance to Arab guerrilla fighting (which since late 1947 had already become a shooting war) and by formal notice to the U.N. which the Jewish Provisional Government issued in April 1948. In the U.S., machinery for public protest was once again set in motion, but this time the concentration was entirely upon President Truman. If he supported trusteeship, the U.N. would not hesitate to accept it; if he opposed the idea either by public repudiation or by direct intervention at the U.N. the Henderson conspiracy would be defeated.

In Chicago the Zionist Emergency Council decided upon a mass meeting to mobilize community sentiment. To indicate the totality of Jewish community support of the affair, I as President of B'nai Brith was chosen chairman of the meeting. An equally significant reason for choosing me was the fact that even in those critical days, the rivalries between the various Zionist organizations made it more politic to select a chairman not officially affiliated with any of the member organizations of the ZEC. By this time, I felt sufficiently strong with the B'nai Brith Council constituents to bring B'nai Brith participation in the mass meeting to a formal vote. I arranged to have a resolution introduced to accept the honor of having its president preside at the meeting and to vote a generous sum of money to defray the expenses. The resolution passed.

The affair was held in the beautiful Civic Opera house built by the utility tycoon Samuel Insull. More than 4500 people crowded into the 3600 seats and overflowed into the aisles. Our principal speaker was Carlos Granados, U.N. delegate from Guatemala who had been a member of UNSCOP. We knew that he was a passionate partisan in the fight for an independent Jewish nation. He was then in the forefront of the U.N. battle to prevent the trusteeship idea from being formally presented. This mild little round man electrified the audience in his clear heavily Spanish-accented English. He declared that the Jews were a nation and that small nations had the universal right of all mankind to self determination and throw off the dominance of the big powers. Several years later I realized that he was also speaking for his own nation of Guatemala, when big brother U.S., through the CIA, connived to overthrow the liberal government of which he was a leader and install a right wing military dictatorship in Guatemala controlled by wealthy landowners and industrialists.

After the meeting, Rabbi Berman and I with our wives and Dr. Granado's charming senora spent several pleasant hours at Chicago's famous Chez Paree night club. As we chatted, Senor Granados assured us that Israel would surely come into being and that the trusteeship idea would fail. He made it clear that even then the U.N. was a puppet show. He knew that the U.S. would not push the plan and that Truman was furious with Henderson and the State Department, and that Warren Austin also was upset. He observed that he was greatly impressed by the earnestness of the Palestinian Jews and their leaders and knew that they would never back down now that they were so close to their goal. He did urge that the public campaign be kept up at crescendo force because Truman needed the assurance that the American public backed him against the obviously powerful economic interests behind the Henderson plan. Granados shrewdly observed that the fact that Truman was running for president in the fall was very much in our favor.

A few days later President Truman did publicly reject the trusteeship idea in words carefully chosen to save face for Austin and Henderson. A month later, on May 14, 1948, Israel declared its independence. The next day five Arab nations invaded Israel and the War of Independence broke out in full force. The major job of securing the fragile nation and bringing the refugees to its shores still lay ahead.

At the same time that the campaign for independence was going on in 1947 and 1948 Jews were being brought to Palestine legally and illegally, and the Palestine community was preparing itself for war, a war that in fact had already begun. The Jews wer resisting Arab ambushes all over the land. Jerusalem was in a state of siege, and the Jewish extremist underground military armies, the Irgun and the Stern Gang, were harassing the British occupying forces at every turn. Although the ZEC officially took no part in the efforts to arm the authorized Israeli military forces, (the Haganah), covertly and unofficially it was busily engaged in just that activity, with some of us aiding the Irgun as well.

Materials for Israel (MFI) was one operation carried on quite openly in cooperation with the ZEC. This involved collecting and shipping civilian goods — clothing, food, utensils, tents, cots, medicines, tools, hardware, jeeps and other vehicles — to the refugee immigrants. I persuaded my own B'nai Brith lodge members to set an example of MFI work. Since the great majority in the lodge were associated with pharmaceuticals in one way or another our drive focused on collecting tens of thousands of dollars worth of drugs and sundries, which were shipped to Israel in the spring of 1948. Many other B'nai Brith lodges organized similar drives. These campaigns were carried out on a personal basis and not officially sponsored by the B'nai Brith.

Among the B'nai Brith members were many merchants and salesmen. The opportunity to assist the refugees with donations of actual goods instead of money evoked instantaneous enthusiasm, and merchandise started to flow into MFI warehouses from B'nai Brith members. I realized that even more could be achieved if the B'nai Brith had its own identifiable project. I asked the MFI to permit the Chicago B'nai Brith Council to fill a whole trainload of goods and send it out as the "Chicago B'nai Brith Freedom Train." The suggestion was immediately accepted and unanimously approved by formal resolution of the B'nai Brith Council. Committees and chairmen were appointed and the campaign launched with much fanfare and publicity in April, 1948. The results were beyond our most optimistic hopes. B'nai Brith members not only collected goods from their Jewish associates but obtained gifts from numerous non-Jewish individuals and firms. It seemed that everyone wanted the European Jews to get to the Holy Land. Trucking firms donated the use of their trucks and packing facilities. The Pennsylvania Railroad station master, an ardent Irish patriot, persuaded his company to permit him and his co-workers to handle the packing of the freight cars and warehousing the goods without charge. Eventually the railway company moved the cars to New York harbor at its own expense. Other B'nai Brith lodges in the Midwest heard of the Chicago project and sent contributions. The B'nai Brith of Minneapolis for example sent a full carload of flour to Chicago.

In July 1948, seventeen freight cars packed with every conceivable item to make the lives of Jewish DP's more tolerable pulled out of the Chicago loop. Two thousand people turned out at the station to send it on its way. Not all the goods on the train benefitted civilians. The some 40 jeeps were effectively used by the Israel Defense Forces towards the end of the War of Liberation. Also carefully hidden in crates and barrels amongst tons of clothing were hundreds of small arms and carefully disassembled machine guns. The freight cars carried large banners listing the various B'nai Brith units that had participated. It was a great day for the B'nai Brith of Chicago.

The need for military materiel for the Haganah and for its rival guerrilla force, the Irgun, was dire. Throughout 1947 and the greater part of 1948, MFI carried on a covert operation to collect small arms for the Haganah under cover of its public civilian activities. Even more important, a continuous campaign went forward to raise cash to buy arms throughout the world. This was a dangerous activity because of the constant fear that a leak might destroy the standing of MFI as a civilian enterprise. Only the most dedicated donors could be approached for contributions. There was no tax deduction and no glory. Nevertheless substantial amounts of money were raised.

I became involved in collecting arms even before I was aware of the MFI activity. In spring 1947, under the pseudonym of Ben David, Ovadia Rasiel was sent to me by Maurice Davis, a colleague and friend of long standing. Ovadia was then a young stripling, a cousin of David Rasiel, the founder of the Irgun, who was killed in 1943 scouting for the British Army in Palestine. "Ben David" told me of his mission to collect guns and money for the Irgun. I was not entirely receptive at first. The activities of the American committee for Irgun under the flamboyant leadership of Ben Hecht were then recent painful history. My friend Pierre Van Paassen had resigned as its chairman the year before, and he told me a good deal of their misadventures.

There were echoes in the United States of the rivalry between the Irgun and the Haganah. A group of unquestionably sincere but flamboyant, clever Palestine Jewish patriots arrived in the U.S. in 1946 to marshall support for the Irgun. Their leader was Hillel Kook, a talented restless sabra son of the late Rav Kook, the then Ashkenazi Chief Rabbi of Palestine. Kook was a co-founder with David Rasiel of the Irgun in Palestine. In America, Hillel Kook called himself Peter Bergson. They succeeded in persuading the distinguished American Christian Zionist, the late Pierre Van Paassen, whose *The Forgotten Ally* had just been published, to become their titular head, to lend them the dignity and acceptance they sought. Expansively they called their group, "The Committee for a Hebrew Army." In a few short months, Van Paassen discovered that these adventurers were much too interested in pomp and circumstance, self-aggrandizement, paramilitary formality, and chain-of-command attitudes; that their fund-raising activities were not accredited or audited by the Palestine Irgun and that their connection with the Irgun in Palestine was becoming more and more tenuous and one-sided. Van Paassen resigned in sadness and disgust; Ben Hecht, the brilliant erratic American writer succeeded him. Hecht had rather late discovered his Jewish heritage, at the height of Hitler's rise to power in Germany, and had written a book on the subject, *A Guide For the Bedevilled,* a brilliant subjective essay on the trials, tribulations, and triumphs of the 20th Century American Jew. A decade later he debased his awareness by including in his autobiography, *A Child of the Century* a biased inaccurate account of the Irgun and a vicious attack on Ben-Gurion and other Israeli leaders.

Sadly enough, Hecht died embittered without ever having visited Israel. Much of the help the Bergson-Hecht group contributed to the campaign to marshall support in the United States for the establishment of the new state and the rescue of the survivors was vitiated by their wild, tasteless propaganda extravagances, full page ads in the New York Times and other national newspapers, glorying in the revenge attacks on British soldiers in Palestine.

The proliferation of committees for Arab liberation in the 1960's and 1970's was apparently modeled on the Hecht-Bergson scenarios, with some one-upmanship in violence, murder, kidnapping, similar "refinements." What a twist!

Young Rasiel assured me that he was a direct emissary of the Palestine Irgun and had nothing to do with the American group, which, he told me, was no longer authorized to act for the Irgun. Rasiel was under direction to return to Europe with the funds he collected and to direct delivery of the guns through an underground route operated by Palestine Irgun leaders and undercover American friends. He told me in detail the Palestinian Irgun's feelings of anger and betrayal towards the Hecht group which had raised thousands of dollars that had never been turned over to the Irgun. This confirmed Van Paassen's assessment, and I sensed that Ovadia knew what he was talking about. During the week he spent in Chicago, I rounded up some of the members of my B'nai Brith lodge recently returned from World War II and other veterans whom we knew well enough to trust with the delicate mission of gun running. We garnered an amazing collection of weapons, mostly German lugers brought back from Europe as souvenirs. We sent Ovadia on his way to Paris with several thousands of dollars. At the time of his first visit to Chicago, I did not know his relationship to David Rasiel. I knew him only as a thoroughly dedicated bright young man. He later became my closest Israeli friend.

Several months later, after I became associated with MFI I once again became a gun collector, this time for the Haganah, and on a much larger scale. For months, the trunk of my car was frequently filled with weapons, and I took special pains to observe all the traffic rules and luckily was never stopped for speeding or for any other traffic violation.

During the same period I was introduced to another on-going enterprise, informally under the direction of the ZEC. This activity was blandly designated as "Land and Labor for Palestine." It operated out of a small office in an obscure office building in the center of the Chicago Loop under the direction of the late Milton Silberman. Silberman had been a leader of the Chicago General Zionist Organization for years and was at that time its president and a member of the ZEC executive. He told me about the "Land and Labor" mission, which was no less than the midwest recruiting office of the Haganah. He invited me to become a member of the screening committee, assuring me that it operated quite anonymously and safely.

For five months in 1948, I sat with Silberman and several other ZEC members once a week interviewing prospective candidates who had volunteered to join the Haganah. The atmosphere was strictly cloak and dagger. The panel sat behind a long desk in total darkness. We could only be identified by our voices. The applicant was ushered into the room and seated in a chair under a spotlight so that he could be clearly seen. Before each candidate was interviewed, his curriculum vitae was checked by the panel. Interestingly enough there were many more applicants than places to fill due to the limited amount of funds available.

Almost all of these young men were veterans of World War II with records of combat service. Most, but not all were Jewish, but very few of them observant religious Jews. They had all been found by word of mouth, one-to-one solicitation, in most cases sent by war buddies. There were a number of sine qua non rules for eligibility: no married men; no one over 30 years old; no one without at least two years of service overseas; and none exhibiting too much pious dedication. Zealots were out. We had enough of them in the organizations.

The most important recruits needed were pilots, bombardiers, air force ground crew personnel, navigators, artillerymen, sharpshooters, field medical assistants, drivers, radio operators, and specialized small craft navy personnel. During most of the months of the Independence War Israel had to rely on these recruits to fly the nondescript airplanes being acquired from all over the world. It was these foreign volunteers who flew to Europe to pick up munitions and who thereafter trained the fledgling Israel Air Force.

A B'nai Brith lodge brother and close friend, Jules Cuburnek, who flew as a navigator for Israel, did not learn until many years later when we were neighbors in Israel, that I was a member of the committee that had screened his application. It was interesting that the most acceptable candidates proved to possess a healthy mix of genuine interest in helping Israel, a yen for adventure, and a desire to make a buck (although the pay wasn't that good). The best candidates were youngsters who had returned from the war restless and not yet ready to settle down. Killers were out, and there were not a few of them. Because of the limitations of funds, the specialized areas of experience we were seeking and the large number of applicants, we could afford to be choosy, and we were. About one in five were accepted.

In late April, 1948, Max Swiren called me to help formulate plans for a Chicago celebration of the birth of Israel as a nation. We agreed that any celebration we arranged must include the entire Jewish community and not just a few organizations. Swiren was local chairman of "Americans for Haganah," which was in reality a part of the MFI operation. We further agreed that the Haganah organization would be the chief sponsor in order to emphasize to the general public that a hot shooting war was on in Israel and would inevitably escalate after May 15.

We rented the Chicago Stadium for the Sunday evening of May 16, though we had no funds for the purpose. Swiren and I co-opted Morris Bromberg, a vice-president of the Zionist organization in Chicago, and the three of us planned the celebration which we named "Chicago Salute to Israel." We estimated the funds needed and arbitrarily assessed a group of sponsoring organizations, including the ZEC. I pledged a large amount for B'nai Brith and called an emergency meeting of the Council to obtain formal sponsorship and to appropriate funds. Both were voted in enthusiastically.

We called every Jewish organization in Chicago — left, right, center, religious, labor, war veteran, fraternal, men, women, youth, professional, some 60 in all — requesting endorsements for "The Salute," They all agreed. The only organization we did not invite was "The Council for Judaism" an anti-Zionist group.

We lined up an impressive list of speakers. Scores of young volunteers decorated the stadium with banners and flags and served as ushers. We even arranged for a loud speaker mobile platform in the event of an overflow crowd, although we doubted that we would fill the hall, which seated over 23,000 people. On Saturday morning, the 15th of May, we learned that an Israel Declaration of Independence had been issued, the text of which we did not receive until the following morning. The Saturday papers carried banner headlines: "Israel invaded by 5 Arab countries." Our arrangements were complete; we had given the Chicago Jews a chance to publicly declare their support of the embattled new nation.

On late Sunday afternoon, the speakers and platform guests met for a reception and then proceeded in a parade of limousines through the Loop to the stadium three miles away. The excitement of the moment infected everyone. We were ecstatic. The newspapers and radio had given us full publicity and we had little doubt that we would have a full house. We arranged for the doors to be opened at seven o'clock and decided to wait until 7:30 to start the parade. A mile from the Stadium, we were met with a sight we could hardly believe. The streets leading to the Stadium were filled with tens of thousands of people who could not get in! It took a cordon of police to maneuver the limousines through the roaring, joyous crowd and to shepherd the platform guests into the stadium which had been filled since four o'clock with the largest audience in its history, some 25,000 people.

The aisles were filled with old bearded men and youngsters dancing, shouting, singing, laughing, crying. As soon as everyone was seated on the platform, I went outside to the loudspeaker platform and in every direction I saw a sea of faces as far as my vision could reach, tens of thousands of people. The crowd was happy even though they couldn't get into the stadium. They were just glad to be there. I announced over the microphone that the speakers would come outside to address the throngs in the streets as soon as they finished speaking inside. We were glad that we had had enough foresight to arrange for an outside platform even though the cost had put us well over our budget.

Rabbi Wolf Gold, the head of the World Mizrachi, the largest organization of Orthodox Jews, spoke in Yiddish. An impressive black-bearded man, he was the most important Jewish religious political figure of the time and a member of the executive of the Jewish Agency, the official representative body of Zionist organizations throughout the world.

But two speakers stole the show and for the same reason — they talked about the war in Israel and the need to support the war. One was Reuven Dafni, a young commander of Haganah, who had distinguished himself as an officer in the British Army in Palestine during World War II. He apologized for not being with his comrades whom he was flying to join the following morning. The audience cheered him for 10 minutes.

The other "star" was C. Wayland Brooks, Republican Senator from Illinois. Brooks was a practicing isolationist, a protege of Colonel Robert McCormick, owner of the Chicago Tribune, and was not popular with the largely Democratic Jewish audience. He had never expressed himself on the issue of Jewish independence in Palestine. I had arranged for his appearance on the program, and had helped write his speech. Before Brooks arose to speak I whispered to him, "You may hear a few boos. Don't let it bother you, they'll cheer you when you finish." There was in fact some booing, interspersed with polite but unenthusiastic applause. Brooks was a handsome man and a powerful orator. The thrust of his address was a call for the immediate lifting of the arms embargo so that Israel could acquire U.S. armaments to defend itself, and he pledged his support for this objective in the Senate. He concluded his talk in a thunder of applause. The audience had not expected such unequivocal support for Israel from this unlikely source.

The principal speaker was the late Bartley Crum, a charismatic Catholic lawyer from San Francisco. In 1946 he was appointed to an Anglo-American Commission of Inquiry, which had recommended that 100,000 Jewish DP's be permitted to go to Palestine. When the British government repudiated its agreement to abide by the decision of the Commission, Crum became an ardent Zionist and National Chairman of Americans for Haganah. He was as happy as any person in the stadium. When the time approached for him to address the audience, he said to me: "I'm throwing my speech away. It has all been said!" He received a tremendous standing ovation from the audience. When the applause died down, he said simply, "Shalom. This is a great moment in Jewish history. I rejoice with you. All the decent people of the earth share this moment. The new State of Israel will be a light to all nations."

I had the privilege of reading Israel's Declaration of Independence to the people in the Stadium and in the streets. I shall never forget the roars of acclamation each time I concluded the readings. I heard the ancient battle cry of the Jews in the Stadium and from the sea of faces below me in the streets. AM YISROEL CHAI! (The Nation of Israel Lives!).

Two weeks later the U.S. Senate began debate on a resolution to lift the arms embargo. There was much opposition from the "neutralists" and it appeared that the vote would be close. I was asked to call Senator Brooks to appeal for his active support. His record as an isolationist conservative Republican would make him an effective advocate. I reached him in the Senate cloakroom. The conversation went somewhat as follows:

Alexander: Hello, Curly, this is Morrie Alexander, how are you?

Brooks: Fine, Morrie, how are you? What's up?

Alexander: Curly, I hate to disturb you but it's very urgent. It's about the debate on the arms embargo.

Brooks: Yeh, what about it?

Alexander: You made a great speech in Chicago. Would you talk in the same vein on the floor? It would be very helpful.

Brooks: Morrie, I just knew that if I made that speech you guys would be after me. Wasn't the speech enough?

Alexander: Curly, you said you'd work to lift the embargo. You'll be a big hero with the Jewish community and with many others, too. It'd help in your future campaigns.

Brooks: Listen, Morrie, I don't touch foreign affairs. I'll have to talk to Bob Taft on that. He calls the shots for us Republicans.

Alexander: Well, we know that Taft is in favor of lifting the embargo. I'm sure he'll tell you to speak out.
Brooks: Well, I'll talk to him. That's all I can do.
Alexander: O.K., and thanks, Curly.
Brooks: Not at all, Morrie. Good bye.
Alexander: Good bye.

Brooks did not speak out on the embargo, but it was lifted thanks mostly to the late Senator Robert Taft who led an effective bi-partisan effort.

Fund Raising

By the end of that year of 1948 the shooting war was over, and Israel and the Jews of the world proceeded with the task of immigration and rehabilitation. During the balance of the year and through the two years that followed, I continued to work in CJA campaigns, realizing that the United Israel Appeal, which was the chief beneficiary of the CJA, was the most significant agency providing funds for the ongoing resettlement activities. During my term as president of the Chicago B'nai Brith Council we had worked out an alliance with the CJA to persuade B'nai Brith members to become donors to the CJA cause. The majority of B'nai Brith, middle class merchants and salaried employees, had not previously contributed to the CJA or its partner, the Welfare Fund, and the alliance, though short lived, did have a wholesome educational result. During 1949 and 1950, I was a kind of unofficial liaison officer between B'nai Brith and CJA. But my main interests and personal commitments lay elsewhere. Like most of the younger men and women who were interested in aiding the new nation in those pioneering years, I wanted to build new pathways for Americans to relate to the existence of an independent territorial Jewish country. To us, as well as to many of the older Zionists and friends of Israel, the existing organizations and institutions seemed inadequate, outmoded, vested. Above all they were under the control of Brahmins, many of whom were more interested in American hospitals and old peoples homes than in the exciting gestation occurring in Eretz Yisroel, the Land of Israel.

Top: The author, far left, and Philip Klutznick, fourth from left, former ambassador to the United Nations and former president of B'nai Brith, 1957. Others are Chicago B'nai Brith leaders.

Bottom: B'nai Brith introduces baseball to Israel by contributing equipment to Mrs. Ogden Reid, wife of the former U.S. ambassador, 1959.

3. B'nai Brith and Israel

The success of the "Freedom Train" and similar Israeli oriented campaigns throughout America had made a profound impact on the B'nai Brith's rank and file membership and on many of its national leaders. President Frank Goldman was eager to sustain the interest that had been engendered in Israel. Goldman visited Israel early in 1949 and was cordially received by the leaders of the new government, especially by President Chaim Weizmann and his wife Vera. Weizmann was knowledgeable about B'nai Brith in Europe and the U.S., having once been president of a B'nai Brith Lodge in Manchester, England. He had known Henry Monsky and Monsky's great ambition to lead B'nai Brith into the struggle to create a Jewish state. Weizmann knew, too, that Frank Goldman and Henry Monsky were cut out of the same cloth, though Goldman did not have Monsky's drive and charisma.

Mrs. Weizmann easily persuaded Frank Goldman to commit B'nai Brith to raise funds for an occupational therapy unit at the veterans' hospital near Tel Aviv, then called *Tel Levinsky* and later *Tel Hashomer.*

Upon his return to the U.S., Goldman asked me to help him raise the money for Mrs. Weizman's project. I agreed with alacrity, realizing that such ad hoc projects would help to launch an Israel B'nai Brith program. Thus came into being, quite casually, an activity known as "Aid to the People of Israel," the forerunner of the permanent Israel Committee of B'nai Brith created in 1953. Before the end of 1950, $150,000 had been contributed to the therapy project, more than half from the B'nai Brith of Chicago and the middle west.

In January, 1950, I visited Israel for the first of many times. Though I had no official status, I wanted to survey the activities and projects of

B'nai Brith in Israel and to become acquainted with the Israel B'nai Brith leaders. I had been encouraged in this by Frank Goldman who asked me especially to visit the therapy project and to become better acquainted with its director, the late Dr. Chaim Sheba.

I visited Moledet on this initial trip. I had known of the two settlements, Moledet B'nai Brith and adjoining it, Ramat Zvi (named in honor of Henry Monsky) which had been established by B'nai Brith, and I was curious about them.

I was especially intrigued by Moledet, as Chanan Prinz, a member visiting in Chicago, had told me about his settlement and had urged me to visit there and to bring greetings to his family and friends. He also had told me first to seek out Dora Lanir, the historian of the new settlement.

Though the B'nai Brith gift that bought the land on which the village was located had been made fourteen years before, I was amazed to learn that I was the first member of the organization from outside of Israel ever to visit there. Dora expressed regret that her husband Meir was not there. As usual, he was traveling around the country for the village. In fact, I did not meet him until three years afterwards, but during the next fifteen years and until his death we were fast friends. Dora had succeeded Meir as secretary of Moledet and during the next several hours she vividly described the history of the colony, the themes on which the community was based and their plans for the future. We trudged in knee high boots to see the farm (meshek) over deep rutted mud paths.

This first meeting with Dora Lanir marked the beginning of a relationship between B'nai Brith and Moledet B'nai Brith that over the years has resulted in many programs of mutual cooperation and interest.

I returned from Israel in February, excited and thrilled. I had seen the devastation in Haifa and Jaffa, the mean makeshift tent camps on the seashore, the grinding, back-breaking effort to restore the soil in the agricultural settlements, and the hustle-bustle of construction in the cities. My most vivid impression was the combination of fear and hope I saw in the eyes of the new immigrants and their children, not only the Europeans but the thousands of dark-skinned Jews coming from the Arab lands. I realized for the first time that all of us American and European Jews insulated in the western world for generations were abysmally ignorant of their existence. Statistics and oratory, polemics and exhortation could never evoke the three dimensionalism of their flesh and blood reality.

Dirt and squalor, the immediacy of near starvation, the insufficiency of blankets, tools, lamps, medicine, vehicles — all the lacks I had seen, I had recorded on several thousand feet of badly filmed, out-of-focus motion pictures. I showed my films to every audience willing to view them.

I was consumed with impatience to start a campaign at the forthcoming B'nai Brith triennial convention to create a program for Israel within B'nai Brith, that service organization of a half million Jews in America and throughout the world. I knew that there existed kneejerk response among the rank and file B'nai Brith members, peripheral Jews for the most part, to every campaign to aid Israel.

In the fall of 1950 an extraordinary convention of organizations and individuals was brought together in Washington to organize support for the first Israel bond issue, launched at a world-wide economic conference in Israel a few months earlier. President Goldman had appointed me and several other pro-Israel activists to represent B'nai Brith at the convention. In a statement that electrified the assemblage, he declared that since the B'nai Brith membership constituted approximately ten per cent of the Jews of America, B'nai Brith would, therefore, commit itself to buy ten per cent of the Israel bond issue. We knew, as the delegates to the bond convocation did not, that Goldman had made this commitment without the approval of the B'nai Brith Board of Governors. But Goldman's commitment was not repudiated. The progress of Israel during the years had captured the admiration of the entire world, and all Jews were basking in the reflected glory of that progress.

The Israel bond campaign did not progress well in B'nai Brith in the United States at the beginning, except in areas like Chicago and a few other cities where the community bond leadership was also connected with B'nai Brith. The organization had lost the impetus for Israel that looked so promising in 1948 and 1949. Despite my pre-occupation with B.I.G. (Bond of The Israel Government) in Chicago, I was concerned with the national B'nai Brith inactivity and felt a strong personal obligation to do something about it, especially because Frank Goldman had named me national chairman for Israel Bonds. I offered to convene a meeting of B'nai Brith Israel activists from all over the U.S. To give the meeting official status, Goldman sent the national treasurer, Sidney Kusworm, to address our meeting in Chicago.

I knew most all of the real Israel afficianados in B'nai Brith. I had met them at many meetings and conventions over the years and many of us had become warm friends during our losing battle to create an Israel Committee in 1950. Some fifty stalwarts showed up in early November 1952 and we had two fruitful days of skull sessions ending with a public dinner meeting.

Israel President Chaim Weizmann had died several weeks earlier and protocol prohibited Israeli officials from making public appearances during the month of mourning. However, I prevailed upon Israel's Consul General in Chicago to attend our meeting by assuring him that the meeting would be held as a B'nai Brith memorial for the late President and I promised him the affair would be conducted in good taste. Consul General "Bobbie" Yaron and I had become intimate since the consulate had been established and over the years that followed we forged a deep friendship that has continued until the present. Despite his official misgivings, he acceded to my request.

One of the speakers was Mayor Ben-Ami of Netanya who was to become a close colleague of mine in later years. Sidney Kusworm spoke before Ben-Ami and after a "bad start" delivered a warm and eloquent speech about Mr. Weizmann whom he had known and admired, particularly because of Weizmann's friendship with Henry Monsky. Then Oved Ben-Ami, a third generation sabra (native born Israeli), spoke. He had come to the United States at the request of Israel's Ministry of Finance to help promote the sale of bonds. He was even at that time probably the best informed industrialist and land developer of Israel and he clearly delineated the economic problems of the new nation and the limitless possibilities for growth if sufficient investment capital could be made available. The evening ended on a high note.

In May, 1953 the long hoped for Israel committee was established within B'nai Brith, charged with the responsibility of creating a program of activities for approval by the Board of Governors in November. Though not stated explicitly, our mandate was limited. The B'nai Brith organization was more than 100 years old. During that hundred years it had developed institutions and agencies that were sacrosanct to many of the older members and officers. It was essential for our success that this new agency would pose no threat to these sacred cows, some of which had long outlived their usefulness. We were constantly reminded that there remained in B'nai Brith a powerful element of unreconstructed isolationists who abhorred the notion that their American organization might become subverted into an adjunct of the Zionist movement — Israel or no Israel. Our mandate included a requirement to woo these stoneagers. The new President, Phillip Klutznick, had even appointed one of them, the late Harry K. Wolff of San Francisco, to our seven man committee.

I invited the committee to accompany me to Israel on a fact-finding mission to research on-site activities that B'nai Brith might adopt for its future Israel program. Three members of the committee and I made the trip. We four began the mission in Jerusalem as B'nai Brith representatives to an international economic conference, convened by Prime Minister Ben-Gurion to stimulate Israel bond sales throughout the world. We were impressed and not a little embarrassed by the importance the assemblage attached to the role of B'nai Brith in the campaigns, since our record of bond sales at that time hardly merited the attention paid to us.

Most of the institutions we visited did not seem to fit the criteria for new international B'nai Brith activity in Israel that we were seeking to establish. They were indeed much like the many institutions that B'nai Brith had created and maintained for the Jewish communities in America and Europe in the 19th and early 20th Centuries. However, a children's club at Pardess Hannah and the kindergartens in Tel Aviv were activities for new immigrants that were performing the kind of service that had to command attention in any significant program of B'nai Brith Israel activity. Similarly two institutions recently established by the American B'nai Brith impressed us as meriting much more publicity amongst B'nai Brith members than had so far been given. B'nai Brith women had created a home for maladjusted children in 1948 in an old building in the slums of Jerusalem, and at the time of our visit was completing a new home in the Judean Hills near the new site of the Hebrew University. The children's home has continued over the years to be an important well run institution, serving to alleviate problems of emotionally disturbed youngsters. Also, the Hillel House at the Hebrew University, started by the B'nai Brith in 1950, served foreign students, and was just about the only place where the few Israeli Arab students could meet and mingle with their fellow students in a non-supercharged political atmosphere. These two institutions have continued over the years to be major B'nai Brith contributions to the Israeli scene.

We were wined and dined by government bigwigs and the heads of institutions and agencies who knew of our mission and hoped that they might persuade the B'nai Brith to support their activities. Not all of the officials we met wanted to sell us something. Some realized the value of acquainting the largest non-Zionist Jewish organization in the world with the government and people of Israel and merely briefed us on the nation as it then was and as they hoped it would be in the future. The most thoughtful Israelis — officials and private citizens — realized that the future of Israel to a great extent lay in creating a sense of partnership and mutuality with Jewish communities outside of Israel, especially with the Jews of America.

The four of us met with Mordechai Namir, the secretary general of the Histadrut, the powerful labor union which was then and still is to a great extent an alter ego of the government. The Histradrut headquarters was located in an imposing new office building far out on the outskirts of north Tel Aviv, called by irreverent Israelis, "The Kremlin." Today the building is in the center of town, surrounded by many equally large and impressive edifices. Namir, with his shaven bullet head and brusque imperious manner seemed a worthy "commissar" to preside in the "Kremlin." Actually, he was an affable and gentle man, as I found out years later when he was the Mayor of Tel Aviv. He spoke Hebrew, translated by a young assistant into impeccable British English, and our English was likewise translated into what we assumed was equally impeccable Hebrew. He was eager to convince us that there was nothing his union desired more than substantial private foreign capital to invest in the building of the nation.

We were impressed by his sincerity, but as we left his office Monosson chuckled, "He's a wise old fox. Namir understands and speaks English very well. I've talked to him many times in English."

"Then why did he insist on Hebrew and an English interpreter?" we asked.

"Because," Monosson replied, "it gave him more time to consider his answer. They're a clever bunch, those Jewish labor guys. I was one of them myself, you know."

I had been mystified by the appointment of Monosson to our committee. Though he was well known in Zionist circles, he was entirely unknown in B'nai Brith, and although I had heard of him for years, I had never met him before, I could not understand why a man as completely involved with Israel affairs, especially with the Jewish National Fund and more significantly, with the Soldiers' Welfare Committee, should seek a position in an organization in which he had little interest, and even less status. I had no personal objection to his appointment. He was a likable, crusty little burr of a man, and his knowledge of the country and its personalities was invaluable to our mission. However, Monosson's main purpose soon became clear. He had been a one-man committee in America for the Israel Soldiers' Welfare Committee (*the Va'ad Leman Hachayil*) — a sort of Israel USO, started during the war of independence in 1948. Monosson saw a golden opportunity to marshall massive support for the Va'ad if B'nai Brith made it a part of its Israel program.

Monosson had done his homework well. On the second day in Jerusalem, even before all of our committee had arrived, he introduced me to Pinchas Lavon, then the Minister of Defense. Lavon proved to be a charming, sophisticated, vigorous man in his early forties. He told me that the Government and the Israel Defense Forces were keenly interested in the mission and were impressed that this largest organization of Jews in the world was undertaking to create a program of Israel activities as a part of its service posture. He and his colleagues were eager to give us the opportunity to see at first hand Israeli defense establishments throughout the country. Unfortunately, he was too busy personally to conduct us, but assigned his wife to act as our hostess. Mrs. Lavon was present at our meetng. She was as charming as her husband, a young woman who had come to Palestine as an immigrant shortly before Hitler invaded Poland. The Lavons produced a scheduled itinerary for our planned visits. I asked Lavon if he expected the B'nai Brith to become an important source of armaments for the Israel army. He laughed.

We agreed to accept the invitation to visit all the places suggested, which included the soldier's rest homes and clubs of the Soldiers' Welfare Committee on condition that no commitment for B'nai Brith involvement would be implied. The Lavons graciously accepted this stricture.

The visits to the defense establishments proved to be the highlight of our mission. In addition to Mrs. Lavon, we were accompanied on all these trips by the late Joseph Baratz, the Israel head of the Soldiers' Committee. Baratz was a tough, blue-eyed *vatik* (old timer) who was one of the founders of DEGANIA, the first Israel kibbutz, near the southern end of the Sea of Galilee. His genuine passion for the welfare of his beloved soldiers was awesome. We witnessed specially arranged maneuvers in the Negev and were shown secret camouflaged tank and air force emplacements in the desert. At Eilat on the Red Sea we were taken sailing.

In each section of the country our hosts and guides were the local commanders. One of these was a young dark beetle-browed colonel from Yugoslavia, David Elazar by name. He later became Chief of Staff of the I.D.F. (Israel Defense Forces) and was commander in chief during the Yom Kippur War. Poor Elazar became the fall guy for the lack of preparedness at the beginning of that war.

All of us were impressed by the dedication and gentle decentness of the I.D.F. people we met and by the defense establishment that had been created in a short five years. At the end of our mission Lavon hosted a cocktail party for us in Jerusalem. In a toast to the I.D.F. and the Va'ad, I observed, "we have been willing victims of a most pleasant conspiracy. Mr. Lavon is undoubtedly a master conspirator." The irony of this innocent statement was brought home to me when the conspiratorial "Lavon Affair" made headline news a year or so later.

The Jewish National Fund (Keren Kayemet) had been raising money to buy land, establish agricultural settlements, and plant trees in Palestine and Israel for half a century. I can remember dropping pennies into the little blue and white box in my mother's kitchen even before I started kindergarten. For years its national director in the U.S., Mendel Fisher, had maintained cordial relationships with the B'nai Brith. It was Mendel Fisher who persuaded the organization to buy the land on which Moledet and Remat Zvi were established before Israel's independence. Perhaps more than any other American Zionist, Fisher realized the potential value of B'nai Brith in the work of the National Fund. Our committee, of course, had planned to consult with the National Fund people while in

Israel. But consultation is far too passive a word for the campaign the JNF people conducted to engage our mission in Israel. Mendel Fisher, too, had done his homework well.

One day we drove out of Jerusalem with the chiefs of the JNF to the foot of the Judean Hills to a crossroad called Shimshon (Samson) which is the legendary birthplace of that great Biblical warrior. We traveled into the hills on a narrow dirt and gravel road scarcely wide enough to accommodate one vehicle. As we ascended, the thick forest of pines became scraggly and soon we were looking up at high stony promontories almost bare of vegetation. About three miles up the road we entered a wide round cavern. On the steep hills surrounding it were a few little groves of recently planted trees, but as far as our eyes could see, most of the hills were bare. We got out of the cars and walked a few paces in the widest part of the cavern to the side of a rock hill that served as one of its walls. Weitz said, "We are here." We didn't know where "here" was, but soon found out.

After World War II ended the JNF had planned a forest of six million trees to restore the ancient greenness on the denuded hills of Judea in memory of the Jews killed in the European holocaust. It was named, "The Martyrs Forest," *Yar Ha K'Dosheem.* The project had not progressed, and after six years only about a million trees had been planted. Joseph Weitz, the Chief of Land Development, unrolled a large map on the ground and showed the plan for dividing the forest into discrete national sections — Poland, Romania, Hungary, France, Germany, Czechoslovakia, Yugoslavia, Italy, Russia, Bulgaria, Turkey, Greece, Holland, Belgium, and others.

"The trees are mostly still on the map," he said wistfully. He handed a smaller map to Abraham Granott, the JNF Chairman, who opened it for us. It was the same area on a smaller scale, and in the very center was a rectangular section in color with the words, "B'nai Brith Forest" printed over it. Granott pointed to that area and said, "We are standing n the center of this section. It is our hope that you will accept our suggestion and plant one-half million trees here to commemorate the B'nai Brith martyrs in the lands where they died, and also all your B'nai Brith honored dead. If you will undertake this task, you will give the entire project an impetus that will rescue it from almost certain failure. If you will do this, we will be able to build a sanctuary here on this spot. We will carve out a cave in these rocks where the names of those you commemorate will be placed."

The concept was magnificent and all of us immediately realized that this project was eminently fitting as the first new Israel venture for B'nai Brith. It combined the desire of all Jews to remember Hitler's Jewish victims, to help build Israel, to provide work for newcomers, and to personalize the B'nai Brith's involvement in Israeli activity. In the future it would provide a focal point in Israel, a shrine to be visited by B'nai Brith tourists. We thanked Granott and Weitz and assured them that we would recommend the B'nai Brith Martyrs Forest as part of our new program. We had no doubt that it would be accepted.

Our mission ended in mid-November, 1953. I remained behind for a few days to meet with Oved Ben-Ami about a project I was personally interested in at Caesarea and to visit friends.

At the BIG Conference party in Jerusalem, Golda Meir had asked me to come to see her before I left Israel. One rainy cold day I drove to her office in Jerusalem. She was then busily engaged as Minister of Labor. Her principal preoccupation as Minister consisted of building housing for new immigrants and finding work for them. She recalled our meetings when I was chairman of Bonds for Israel in Chicago. She remembered when we met for the first time, Julius Ginsberg, an old time Zionist labor comrade of hers introduced me by saying in Yiddish, "He's O.K., Golda, *Ehr izz ehner foon unzehrer*" (He's one of ours.) I wasn't, of course. She was most emphatic in encouraging me to develop the B'nai Brith programs. Characteristically blunt, Mrs. Meir said, "Israel needs new Zionists most of all. If we cannot interest the noncommitted Jews in helping us, we will not succeed. You know better than I that the bonds are not being bought by the Zionists. The Zionists, God bless them, are all old people. Their day is gone. Israel needs friends. Jewish friends. Your B'nai Brith is very important."

My most lasting memory of our 1953 mission is the final encounter I had one drab wet November day before I left Israel for Washington. I visited with the late Yaacov Herzog whose premature death several years ago removed from the scene one of the most able statesmen and scholars of modern Israel. At the time of his death he was only in his late forties and was at the height of his career as the chief of the Prime Minister's office. He had served as Minister of the Israel Embassy in Washington and as Ambassador to Canada. A distinguished rabbi and son of the former chief Rabbi of the new State of Israel, he had shortly before his death declined appointment as Chief Rabbi of Great Britain.

I went to visit him in his capacity as head of the American desk of the Israeli Foreign Ministry. I had never met Yaacov Herzog and was surprised that he was so young, only in his late twenties. He was fully informed about our B'nai Brith mission and spoke with intimate knowledge about the American Jewish community. The thrust of his concern was the status of the city of Jerusalem. He outlined for me the ongoing campaign of the Vatican to internationalize Jerusalem, not only the old city held by

Jordan but the new city as well. The Israel Foreign Minisry had not dared to establish its official headquarters in Jerusalem because of the reluctance of most countries to recognize Jerusalem as the capial of Israel. He urged me to mobilize American public opinion through B'nai Brith to oppose the drive for internationalizing Jerusalem, which he felt would be disastrous for the future of Israel.

He walked me down the corridor as I took my leave, pressed my hand and said solemnly, but with a twinkle in his eyes, "You must never forget the Biblical injunction, 'If I forget thee O Jerusalem, may my right hand wither and may my tongue cleave to the roof of my mouth'." I got the message.

I returned to Washington and met with our committee to prepare a report and a program for approval by the B'nai Brith Board of Governors, which was then holding its annual meetings. We had been presented with a score of projects in Israel, literally from A-ales (everything) to Z-zoo. During the mission I had met with Simon Agranat, then a justice of the Supreme Court and now for many years its chief justice. He was a former Chicagoan whom I had met at the home of his brother-in-law, Herzl Friedelander, a neighbor of mine in Chicago. Judge Agranat was the head of an Israel organization concerned with juvenile delinquency, which was then a burgeoning social problem in Israel (today it is even more serious), aggravated by the tremendous immigration since 1948. He argued, perhaps rightly, that nothing we could do for Israel was more important than to help ameliorate the problems of youngsters thrust into a strange new environment.

In the course of our talks I asked him if he was a member of the Israel B'nai Brith. He answered that he was not and had no desire to become a member though, of course, he had been invited to join may times. He candidly stated that the B'nai Brith members in Israel were living in their European past. Even after the state of Israel was created, they did not show any signs of becoming a service order on the American pattern. He said he hoped that the example being set by our American Israel Committee would stimulate the organization in Israel. "They could do a lot of good," he said. "Your mission has seen the number of problems facing our country. When your Israeli brothers stop the 'coffee klatching' and start to realize that they are no longer living in Berlin or Warsaw, I'll be happy to join them."

People we met on our mission had delineated needs in almost every field of human activity — medical and vocational training; hygiene; industrial and economic development; child care; family welfare; art; music; elementary, secondary, and higher education; housing; agriculture, entertainment. Almost all of them had the mistaken notion that we had access to unlimited funds, that we represented a constituency of hundreds of thousands of affluent Jews who could respond to the needs of Israeli newcomers with unlimited understanding. It had been painful to explain to them that we were just beginning our work and that the job of pioneering in our own organization was almost as difficult as that of the early Palestine Zionists.

Our committee reported all of this during two days of meetings in Washington in late Novemer 1953, especially the heartbreak of having to say "no" to most of the earnest, public spirited, informed Israelis we had met. We recommended the adoption of the "B'nai Brith Martyrs Forest" project as the only wholly new activity, and we urged support of the Israel Soldiers' Welfare Committee on an individual, non-organizational basis. We also decided to set up subcommittees to keep in touch with several of the other agencies that appeared to be especially worthy of our support and to continually review the B'nai Brith membership's interest in Israel in order to add new activities to the Israel program.

I carried on as Chairman of the Israel Committee until 1965. During those twelve years the program of activities expanded by the addition of new projects, including several shelved in 1953. In 1956, the impact of the Sinai War opened the way for our committee to launch a campaign for the Soldiers' Welfare Committee, which resulted in several millions of dollars of contributions to that organization, directly through B'nai Brith, especially from B'nai Brith supporters in Canada and Chicago, and by wealthy donors whom we had interested in the Va'ad. Our cooperative conspiracy with Pinchas Lavon and Joseph Baratz finally paid off handsomely.

In 1957 we inaugurated B'nai Brith chartered tours to Israel which proved so successful that the B'nai Brith held its international convention in Jerusalem and Tel Aviv in 1959. I was particularly pleased that one of the sessions was held in the reconstructed Roman arena in Caesarea. The success of this convention, attended by more than 1000 members from all over the world, marked the beginning of international conventions in Israel which have become an important source of foreign currency income to the new nation. The program later proved to be an important source of income for B'nai Brith through tours that the organization now arranges to areas all over the world.

Our golden years of the B'nai Brith Israel program were the years when the late Label Katz was president of the B'nai Brith Supreme Lodge from 1959 to 1965. Katz was a committed Zionist who had become a member of the Israel Committee soon after its inception. As chairman of the B'nai Brith Youth Organization he stimulated youth summer tours to Israel, with Moledet as the focal point of the young peoples' visits. As

President of B'nai Brith he supported our Israel work despite continuing rear-guard opposition from many unreconstructed B'nai Brith leaders. It was his unremitting backing that made it possible to convert the Israel Committee into a constitutional B'nai Brith Commission. This achievement at a convention in Washington in 1962 precipitated a bitter debate, revealing a schism within the leadership and a dichotomy of attitudes concerning the connection between B'nai Brith and Israel. Our victory was decisive but not happy and presaged the eventual failure to make Israel a central factor of the B'nai Brith *raison d'etre.*

In the early 1960's, the problem of free high school education in Israel became acute. Sephardic Jews in Israel by then constituted almost half of the entire population, but their children for a number of reasons — mainly poverty — represented a disproportionately small percentage of the students in the high schools and colleges. Our Commission undertook a modest campaign to obtain scholarships for youngsters who could not afford to attend high school. This campaign was undertaken at the express request of Abba Eban, who was then Minister of Education. As our campaign gathered momentum, we began to meet with opposition within B'nai Brith. We were accused of threatening the sacred cows of B'nai Brith generosity — the Anti-Defamation League, and other traditional agencies. Label Katz backed us, however, until he met with unexpected opposition from the Israel Establishment itself. The Jewish Agency people in the U.S. felt that this new B'nai Brith activity impinged on their "exclusive" right to raise funds for Israel in the U.S. I had run into the late Moshe Sharett at a meeting in New York and had solicited his support for this new (for B'nai Brith) activity. He was then the world head of the Jewish Agency. He readily agreed to help us gain permission to proceed with our efforts. But the Agency people in the U.S. continued to bug Label Katz, claiming that we were interfering with their larger efforts to mobilize funds for free schooling in Israel.

Several months later, Philip Katz, the director of the Israel Commission, and I were in Israel at the time that the Jewish Agency Executive Council was meeting. Philip and I met with Sharett and I reminded him of the promise of support he had given me in New York. He remembered the promise, but pointed out that he did not want to interfere with the autonomy of the American section of the Agency. I told him of the efforts our Commission had made for years to interest the rank and file of B'nai Brith in Israel and rather too bluntly stated that if Israel was to remain the exclusive province of Agency Brahmins, it would never gain the partnership status with Diaspora Jews that was essential for the future of all the Jews of the world, *qua* Jews, including and especially the Israelis. I had touched a sore point and he reacted with anger.

"I'm sorry," he said. "I don't think anything useful can result from continuing this discussion."

"I completely agree," I replied and rose to leave, Philip Katz, terribly distressed, behind me. It was an awful moment, I was sick with the feeling that I had offended this great Jewish leader and former Israel Prime Minister, but even more upset that establishment status seemed to be more important to him than the totality of Jewry, the little Jew as well as the big one. As we reached the door, he stopped us.

"Wait a minute," he said, "I understand how strongly you feel. Perhaps we can work this out. Come, sit down."

I apologized for my rude forthrightness, and made it clear that I had the deepest respect and admiration for him. He responded by saying he would arrange a meeting for us with the American Agency people and with (the late) Aryeh Pincus, then the treasurer of the Agency, who succeeded Sharett when he died in 1956.

"People of good will can always work things out," he said. "And when it comes to Israel, Jews musn't quarrel."

Several days later we met with the American members of the Agency. We again tried to explain to them that our scholarship program did not constitute a threat to the campaign for capital funds for free education in Israel, and that they should encourage our efforts to engage the "smaller" people in Israel problems. They agreed to reconsider their opposition to our efforts, but within a few months they notified Label Katz in unequivocal terms that we must drop our scholarship program. Reluctantly we abandoned our campaign. We did have the satisfaction, however, of knowing that our work had publicized the problem of unequal educational opportunities in Israel and had served to accelerate the Jewish Agency's concern for the problem, which over the years has made free high school education a near reality in Israel.

As the term of Label Katz as B'nai Brith President drew to a close we began to realize that a gradualist long view connection between B'nai Brith and Israel was not productive. Israel Bonds and the Martyrs Forest had become so well established that they needed little stimulation from the Israel Commission staff. We had so carefully managed our administrative budget, with grants from the Israel agencies with which we worked, that we had required almost no funds from the B'nai Brith treasury. As a result, whenever we asked for allocations to expand our work, we were turned down and were told to continue to raise our moneys without burdening the B'nai Brith budget.

Our Commission had brought prestige to the B'nai Brith because of its aid to Israel and had helped to make the leadership politically powerful in the Jewish world far beyond our rather peripheral accomplishments.

But the Israel Commission had enlisted few new B'nai Brith adherents willing to assume leadership roles in the Israeli programs. For the most part, the same devoted afficionados who initiated the Israel Committee were still running the show. I determined to resign when my current term of office concluded in 1965 — to end the one-man showmanship.

In anticipation of this move I convened an annual meeting of our Commission in Toronto in the summer of 1964 at which we hammered out a future program that was as bold as the program we projected in 1953 had been cautious. The "Toronto Program," as it became known envisioned several new areas of activity relevant to Israel as it was in the mid-1960's, such as problems of Israeli Arabs and the increasing divisiveness between Israel and the Diaspora. The plan emphasized the fact that B'nai Brith could not carry on a meaningful Israel connection without paying for it with B'nai Brith funds. And this time around we didn't ask for the Board of Governors' approval.

After heading the Israel service work in B'nai Brith for almost 20 years, I was determined to step down and help to develop new leadership. Dr. Wexler, the new President, urged me to stay on for the three years of his first term, but I pointed out to him that I could retain my interest in the Commission's work as honorary chairman — a position to which I had been elected by the incoming administration. I also had begun to think seriously of emigrating to Israel and believed that the chairman of the B'nai Brith Commission should be based in the U.S. I was succeeded as chairman by Samuel Levitsky, whose devotion to our program was deep and abiding. I was certain that the Israel Commission would prosper under the sympathetic interest of the new executive vice president, the late Rabbi Jay Kaufman, whose identification with Israel as a long time Zionist was well known.

However, the next three years did not evince any appreciable growth in the B'nai Brith Israel program. Kaufman set out to prove that he was a man for all seasons and not a Zionist first. Wexler began to fancy himself as a Jewish statesman and showed more interest in the public relations aspect of B'nai Brith support of Israel than in enhancing the organization's service relationships with the Jewish State. In 1959, an International Council had been created by Phillip Klutznick, designed to serve as the umbrella for B'nai Brith's international activities, including the Israel work. Label Katz had thwarted this grand concept by making himself the head of the International Council. As a result, the Council remained a shell agency without any real function. At the 1968 Triennial Convention Kaufman and Wexler decided to reactivate Klutznick's original idea and began a campaign that ended up in the elimination of the Israel Commission and a take-over of all its functions by the International Council. A subagency of the International Council was created, an Israel "cabinet" to handle the work of the Israel Commission. Philip Katz, the Commission's able director for 12 years was forced to resign. Rabbi Kaufman died soon afterward and the Israel service program declined. The only part of the "Toronto Plan" to be effectively implemented was the creation of a number of Israel investment clubs in B'nai Brith lodges throughout the U.S. and Canada.

Six years after the demise of the Israel Commission for Israel B'nai Brith had a change of heart. The shock of the Yom Kippur War in 1973 undoubtedly had a galvanizing effect on both the leadership and the rank and file. The indifferent record of the Israel Cabinet following the discarding of the Commission, and the alarming decline in B'nai Brith membership in the U.S. persuaded the delegates to the Triennial Convention in Jerusalem in 1974 to reinstate the Commission for Israel despite the opposition of the former president William Wexler.

Scroll of Fire

Many lasting accomplishments of our work remain in Israel, and institutions we initiated, supported and stimulated will remain for generations as evidence of the fruits of rapprochement between the Jews of the diaspora and the Israelis. Certainly a most visible evidence is the great Scroll of Fire proudly placed on the highest mount of the Judean Hills in the center of the now almost completed Martyrs Forest of six million trees. This imposing bas relief in the form of a 25-foot-high half-open scroll depicts in sculptured intensity the story of the destruction of the Jews of Europe, the battle of the Warsaw Ghetto, and the migration to Israel of Europe's surviving Jewry. Our Israel Commission decided to commission this work in 1965. We had asked the late Jacques Lipshutz to sculpt a fitting memorial. He told us that Natan Rapaport was our man.

Rapaport had created the striking Warsaw Ghetto monument for the Polish Government that now stands on the site of the Warsaw Ghetto. He had created the heroic bronze statue of Mordechai Anilevich, the leader of the Jews in Warsaw in their last stand against the Nazis, now standing at *Yad Mordechai,* the kibbutz in the Negev where survivors of the Warsaw Ghetto had held off the invading Egyptians in the 1948 War of Independence. Rapaport had originally designed our Israel scroll for the City of New York. The New York City fathers had rejected it on the specious grounds that it was too "ethnic." For six years Rapaport labored with passionate artistry to commemorate his Polish Jewish brethren and to depict the Jewish victory over defeat first in his studio in New York and finally casting his masterpiece in Italy. After the Six-Day War of 1967 Natan added that great victory to his Scroll.*

The Scroll of Fire memorial was dedicated at a ceremony in 1971. The B'nai Brith leadership from the U.S. was present for the dedication as were many Israeli B'nai Brith members. By a lucky coincidence, Philip Katz was in Israel at the time. I suggested that he invite Natan Rapaport to drive up to Judea with us. As we drove into the hills, all three of us became sentimental. We reminisced about the early days when the project was only an idea and we didn't know if we could get the necessary funds from the B'nai Brith or from the Jewish National Fund.

Natan, from the first time we mentioned the project to him, was convinced that it would be done. He considered the "Scroll" the culmination of his life's work and he had set to work immediately on the early models. When Philip and I visited him in his New York studio to tell him of our problems, he would reassure us, "You will find the money. It is *bashert* (preordained)," he would say. Driving into the Judean Hills he recounted to us the early years in Italy, supervising the casting of the final work in bronze and the engineering problems in shipping the work to Israel and erecting the platforms and bases required to set it up.

As we climbed the winding road through the hills, Natan spotted the monument from time to time and showed us how visible it was from many miles away crowning the highest hill in the Martyrs Forest. Just before we arrived, Natan said once again, "It was bashert that this memorial be done by me, also bashert that on this day of its dedication we three should be together once again and in Israel to witness our accomplishment."

The Jewish National Fund had leveled a plateau for the monument and had tastefully landscaped the area and built approaches, all of which created a fitting setting for Rapaport's remarkable work. Jacob Tsur, the world head of the JNF spoke eloquently of the significance of the monument as a shrine to dramatize the connection of all Jews in the world with Israel. I was pleased to hear his words, recalling that he had been rather dubious about the project when we first broached it to him. When the ceremonies were over, Natan Rapaport was surrounded by people congratulating him on his achievement. He turned to me and said, "I haven't heard a word from you. What do you think of it?" I answered, "Natan, I

*In March 1976, his bust of Artur Rubinstein was unveiled in Carnegie Hall, and in April a replica of his Warsaw Memorial was erected in Jerusalem.

have no words to describe my feelings. It is too beautiful for words — too beautiful!" He put his arms around my shoulders and kissed me. Both of us were too choked to say anything more. For me and my dedicated colleagues of the B'nai Brith Commission and our devoted staff, the Scroll of Fire will forever stand as a fitting epitaph of our faulted dream.

The author and Avrum Harmon, former Israeli ambassador to the United States and presently chancellor of the Hebrew University in Jerusalem. At the far left is Rabbi Jay Kaufman, director of B'nai Brith. Behind the author from right to left are Samuel Levitsky, who succeeded the author as chairman of B'nai Brith Israel Commission, Dr. William Wexler, former president of B'nai Brith, and Philip Katz, then director of B'nai Brith Israel Commission, at the Israeli Embassy in Washington, 1962.

Late Prime Minister David Ben-Gurion challenging Mrs. Irene Alexander (the author's second wife) on her assertion that Mr. Ben-Gurion's daughter had not spoken at an Israel meeting in Chicago. Photograph taken at dedication of the famous Mann Auditorium in Tel Aviv, 1957. The man at far right is the son-in-law of the prime minister and the husband of the daughter in question.

4. B.I.G.

A generation after the creation of the State, the Israeli labor government establishment succeeded in dominating the diaspora communities' relationship to Israel almost as completely as they have controlled the political processes in Israel since its inception. The most effective apparatus in accomplishing this domination has been the Israel bond organization. In 1950 a genuinely professional establishment was created to sell Israel Government bonds throughout the United States and in Canada, Central America, South America, England, Western Europe, Australia, South Africa.

The architects of the bond drive in the Israeli government were Ben-Gurion, Levi Eshkol (then finance minister, later prime minister), and Golda Meir. The importance they attached to this new dimension of diaspora support is indicated by the prominence of the Americans whom they co-opted to the program and the elaborate arrangements made to launch bond sales. The first chairman of the board of the bond corporation in the United States was Henry Morgenthau, Jr., Franklin Roosevelt's Secretary of the Treasury. Abraham Feinberg, an intimate friend and supporter of President Truman, was the first campaign chairman. Samuel Rothberg, like Feinberg, one of the younger new leaders of the UJA, was co-chairman. Both of these men were successful industrialists. James MacDonald, first United States ambassador to Israel, was given a prominent cosmetic position.

The appointment of Henry Montor as executive director further emphasized the importance to Ben-Gurion and his associates of this new venture. Montor resigned his position as director general of the UJA to take the job. This dedicated, complicated, morose genius, a former rabbi, had molded the UJA, in the years before Israel was created and during the first two years of its existence into one of the largest special interest fund-raising apparati in the history of the United States. It was Montor who understood most clearly the guts appeal of Israel to American Jews. That he was willing to leave his secure perch in the UJA to accept the uncharted bond effort, which was supported by very few of the old time American philanthropists and was considered by most of them to be an unnecessary and divisive gimmick, offers evidence of his prescience and the persuasive powers of the Israeli leaders.

Montor and his staff lost no time in attracting to their organization a cadre of younger enthusiasts whose commitment to the concept of Israel was pristine. They lived in the big cities and small towns of America these young businessmen, doctors, lawyers, accountants, rabbis, mostly sons of Eastern European Jews who rather resented the control of their communities by the descendants of German Jewish immigrants of the 19th century. They were supported and encouraged by wise, seasoned labor Zionist veterans whom they had not previously known and whose charm and sincerity were refreshing. By the middle 1950's the free wheeling Israel bond organization in the urban communities became an exciting and interesting diversion. Entertainers, senators, comedians, movie stars, beauty queens, pundits, were made available for the meetings together with a steady stream of Israeli cabinet ministers, war heroes and famous figures.

The Israel bond drive was launched early in 1951. In Chicago, the organizing efforts proceeded at a furious pace. I enthusiastically immersed myself in the job of helping to put together a framework of workers from Jewish community organizations interested in Israel and individuals who had worked with MFI and other Israel projects during the previous years. At the beginning, we were faced with opposition from the CJA and Welfare Fund people who saw the bond drive as a threat to their previous hegemony. Those of us who had been officers of the CJA were looked upon as traitors to the cause of honest philanthropy. Many CJA people considered the Bond Drive to be a device of Zionist manipulators to obtain contributions for Israel under the guise of an investment instead of a contribution.

The Bond Organization, realizing the importance of assuring the public of the validity of Israeli bond investments persuaded Prime Minister David Ben-Gurion to come to the United States personally to launch the campaign. In May of 1951, the Prime Minister arrived in Chicago where he and his wife Paula were met at Midway Airport by a crowd of admirers that escorted him to city hall in a parade of automobiles. On a platform in front of "The Hall" Mayor Kennelly introduced Ben-Gurion to several thousand enthusiasts and casual bystanders. During his 24 hour stay in Chicago his appearance at several small meetings of wealthy Israel supporters resulted in sales of several hundred thousand dollars.

But after Ben-Gurion left and the tumult and the shouting died, the going got rough. We had established an ad hoc committee to run the Bond show, but there was no clear-cut delineation of authority. The chairman of the committee was the late Max Bressler, a sincere Zionist, but a tartar of an impatient man who had no talent for relating to people. He was a self-made business man, an immigrant from Poland who had made many enemies, especially among the CJA people. Our problem was compounded by the professional manager of bonds who was a stranger to Chicago and had little experience in fund raising. It was feared that if Bressler became the permanent chairman, the bond drive in Chicago would never get off the ground.

I suggested Samuel Katzin as chairman. Katzin was a wealthy automobile dealer and builder whose interest in Israel was well-known and who was also respected in CJA and Welfare Fund circles. He was a natural for the job. I was delegated to offer the position to him, and after a discussion in which I persuaded him of the need in Chicago as in all the large Jewish communities, for fresh approaches to mobilizing the effort to build Israel, he accepted. I convinced him that Israel needed investment dollars more than charity to develop its economy.

Lacking any organizational base in Chicago the National office of B.I.G. in New York had arranged for the city manager to call a meeting of representatives of organizations interested in the Bond drive, at which a chairman would be "democratically" elected. Bressler had indicated that Sam Katzin was acceptable to him, and that he would not contest his election. The stage was set and it seemed that we would be able to get to work. In promising to be Katzin's chairman of trades and professions and to bring the B'nai Brith Council into the campaign, I looked forward to pleasant and productive personal activity in an area where I had gained experience through my CJA activities and as President of the B'nai Brith Chicago Council.

A week before the "election" was scheduled to take place, Katzin informed us that he could not accept the bond chairmanship as he had been offered the chairmanship of the CJA campaign. He explained that he could do a better job for Israel in that position, and that he felt he lacked the experience to organize the new venture of Israel bonds. I didn't tell him that I was certain the CJA had coopted him when they heard that he, one of "their men," was about to become chairman of bonds. He also told me that he had called Colonel Arvey to suggest that I was a much more logical choice for bond chairman, in any event.

During the days that followed I was importuned to stand for election as chairman. Not only did Arvey and the local Zionist leadership work on me, but the late Henry Morgenthau, Henry Montor, Phillip Klutznick, Sam Rothberg and others called to persuade me. I was in a genuine dilemma. Max Bressler was a friend of mine. We had worked together for years in the Jewish refugee cause. He had devoted himself diligently to Israel bonds since early spring, and I knew that he had his heart set on becoming chairman. But, I also knew that at this "point in time" his personal unpopularity would be disastrous for the job ahead of us.

I agreed to accept the chairmanship if my election were unanimous and if Max Bressler seconded my nomination. Henry Montor agreed to my conditions and flew to Chicago personally to take charge of the election meeting. I was nominated by Col. Arvey and seconded by a half dozen of my Zionist organization chaverim (comrades). Someone nominated Bressler. It was a tense moment. Bressler arose flushed and angry and delivered a short bitter statement in which he barely concealed his belief that he was the victim of a conspiracy to unseat him. He ended by stating that for the good of Israel, he would not precipitate a contest, that he knew I would make a good chairman. He then withdrew his nomination and seconded my nomination. Montor had done his job well. I was not happy. I felt that I had been involved in a surgical operation, not an election.

For the next year and a half until the spring of 1953, I lived, slept, and dreamed Israel bonds, both as Chicago chairman of the drive and in B'nai Brith. I had the able cooperation of a hard-driving new professional city manager, Seymour Fishman. The two of us worked with a singleness of purpose. I also had the backing of all the Zionist organizations, especially the Labor Zionist group, and of course my B'nai Brith associates. We determined to avoid any schism with the CJA and succeeded in this objective with the cooperation of Sam Katzin and many friends in the CJA leadership. Jacob Arvey's quiet steady encouragement and his ability to open many important doors was always available. The national organization was deeply interested in the success of Chicago, the second largest Jewish community in the U.S. Sam Rothberg the National campaign chairman, frequently came to Chicago to lend a hand. Slowly but surely, we began to convince the Chicago community that bonds of the Israel Government was not a charity enterprise, that principal and interest would be paid when due.

In late winter we ran our first big city-wide bond drive dinner. Eddie Cantor was scheduled to be the principal speaker. Two days before the dinner, Cantor became ill and Edward G. Robinson flew out from Hollywood to take his place. To help insure the success of this first venture Sam Levenson, the comedian and pundit was sent out from New York.

Robinson flew in at 3 a.m. on a Sunday morning and I met him at the airport. He was hungry, so I took him to an all night restaurant on the near north side, favorite eating place of Rush Street late nighters and the more affluent Mafiosi. When I told Robinson this, his eyes glittered with excitement. "You know," he confided, "I've never met any of those guys. I don't think I ever saw a real gangster."

When we walked in, he was immediately recognized by the "inmates." Amazingly, this little Romanian Jew who had started his career as an actor on the Yiddish stage, was a favorite of "the boys." He had unwittingly made them bigger than life in his early movies. When we were finally seated, many of them came over to our table to shake his hand. He told them he was in Chicago to help the State of Israel sell their government's bonds and expected them all to buy. After a couple of drinks, the actor in him emerged. He stuck a cigar in the corner of his mouth, assumed his "Scarface" pose, looked quizzically around the crowded room, and said in his gravelly voice, "These guys are the mob, you say. Hell, I taught them all they know."

"Eddie," I implored. "Smile and wave and let them know you're acting. These guys are half drunk — they don't like to be kidded. The big bosses of the Chicago mob are in this room. Please don't make with the jokes."

He became very sober, smiled his infectious grin and the moment passed. In private life he was far removed from the roles that had made him famous. In fact for years he had striven to escape the gangster stereotype. Actually, he was a mild, shy introverted man and a serious intellectual, as I discovered the next day.

Sam Levenson arrived in the morning. He was a funny roly-poly fellow, gentle and bright and easy to be with. He could hardly believe his popular success as a performer that in a few years had catapulted him from a high school Spanish teacher to the top of the entertainment world. He and Robinson and I spent all day preparing for the evening affair. Both Levenson and I were surprised that Robinson was genuinely worried about his address which he had written himself. He rehearsed it assiduously, and Levenson and I found ourselves assuring him that it was first rate, and it was.

The evening was an unqualified success. Many of Chicago's affluent Jews and non-Jews as well, bought a substantial number of bonds, stimulated by Robinson's thoughtful address and Levenson's ad lib good humor interspersed with knowledgeable concern for Israel and its problems. The dinner was the auspicious beginning of steady community-wide buying of Israel bonds in Chicago.

In the spring of 1952, my colleagues and I felt confident enough in the appeal of Israel bonds to attempt to reach purchasers through the device of a one-day bell-pushing campaign. I saw this idea also as an opportunity actively to involve the rank-and-file membership of B'nai Brith and the Zionist organizations in helping Israel. As a kick-off we arranged a gala entertainment and "big name" rally for bonds at the Chicago Stadium. The line-up of "stars" who agreed to appear insured that we would fill the hall — which we did.

Georgie Jessel and Irving Kupcinet, the columnist, were the masters of ceremonies for the entertainment portion of the evening. Among the many entertainers who volunteered to appear was Rosalind Russell, then appearing in Chicago in "Bell, Book, and Candle." Gracious Miss Russell wanted to participate in the serious part of the program, and I suggested she read the Israel Declaration of Independence, which had made a tremendous impression at the Independence Day Rally four years before. The biggest names of the evening were Illinois Governor Adlai Stevenson and Israel's Ambassador to the U.S., Abba Eban.

Jessel arrived an hour late and more than a little drunk, giving us a scare as the capacity audience grew restive. But Jessel sobered up and Kup kept him in line, and the evening became electric. The great Jewish cantor, Moshe Koussevitsky sang the sad Hebrew lament for the dead to commemorate Hitler's victims. As Koussevitsky sang, weeping and anguish filled the hall. I stood in the wings with Miss Russell who was to follow him. When the cantor finished, she turned to me and said, "I'm not going on. Nobody can follow that act." This experienced and talented and beautiful woman actually had stagefright! I assured her that the audience would love her and gently nudged her front stage center as she was introduced to a great burst of applause. The affirmation of the living she delivered was exactly the appropriate counterpoint for Koussevitsky's lament and she left the stage in triumph.

It was almost midnight, but the audience had been aroused to a high pitch of excitement and stayed to hear from the governor and ambassador. Adlai Stevenson was already being mentioned as a possible presidential candidate. I introduced him with this sentence: "Ladies and gentlemen, our beloved Governor of Illinois, a great friend of Israel, and the next President of the United States!" I had made his first nominating speech.

The Governor was obviously pleased. He acknowledged my introduction with the comment that he appreciated my very premature compliment, but he was there not to run for president but to introduce a great Israeli and he then proceeded in his inimitable elegant style to talk about Abba Eban, whom Stevenson had known during his years in the state department. Eban was very impressed by the huge audience and the enthusiasm of the long evening. In his impeccable Cambridge style he quickly brought the thrust of the meeting into focus. It was an altogether glorious night. One Sunday several weeks later, the almost anti-climactic house-to-house "Big Day" came off. In terms of bond sales, it was not particularly successful, but the day did serve to reach many hitherto uninvolved Jews in Chicago, giving them a chance to express their interest in Israel and to discover that many of their non-Jewish neighbors were willing to buy Israel bonds. My most vivid recollection of that day was shepherding Senator Hubert Humphrey from early morning to late afternoon to a series of meetings all over Chicago to stimulate the solicitors. Humphrey was cheerful, ebullient and indefatigable. In the late afternoon, we arrived at a hotel on the south side of Chicago. I knew Humphrey was tired, and I was exhausted. I peered into the hall. There were no more than ten people there. We had already attended about 15 meetings. "Senator," I said, "There's only a handful of people here. You've had an exhausting day. We can skip this one. Let's go have a drink and a bite to eat, and I'll take you to the airport. You've done more than enough today, and we're deeply grateful."

"Oh, no," he said, "These people have been waiting to see us. I don't want to disappoint them." And the unsinkable "Hubie" walked briskly into the room and made his best talk of the day. Many years later in 1968, I recalled that day with this remarkable man, and went to the American Embassy in Tel Aviv to cast an absentee ballot for him.

In 1955 Henry Montor was fired. He had believed that his position was too secure to accept directives from Israel with which he disagreed. The great majority of the volunteer Jewish leaders who were associated with B.I.G. were Montor partisans, devoted to this acerbic, sarcastic little giant. Even those who didn't like him respected his unquestionable capabilities and sincerity of purpose. Montor was certain that his allies were adequate buffers between him and the Israel Mapai hierarchy. He was wrong. The immediate quarrel over policies and tactics involved comparatively minor abrasions. The fundament of the battle between Montor, Prime Minister Ben-Gurion, and his finance minister Eshkol, was political. The labor government establishment wanted to control B.I.G. not only in the sale of Israel bonds but in nudging the American Jewish community towards the interests of the labor establishment. Montor was opposed to what he considered intolerable domestic interference. He refused to be an errand boy for partisan policies and politics.

Behind the scenes there were frenzied efforts to persuade the Israeli Government not to let Montor go. In addition to Montor's active backers, I and many other American participants in B.I.G. hoped that he would continue to head the Israel Bond Organization. I had come to respect the man himself as well as his talents. I had learned how to communicate with him despite his maddening taciturnity. Very few of us at that time were aware of the political stakes involved. To no avail, Montor left and with him several of his key staff and a cadre of the most devoted volunteer leaders, including Sam Rothberg, the national campaign chairman.

Montor was succeeded by Dr. Joseph Schwartz, the man who had followed him several years before as head of the UJA. Schwartz had been for many years the director of the Joint Distribution Committee and in that position had been a key figure in the rescue and movement of Jewish refugees immediately after World War II. I found him easier to work with than Montor. Schwartz understood and accepted the political implications of his new position and with his appointment, the Israeli labor government assumed complete control of B.I.G. Ben-Gurion and Eshkol were the bosses. When Eshkol became prime minister in 1963, Pinchas Sapir his successor as finance minister took over control of B.I.G. Sapir a short while later also became secretary general of Mapai, and for years until his death in 1975 he was the political boss of the ruling alignment in Israel.

The main function of B.I.G. has always been sales of Israel bonds, as many as possible. The yardstick of achievement is easily measured — the total of sales at the bottom of the line. But subtly a new dimension of purpose was added in the middle 1950's. By the 1960's a political manipulative process could be discerned in the hard sell style of promoting Israel bonds as practiced in New York, Chicago, Los Angeles, Miami and other centers of large Jewish populations.

The later history of B.I.G. in Chicago provides a case study. The Welfare Fund and the UJA were entrenched there when Israel Bond sales were introduced in 1951. The early years of the campaigns when I was an active participant, were grudgingly difficult. Most Jews doubted that Israel Bonds would ever be redeemed, and few of the well-known community leaders were willing to involve themselves in the effort to sell the bonds. By the time the Schwartz administration moved into control of the national apparatus, B.I.G. was well established in Chicago. All elements of the Jewish community were participating and B.I.G. had become a force attracting successful businessmen and professionals who had never before participated in Jewish communal work. Jacob Arvey, the powerful leader of the Democratic Party, had always been a committed Zionist. He had interested himself in Israel Bonds from the start of the campaigns, and through his prestige and influence, he brought a number of important figures into B.I.G. and not a few of his henchmen. However, there was no political coloration to B.I.G. in Chicago in the Montor days. This was to come later.

David Zysman, a hard-driving experienced staff member was sent to Chicago by Dr. Schwartz to take over the management of B.I.G. He succeeded Seymour Fishman, the able manager who started with me and had been one of a number of officials and lay officers who resigned when Montor left Israel Bonds. Zysman realized that his solid turf of Brooklyn was very different from that of sprawling midwestern Chicago and its score of suburban towns to which the prosperous Jews were moving. He had been advised to attach himself to Colonel Arvey who enjoyed the friendship and respect of Ben-Gurion, Eshkol, and especially Golda Meir, herself originally from neighboring Milwaukee.

Arvey has never been identified with the labor Zionists nor with any partisan Zionist political position. He had played a central role in influencing the Truman Administration to back the U.N. Partition Resolution and to persuade President Truman to recognize the State of Israel in 1948. I was witness to his dedication to Israel and his personal courage. One late afternoon in March 1948 I received a call from Arvey's secretary to come to a very important meeting in Arvey's office within the hour. When I arrived I found Rabbi Berman there with members of the executive committee of the Zionist Emergency Council and several prominent Jewish politicians of both the Democratic and Republican parties. I, too, was identified as a Jewish Republican at that time because I was a friend of the then incumbent governor of Illinois, Dwight Green. Col. Arvey wasted no time in coming to the point.

"We know Truman is against the trusteeship plan. But he hasn't spoken out publicly yet and if he doesn't soon, partition may fail. None of you are partisan politicians when it comes to the battle to fulfill the dream of Jewish statehood. You are all Jews and so am I. I've arranged to be called by President Truman. The call will come in a few minutes and I want you to hear what I have to say to him."

It was even then an open secret that some of the Democrats were wavering in their support of Truman for the presidency, and Arvey was one of them. It had even been mentioned in the press that Arvey had suggested General Eisenhower as a possible Democratic candidate for president.

The call from the President came in and we all listened transfixed. After an exchange of a few pleasantries, Arvey said, "Mr. President, I think you know what I'm calling you about, and I want to lay it on the line. I'm speaking not only as the Illinois Committeeman, but as an American Jew. Sitting in this room are leaders of the Jewish community of Illinois and several important Jewish political leaders, Democrats and Republicans. We know you are opposed to the trusteeship idea for Palestine and that it was shoved on you. It's bullshit and the Jews in Palestine will never accept it and not in the U.S. either."

He stopped and listened while President Truman replied. Arvey seemed to be pleased with what the President was saying. Then Arvey continued, "That's fine, but you must speak out publicly. I know the pressure being put on you here and from abroad, too; but we also know how tough you can be when you want to, and we know where you stand on this issue." He paused again to listen to Truman's reply and then continued. "Harry, I must be completely candid with you. If the Partition Plan does not go through in May as scheduled, you can kiss the Jewish vote in Illinois good-by, in fact in the whole country. If you knock the trusteeship idea on the head you'll have the Jewish vote for sure, the Republicans as well as the Democrats. There's no question about it — you've got to realize how strongly united the Jews in America are on this matter."

The President spoke again and Arvey finished by saying, "Thank you, Mr. President, I will. And God bless you."

He hung up and turned to us with a grin and said.

"The President told me to tell you that the trusteeship proposal will never be brought to a vote at the U.N. He was definite about it. He did not promise that he would speak out publicly. He hasn't made up his mind on that. But he said there are many ways to skin a cat. His word is good.

"I hated to talk so tough to him, but Harry Truman understands and appreciates straight talk. I know him. I think we can all rest easier now." Ten years later at an Israel Bond meeting in Chicago, Jacob Arvey publicly apologized with great humility to former President Truman for having entertained the idea, even for a short time, that Truman in 1948 should be replaced by another candidate. Arvey said at that meeting that he shuddered at the thought that he could have been guilty of depriving the country of one of the greatest presidents of all time. Mr. Truman replied graciously and lightly, "All men make mistakes, even great men like Jake Arvey!"

During the early years of the State of Israel a close friendship had been welded between Arvey and Ben-Gurion. These two professionals stemmed from the same generation of Eastern European Jewry and both of them had succeeded to positions of stature as consummate politicians. It is not likely that they ever discussed the use of B.I.G. for political purposes. It was not necessary. Arvey understood and accepted the design of the labor government hierarchy to strengthen its position on the American Jewish scene and the Old Man would not have objected to furthering the careers of Jewish politicians by B.I.G. Zysman was sent to the right man.

The twentieth anniversary of B.I.G. was celebrated by a festive convention in Israel in the summer of 1970. These meetings gave me a welcome opportunity to meet many old friends and colleagues from all over the world, especially men and women with whom I had worked in Chicago and throughout the U.S. I also saw many Israelis whom I had known in the U.S. and in Israel, most of whom were surprised to learn I was living in Israel.

Some two thousand representatives from Jewish communities in North America and all over the world attended the meetings. Many of them were not only Israel Bond leaders but also leaders of the United Jewish Appeals in their communities. Over the years the dichotomy of these two major diaspora supports of Israel had evaporated.

Sam Rothberg, the young man from Peoria who in 1950 had left U.J.A. with Henry Montor to inaugurate Israel Bonds — now Chairman of the Boards of Hebrew University and Israel Investment Corporation (an Israel conglomerate) — was installed as Chairman of the Board of B.I.G. by his friend, Pinchas Sapir, the Israel Finance Minister.

Top: The author being greeted by Mayor Oved Ben-Ami and other Israeli leaders at the Israeli airport, 1953.
Bottom: The author with Pinchas Lavon and members of the B'nai Brith Israel Commission in Jerusalem, 1953.

5. More Involvement

Caesarea and Ashod

My encounter in the fall of 1952 with Oved Ben-Ami, founder and Mayor of the City of Netanya, resulted in my involvement for the next several years with an effort to build a new city in Israel. Ben-Ami's pioneer work in Netanya was then coming to an end. He was seeking new worlds to build. When he discovered that I was a real estate lawyer involved in the construction industry, he told me about a project he was then exploring; in fact he had come to the U.S. primarily to seek partners for this new project.

The Rothschilds of France and England, in connection with colonizing activities they began in the 1880's, had acquired ownership of much of the dune land and sea-shore at the site of Caesarea, the Roman capital of the Middle East built in the days of Herod. After the War of 1948 their company PICA (Palestine Colonization Association) was granted options by the Israeli government to acquire additional land adjoining the site of the old city. This would enable PICA to build a modern Caesarea in Israel.

Caesarea is ideally situated on the Mediterranean Sea about 20 miles south of Haifa and 20 miles north of Netanya. It flourished as a Roman playground and capital for several centuries after the beginning of the Christian era. As the Roman dominance of the area declined, it fell into disuse. During the Arab ascendancy in the Middle East, from the 7th to 11th Centuries, it again became an important Mediterranean seaport and a chief objective of conquest during the crusades. One of the most important crusader forts in the Holy Land was built there in the 12th Century and flourished for several hundred years. After the Crusader period, the place denigrated into an Arab fishing village and finally during the Middle Ages reverted once again into the empty sand dunes of the pre-Roman era. For half a millenium, it lay deserted and isolated, its former glory marked only by the tower of a mosque three-quarters immersed in the sea. And thus it remained until the 1950's.

The Rothschilds invited Ben-Ami to participate in a joint venture with PICA in building a new city at Caesarea, and to excavate the site of the Roman city and the Crusader fort as international tourist attractions. He asked me if I knew of any Americans who might be interested. I immediately suggested Phillip Klutznick. At that time Klutznick was completing Park Forest, an organically planned and structured suburb of Chicago. A lawyer and town planner, he had been Federal Public Housing Commissioner in the Roosevelt and Truman administrations and was then the unopposed candidate to succeed Frank Goldman as International President of B'nai Brith. Klutznick's interest in Israel was deep and abiding, and I felt certain that Ben-Ami's romantic Caesarea project would appeal to him.

To my amazement, Ben-Ami had never heard of Phillip Klutznick, although he did know of Park Forest as an outstanding post-war prototype of an American planned city. I offered to talk to Klutznick the following day. The Ben-Amis were flying to San Francisco in the morning, but Mr. Ben-Ami was willing to stop in Chicago on his return East to meet Klutznick, if Klutznick were interested.

Phillip Klutznick had never heard of Ben-Ami either, nor even of Netanya, but he was deeply intrigued by the story of Caesarea and agreed to talk to Ben-Ami. One day the following week, I picked up the Ben-Ami's at the airport in Chicago and brought them to the Standard Club. Klutznick, Ben-Ami and I sat together all day long analyzing the project while Ben-Ami described in detail the history of Caesarea and his ideas for the development of the 12,000 dunams (3,000 acres), which the Rothschild's controlled. He also told us that the Israel Government had agreed to handle the excavation of the antiquities, including the Roman arena which lay beneath the sands. Ben-Ami's kineticism and knowledgeability were infectious. Klutznick was impressed by his experience and know-how in town planning and the boldness of his vision and his financial acumen.

The two men were much alike in their drives and ambitions and even in their personal appearance. They were both short compactly built, vigorous, expressive, charming, forceful. They took each other's measure. I sensed that they could become a remarkable team. Before the day was over, Klutznick had agreed to interest his Park Forest associates and others in the project as partners with Ben-Ami if the Rothschilds would agree to a 50-50 joint venture. Ben-Ami felt confident that this was possible in view of the prestige of his new partners. I was to act as American counsel in the forthcoming negotiations and as liaison between Ben-Ami and Klutznick. Our discussion ended on a high euphoric note.

Ben-Ami had warned us that the negotiations would proceed slowly. In hundreds of years as Europe's leading financiers, the Rothschilds had evolved a long dynastic view. They moved leisurely and could not be hurried. Klutznick in turn assured Ben-Ami we were in no hurry. Klutznick in turn assured Ben-Ami we were in no hurry. His business affairs were multitudinous, and he pointed out that the presidency of B'nai Brith would further consume much of his time and attention. I, too, was fully occupied with my law practice and business as well as with Israel Bonds and B'nai Brith Israel programs.

The negotiations did go slowly indeed. Almost two years later, in 1954, on Klutznick's first visit to Israel, he signed a memorandum of intent with the Rothschild company. During the previous two years I had carried on a voluminous correspondence with Ben-Ami and consulted frequently with Klutznick and his associates. On my trip to Israel in 1953 I saw the site of Caesarea for the first time. While there, I tried to move the negotiations along with PICA's meticulous British lawyer. A few weeks before this trip I met the late Dr. Nelson Glueck, the head of Hebrew Union College in Cincinnati, the rabbinical seminary for Reform Judaism. This urbane scholar was the outstanding Palestine archeologist of his time. A profound student of the Old Testament, he had located and excavated many sites using obscure Old Testament clues, very like a Biblical Sherlock Holmes. A notable achievement was locating King Solomon's copper mines, mentioned in the Bible but lost for centuries. Today these same mines are again being worked at Timna in the southern Negev. It was Dr. Glueck's prestige and perseverance that built a Reform Jewish Temple in Jerusalem despite the dogged opposition of the Orthodox religious establishment.

When I mentioned the Caesarea project, Dr. Glueck's eyes lit up. "If you succeed in getting your project going," he said, "you must promise me that you'll let me know before any of the plans for the excavations are made. I must be involved with this. In all modesty, I know more about Caesarea than any living archeologist." He grinned, but he was dead serious. "Caesarea has been a passion of mine since my college days. Do you know that it is the only unexcavated city in history about which everything is known. We know where everything is — the arena, Herod's Palace, the port, even the underground harbor approach into the center of the city — everything!" He then proceeded to sketch the whole city on the tablecloth, telling me how the city had been completely planned from the beginning, even before any work was begun.

"Archeologically speaking," he continued, "Caesarea is very new and very modern. Unfortunately, much was ruined by the ugly crusaders' fort built over part of it. But some of it remains intact, I am sure." He went on to tell me that just a year before, a small preliminary excavation had uncovered two magnificent headless marble statues — a male and female, three times life size.

"You will see them on your visit," he said. "Don't forget, Caesarea's for Glueck." I assured him that I would remember but unfortunately our participation in the project fell through, and to the best of my knowledge Dr. Glueck did not participate in the rather complete excavations undertaken some years later.

Some months after Klutznick and Ben-Ami signed the memorandum, the Rothschild interests advised Ben-Ami that they wanted the agreement revised so that PICA would have majority control of the enterprise. It seemed that it was a long standing tradition for the Rothschilds to own the dominant share of any enterprise in which they participated, and they would not make the Caesarea project an exception. After carefully considering the new proposal, Ben-Ami and Klutznick decided to reject it. Under the original proposal, the Klutznick-Ben-Ami group were to have pulled the laboring oar in the planning and development of the new city. They were also to have been responsible for raising most of the very considerable capital required to carry out the work. Except for making the land available, PICA's role would be a passive one. Klutznick and Ben-Ami were not willing to contribute their know-how as town planners, their energies in marshalling the diverse international crew of architects, engineers, artists, and others, and to give the enterprise their own close personal attention without being at least equal partners in the Caesarea enterprise. All of us were bitterly disappointed at this sad ending to the two years of work and enthusiasm we had devoted to the project. For me it was another break in the Israeli connection I was trying to forge.

Fortunately, the Israel Government Antiquities Department did proceed to excavate and partially restore the old city and crusaders' fort on the seashore, and it has become a lovely spot, visited by thousands of Israelis, many of them school children. And it is a must for all tourists. The most attractive excavation is a splendid coliseum, which has been almost completely restored and is now the setting for an annual summer music, drama, and dance festival. With the Mediterranean Sea and the Holy Land sky as a backdrop, many of the world's finest musicians and artists perform for large audiences seated in the ancient steep arena where Roman gladiators battled lions 2000 years ago.

PICA's properties have for the most part remained sand dunes. The Rothschilds built the fine Caesarea Country Club, the only golf course in Israel. Adjoining the greens they erected a pleasant luxury hotel that is today part of the Dan chain of Israeli hotels. A few kilometers from the sea a village has emerged from a refugee camp inhabited by former North African immigrants. The ma'abera (temporary immigrant housing) character of the town is still painfully visible, interspersed with the deadly public housing developments marring the landscape throughout Israel. The villagers work in a cluster of factories in the center of the drab town. Closer to the sea near the golf course a group of luxury villas have been built by wealthy immigrants and Israelis. They adjoin a complex of semi-attached expensive apartments operated as the Semadar Hotel.

The rest of the area is dotted here and there by small banana plantations, except for a large kibbutz next to the arena. South of the arena a pleasant little cluster of resort cottages and a good modestly-priced restaurant caters to Israelis — mostly honeymooners. Essentially the somnolent feel of the entire area has not changed much in the past two decades. It can be foreseen that in the years ahead the beauty of the seashore, the incomparable climate — the best in all Israel — and the attraction of the excavations will evolve into a megalopolis of buildings, people, and bustle. The Rothschilds can wait — they take a long view.

Though the years of negotiations on the Caesarea project ended up in deep disappointment, the story had an unexpected happy ending. During the three years from our first meeting with Ben-Ami in 1952, Phillip Klutznick had become the President of B'nai Brith and I had been appointed chairman of a permanent B'nai Brith Committee for Israel. We had become well acquainted not only with Mayor Ben-Ami, but with many of the leaders of the Israel government, including the late Levi Eshkol, the finance minister who later succeeded Ben-Gurion as Prime Minister. One day in late 1954, a few months after the Caesarea project was dropped, I received an exciting letter from Ben-Ami. The Israel Government had decided to build a new deep water port on the Mediterranean Sea south of Tel Aviv, at the site of the ancient Philistine city of Ashdod. Ben Gurion and Eshkol had asked Ben-Ami if he and the Klutznick group would be interested in promoting the building of the port and a new planned city as a part of the project.

When I read Ben-Ami's letter to Phillip Klutznick over the telephone, he reacted with immediate enthusiasm and asked me to write for complete details. Ben-Ami's assertion that the Ashdod project dwarfed the Caesarea venture in size, scope, and significance seemed accurate. Moreover, the Ashdod proposal envisioned a direct joint venture with the Israeli Government, which seemed to us to be even more viable than the Caesarea association with the Rothschild interests.

The Israeli Government had acquired 50,000 *dunam* (12,000 acres) of the dune land adjoining the sea, including 8 kilometers of lovely beaches adjoining a natural harbor. The location was ideally situated some 22 miles south of Tel Aviv. The need for a southern port on the Mediterranean had accelerated as the industrial and economic center of Israel began to shift from Haifa to the Tel Aviv area and as the agricultural development of the northern Negev grew in importance. Also, citriculture products, which had become the most important export of Israel and new plantations in the center and south of the country, required a shipping port much closer than Haifa far up the northern coast. Phosphates, potash, and other chemicals from the Dead Sea needed to be shipped from a more accessible deep water Mediterranean port.

A pipeline to Ashkelon just below Ashdod was then being constructed. The Israelis' chief supply of oil comes from Iran through the Persian Gulf to the Red Sea port of Eilat. The oil could be piped into tankers at Ashdod and carried to the Haifa refineries. Eventually oil refineries would be built at Ashdod to handle imported crude oil and Israel oil being explored for throughout the country and already discovered in the northern Negev. A port at Ashdod was a must!

During the next two years we carried on negotiations with the government to a successful conclusion and formed a company called KBA Ltd., to carry out the project. The city of Ashdod, envisioned to be built during the next 20 years, was to be one of Israel's largest cities, with an eventual population of some 200,000 people — the largest fully planned from scratch city in the history of the world. There would be two five-year periods of planning and construction and a ten-year period of final development, after which the city would flesh out organically. The port was to be built by the government in the first five years, with technical and financial assistance from the KBA company.

Klutznick and Ben-Ami marshalled a team of town planners, engineers, and architects from the United States, England, and Israel to prepare a master plan for an integrated municipality which would also be culturally viable, an attractive place to visit or to live in. The main thrust of the project, of course, was to create an important port and industrial city which would attract workers and new industries. The experts brought in by Ben-Ami and Phillip Klutznick produced a plan for a city of the future which, though changed many times because of the need for inexpensive mass housing, and political and bureaucratic fumbling, did establish a farsighted infrastructure that has made Ashdod a handsome spacious city. Some 50,000 people now live and work in Ashdod and the busy port and new industries abuilding presage that it will become the metropolis its planners envisioned in 1954.

The port, long since completed, today handles almost as much shipping tonnage as Haifa. A new road has been built from Tel Aviv which now links the two cities in fifteen minutes of driving. Hotels and villas are being built along the seashore and Ashdod is finally throwing off the construction worker's facade acquired in its early years. The prescience of Ben-Gurion and Eshkol, Klutznick and Ben-Ami, and the dedicated band of planners who designed the city is becoming reality. Ben-Ami once introduced me to a group of Iraeli officials as the matchmaker (*Shadchan*) of Ashdod. I was flattered.

The Jews wandered in the wilderness for 40 years before they came to the promised land. For 20 years I immersed myself in the 20th Century resurrection of the promise. In June 1968 I determined to forge the ultimate link of my connection with Israel — to enter the promised land myself as an immigrant. As a matter of fact, my first choice was to settle in Ashdod, the town I had helped to create. But I never did live there.

Joseph Baratz, one of the founders of Deganiz, the first kibbutz in Israel, and the founder of the Va'as Leman Hachayil (the Israel U.S.O.), with the author. At the right is Ovadia Rasiel.

IV

Life in Israel

1. The Alexander Family in Israel

Between 1950 and 1968 I had visited Israel fourteen times as a tourist, on missions for Israel Bonds and the B'nai Brith, and to handle business and legal matters for associates and clients. Even in my first exposure to the hard winter days of the struggling new nation in 1950 I hoped one day to go to that land not as a tourist or as a *shaliach* (messenger) grandly distributing the largesse of American Jewish organizations to poor country cousins, but as a genuine *oleh* (immigrant). Despite my dislike for the term Zionist, I guess I yearned to become the essential Zionist to conform to Ben-Gurion's definition that the only true Zionist is one who returns to the Homeland to live. When in New York harbor I boarded the Greek flagship "Queen Anna Maria" in June 1968 with my young wife and our son Robert then five years old, and my son, Mark, 12 years old, to go to live in *Eretz Yisroel* (the Land of Israel) the stardust was still in my eyes.

There were two hundred Jewish passengers on the "Anna Maria" going to Israel, almost all of them new immigrants or returning Israelis, and all from the United States. Young and old, families or singles, the returning Israelis and the newcomers were caught up in a sense of excitement that reached a crescendo after we left Greece and the Israel-bound passengers had the ship to themselves for the last day of the voyage to Haifa. During the three weeks of the trip many of us had become well acquainted. In the last days, as the time for debarkation grew near, we were asking each other "Where are you going to live?" "What are you going to do?" "Do you have relatives in Israel?" "Do you have a job?, an apartment?" "Are you going to study Hebrew in an *ulpan?*" Names and addresses were exchanged, solemn promises were made to look each other up.

In addition to the usual chaos it seemed the Jewish Agency and Israeli immigration officials who came aboard to expedite the landing of the new immigrants and welcome them to the "Homeland" were determined to give the newcomers a realistic preview of Israeli bureaucracy in action, enthusiastically aided and abetted by porters and truck drivers and petty officials who swarmed over the ship, confirming that confusion is endemic in Israel. Most of the Israeli officials spoke only Hebrew, and most of the disembarking passengers spoke only English.

After three hours in port we were practically the last to disembark, tired and forlorn, true "immigrants," certain that even our friends had abandoned us. But they had not. Ovadia Rasiel who had never failed to meet me on my various arrivals in Israel was there. Dora Lanir and Joseph and Tova Gadri had traveled by bus from Moledet, their settlement in the Jezreel, to greet the new *olim* (immigrants). Avigdor Warsha had taken time off from his campaign for mayor of Kiryat Ono to welcome us. Although Kitty and I had seen those friends only months before, we behaved as if we had not seen them for a generation.

Chicago friends, Max and Mignon Eisenberg are former Israelis who have become Americans. To maintain their connection with Israel they keep their pleasant little house near Tel-Aviv, which they offered to us as a temporary home. In an hour, comfortably ensconced in a taxi cab provided by the Jewish Agency, we were traveling south on the old Tel-Aviv road following an overloaded truck carrying our luggage to Ramat Hadar, (extravagantly named Lovely Hill) in the Sharon Plain north of Tel-Aviv.

I thought I knew where Ramat Hadar was, even where the Eisenberg house was located, because I had been there the year before visiting with Max Eisenberg. But I had forgotten that Max and I had driven north out of Tel-Aviv towards Petach Tikvah. I was completely lost and it took us an extra hour's driving through unmarked country lanes to find the house.

As the cab and truck lurched along the gravel roads deep into the countryside I began to have misgivings about settling even for a few months in this out of the way setting. I watched my city-bred wife's chin quiver and drop lower and lower. I had painted a picture of a pleasant country villa in a suburban setting, a few minute's drive from Tel-Aviv and the heart of Israel. Instead we found ourselves in a rather desolate agricultural area in the middle of nowhere.

The house itself was nice enough, spare but adequately furnished. The beds and household furnishings we had carefully packed and shipped to accompany us on the "Anna Maria" were still sitting on the dock in New York, courtesy of the Greek Line. By the time our luggage was unloaded from the cab and truck night had fallen, and the electricity was not going to be turned on until the next day. We found ourselves in stygian darkness in a silence emphasized only by barnyard sounds and barking dogs. The moment was grim. I tried to reassure my family by promising that we would move to a hotel in Tel Aviv in the morning and stay there until we acquired an automobile and other things to make our life in the countryside comfortable and mobile. Whereupon we all peacefully fell asleep.

In the brilliant light of the morning we arose rested and mollified to find that the house was genuinely comfortable. The plumbing worked, and the boys reported that there was a lively though uncared for garden with flowers, shrubbery and fruit trees. The neighboring houses were well kept and well appointed. We were delighted to discover that we were not in Hell or in Chelm — the mythical town of "Fiddler on the Roof".

Kitty discovered a well stocked little grocery down the road. The proprietor turned out to be an English Jew who had come to Israel during World War I as a young British soldier. After the War he decided to stay and became a truck and poultry farmer on the same two acres where he still lived. I was complimented by his offer to sell me some excellent ham and bacon. He told me he had to keep the *trafeh* (non-Kosher) food hidden because there were many orthodox Jewish families in the neighborhood who delighted in reporting him to the religious authorities. Encountering this grizzled good humored Cockney in the midst of the *moshav* (freehold agricultural settlement) was an auspicious beginning for our first days in Israel. We had a great feast of a breakfast. The telephone worked and a call to Ovadia Rasiel brought him out to drive us into Tel Aviv.

The same day I bought a German Ford. Since it could not be delivered for a week, I rented a car. It was essential to our well being in those first days that we be mobile. Before we left the States, Kitty and I had registered for Hebrew lessons at Ulpan Akiva in Netanya and classes were to start in two days. We didn't want to miss the beginning of our studies. With a car, we could easily drive back and forth some 20 miles each way and also provide divertissement for Robert and Mark.

The boys did not want to be stuck in the dull environment of Ramat Hadar, sans language and friends, without even a baseball to toss around. They were city boys. The problem was felicitously solved. I owned an interest in a small hotel in Herzliya on the Sea called Validor, which years before a group of Americans from Chicago and Canada had built for a youth camp. The original camp had petered out and Validor was then being operated as a hotel. Its most attractive feature was a large swimming pool. Each morning we deposited the boys at Validor and drove on to Netanya 10 miles north on the Sea Road. Each afternoon on our return trip from the ulpan we picked the boys up. In addition to swimming and playing table tennis they ate a substantial dinner, which, Israeli style, was served at noon. They became the favorites of the good natured Arab chef, Asees, who did not hesitate to make special meals for them in gleeful defiance of the dour Israeli manager. Asees had learned to make the good solid Jewish dishes of Germany and Eastern Europe, even a passable *chollent,* the meat and bean stew prepared on Friday and left in the oven to simmer all night for the Sabbath meal.

Mark left for home after a month. He had come as a visitor and felt no sense of commitment. He had enjoyed the boat trip and the pleasant days at Validor. He was Kitty's ally in the hope that we would return to the United States.

Robert however soon became an Israeli. Directly across the road in Ramat Hadar lived a family that had emigrated from Poland as refugees soon after WW II. Communication with them was difficult for us because they spoke only Hebrew and Yiddish. My Yiddish was wretched and my Hebrew, lower case pidgin. But their beautiful shy 17-year old daughter Esther was avid to improve her high school English, and she became babysitter and Hebrew tutor for Robert. He was about to enter first grade of regular public school in the neighboring village of Ramatayim. The problem of starting out in a country school with classes taught in a language he did not know, by teachers who knew no English, was compounded by the fact that the overwhelming majority of his schoolmates were Sephardi, mostly Yemenites and Iraquis from very poor families. How was this strange platinum blond, blue-eyed creature who knew no Hebrew going to survive the inevitable hazing? Esther proved to be a rescuing angel. Robert had had two years of Montessori schooling in Chicago. He had already acquired learning habits and could read and print English words. He and Esther decided to trade off English and Hebrew lessons. By the time school started in September he had a foundation in Hebrew — a better foundation than I had after two assiduous months at the ulpan. Esther's Hebrew lessons continued to be most helpful. She and Robert had quite a love affair.

The going, nevertheless, was rough for him at Ramatayim school. With his *teek* (brief case) on his shoulder, he trudged the equivalent of two city blocks on unpaved country road. By the time he reached the bus stop, the indigenous dust rising in small clouds at his feet powdered him with a light orange frosting. Each afternoon he returned home like a stalwart soldier. Now and again a welt on his arm or leg or a reddened cheek would attest to his daily trials. We learned to stop inquiring about the cause after several lame evasions. Fortunately he was a strong kid and I knew that when aroused he could give better than he took, with a quiet violent fury. After the first month the welts disappeared, and the beautiful little black-eyed Yemenite youngsters in the neighborhood began hanging around our house looking for "Robbie" (his name was especially intriguing because Robert Kennedy was a national hero to the Israelis in those days). When a half year later "Robbie" left with his mother for the U.S. (so that his baby sister would be born in Chicago as he was), all the neighborhood kids who were his schoolmates assembled to bid him goodbye and to be reassured that he was coming back. None of us had the heart to tell them that when he did return, we would not be living in Ramat Hadar.

Our belongings finally arrived on the next voyage of the "Queen Anna Maria," two months after our arrival. When we received notice that our crates were in Haifa Port, we immediately drove up to claim them. After spending three hours in the customs house and in the harbor warehouses locating our belongings, we were told to return another day because it was "too late" to clear customs. For the first time we learned that we needed another series of stamps on our bills of lading and had to pay a release fee of a few pounds. Having already aranged with a trucker and his helper to cart the stuff back with us, Kitty would not be denied. She was tired, furious, and very pregnant. She had already learned that in Israel one doesn't accept the first "No, it can't be done." With me sheepishly in tow, she stormed into the customs house and demanded to see the manager. Very loudly and in English she proceeded to inform him that if he didn't arrange to release our goods forthwith we would have everything loaded back on the next boat leaving the country, and we would take our five children and the yet unborn one *out* of the country, never ever to return. Then she turned on the tears. More than her tears and feigned hysteria, the possibility of carrying out the threat to remove the children — precious future citizens — worked. The poor manager himself accompanied us back to the warehouse and explained the situation to the few remaining workers there. In a short time our truck was loaded and we were on our way.

When Kitty decided to return to the States to have our baby "at home", I determined to continue on at Ulpan Akiva for most of the fall and winter term. With our belongings stored in a warehouse in Kfar Shmaryahu, I moved to a small hotel in Netanya for several weeks, struggling to complete the second grade of the accelerated course, which I barely managed to do.

I kept occupied fully enough with my classes and homework. I played a round or two of golf each week at Caesarea Country club, a half hour drive north. On the week-ends I drove into Tel Aviv to visit with friends and cadge a good dinner. I was also occupied with a new business in which I had recently become interested as a possible future occupation.

I did not seek out my old friend Oved Ben-Ami, the founder and mayor of Netanya with whom I had been closely associated for many years in the establishment of Ashdod. I was spurred by my desire to accommodate to Israel as an immigrant rather than as a visitor. I enjoyed the sense of complete anonymity as I explored the restaurants and prowled the streets and beaches and the residential enclaves, the nearby villages and settlements.

At the beginning of December, 1968, I flew to Chicago to rejoin my family and remained in the States until the following March. During these four months we celebrated three happy events. In the last week of December our daughter Sara Elizabeth was born, a big robust healthy baby who has been a constant joy. The same week my youngest daughter Diane was married to Jan Wittenber, and I had the rare pleasure of having all my eight children together with me for a few brief days. A few weeks later Mark was bar mitzvahed, which was an occasion for a reunion with many old friends and relatives. In the States Robert and I continued to study our Hebrew with a young Israeli student couple. Robert made steady progress, and I managed to keep up enough to be able to rejoin my class in the spring.

In early March, Kitty, Robert, and I returned to Israel with the new baby and were soon settled in a little furnished house in Herzliya on the Sea in a section called Shikun Progressivi, peopled almost entirely by well established Israelis from the Romanian exodus of the 1950's. The family that owned our house had emigrated to Belgium. They had ensconced the wife's old mother in a little one room cottage at the rear. The old lady was a formdable hulk of a woman and quite obviously enjoyed her role as sentinel of her family's hearth. She assiduously had to assure herself that the dilettante "Amerikaner" invaders were taking care of her daughter's possessions with care. On one pretext or another she frequently came into the house to check everything out. I communicated with her in my meager Yiddish, but only about the immediate business at hand. She remained unfriendly to the day we left. Not even little Sara who was irresistible to everyone else stirred her embittered soul. Israel was obviously exile for her; when her daughter's family left, it became exile squared, even though she had other relatives in the neighborhood and in Tel-Aviv.

During our four month sojourn in Shikun Progressivi I made some progress in Hebrew under the tutelage of my ulpan teacher Moshe, a young man who as a child had emigrated with his family from Argentina where he was born. With Moshe I finally began to catch the rhythm of the language, though I still couldn't master the syntax and grammar and my spelling remained weird. Robert was making great progress in school, and in a few months was indistinguishable from any other Israeli lad, easily jabbering and speaking modern idiomatic Hebrew with his classmates and the youngsters in the neighborhood.

I resumed my studies at Ulpan Akiva and Robert entered the first grade at the regular public school in Kfar Shmaryahu, a five-minute drive across the main highway. Kitty busied herself with the new baby and the pleasant little house. Our life began to become regularized.

One stroke of good luck when we were living in the Eisenberg house was discovering Sarah Sa'adi in Ramat Hadar to help with the cleaning and household chores. She came back to work for us soon after our return in the spring of 1969. Even though this meant a long bus ride instead of a few minutes walk from her home in the neighborhood, Sarah remained with us until we left Israel in 1972.

Though Kitty had dropped out of the ulpan after three weeks, she began to acquire an impressive working knowledge of Hebrew under the tutelage of Sarah Sa'adi who, in turn, was picking up some English. The weather in those spring months in Israel was lovely, and the flowers and blossoms and lush greenery of our area were a joy. Kitty also became involved in house hunting. We had decided to settle in Kfar Shmaryahu if we could find a suitable house to rent, and by the time the spring school term ended for Robert and me, we had found a fine, beautifully designed ranch house on a shaded, well landscaped *dunam* (quarter acre), conveniently located in the older section of the town. We were going to move in at the end of July when the current occupants left, and we busied ourselves with preparations for finally settling down in Israel with some assurance of permanency.

Kfar Shmaryahu and Rishpon

Kfar Shmaryahu is called *The Kfar* (The Village) because it has become one of the most prestigious and exclusive residential suburbs in Israel. (This snob identification is similar to the title *HaEmek*, the great valley in the Galilee that once was a malarial swamp drained by early chalutzim.

Emek simply means valley and there are many valleys in Israel — but only one "*the* valley." Similarly, *HaZaken* means "*the* Old Man." There are many old men in Israel but there was only one "*The* Old Man" — David Ben-Gurion). Thirty years ago, the Kfar looked exactly like Rishpon its neighbor to the north did — and still does — a little village of chicken farms, modest one-story concrete block and wooden houses surrounded by barns and chicken coops and farm implements. Both settlements were founded by Rassco (Rural and Suburban Settlement Corporation), a Jewish agency company set up by European Zionist leaders in 1930 to encourage middle class free enterprise immigration to Palestine.

The average size of a farm in Rishpon is four *dunam* (one acre). Some of the farmers own additional land east of the village on which they grow a variety of vegetables and other crops, including ground nuts. Their main sources of income, however, are eggs, chickens, turkeys, and milk. The settlers are almost all German Jews who have become prosperous by hard work and the good fortune of being close enough to the markets of Tel-Aviv and other large towns and cities where their quality produce always has commanded the best prices. The farmers of Rishpon have retained the *moshav* character of their village and have steadfastly resisted any temptation to change their agricultural zoning which would allow them to sell their land for housing sites, as in the Kfar where land values have risen astronomically.

The attractive grade school on the border between the two communities is maintained and operated jointly. Our son Robert went to school there from the first through the fourth grades. The community school is another persuasive inducement for the Rishpon folk to maintain their rural way of life under favorable circumstances. It is doubtful if the next generations will continue to resist temptation. The growth of the Kfar, where scarcely any vacant plots are available, inevitably will extend north into Rishpon and, predictably, Rishpon will in a few years become a part of the lush suburbia that is Kfar Shmaryahu. The cows and chickens and turkeys and peanuts are surely doomed.

Kfar Shmaryahu (named after Shmaryahu Levin, the great European and American Zionist leader) was also established by Rassco as a moshav of German-Jewish freeholders settled on similar little chicken farms. When Israel became a state in 1948, Kfar Shmaryahu still retained the rusticity of a little *moshav.* Most of the residents were the same style of small Yekke farmers as their Rishpon neighbors. More German was spoken than Hebrew. Over the years, the original rawness of the land has been replaced by the greenery of tall trees, shrubs and flower gardens, all lovingly tended by the settlers who had created, perhaps out of nostalgia, a charming German country village.

The original layout of the village was astutely planned by our friend and neighbor Dr. Louis Pinner, one of the founders of Rassco who came to Israel as an agronomist in 1923 and who today is recognized as an outstanding authority on citrus culture in Israel. Dr. Pinner, as head of Rassco Plantations, now known as Pri-Or (Fruit of Light), is the man most responsible for the development of citrus fruit farming as a major agro-industry of modern Israel. The modesty of this elegant little sprite who bears his more than 80 years lightly, is attested to by the fact that he lives in the Kfar and almost none of his neighbors know he is the founder of the village.

After 1948, the green charm of Kfar Shmaryahu began to attract wealthy Israelis and new immigrants as an ideal location to build homes close to, but outside the concrete harshness of Tel-Aviv. Over the past 15 years, magnificent villas have been erected there, some of them lavish palaces. The diplomatic corps also discovered the place. Today there are scores of beautiful mansions occupied by politial and economic elite. The town fathers recognized that if they controlled the zoning intelligently, the *moshav* flavor could be retained and the village could develop into a suburban paradise and still remain a farm community. They have succeeded. Most of the *nouveau riche* Israeli newcomers, the wealthy South African and American immigrants and the diplomats are of one mind with the original settlers that the village should retain its essential charm as a green country village. Million-pound edifices stand side by side with or face across the street from modest little houses. Those are the homes of the original settlers and their grown children who still farm the land and tend the chicken coops, the cow barns, and the horse stables. The original settlers and their families have become wealthy, almost against their will, selling off sections of their small holdings for housing plots, the prices of which match the most expensive home sites in the western world. Today the Kfar is a prestigious address, sought after by the moneyed types to whom an address is important. Yet the Kfar is also inhabited by many who simply appreciate the pleasure of convenient rural living in houses rather than the apartments in which most Iraelis dwell.

At the entrance to the village there is now a modern shopping center of pleasant stores, well-stocked and altogether in good taste. A few steps away the original flour mill of the *moshav* still operates, as do two small and primitive bakeries from whose ovens the aroma of fresh bread and cakes mingle with the scent of the flowers growing at every turn. In the center of the village on the highest hill, which Dr. Pinner planned as the focal point for the winding streets, there is now an Olympic size swimming pool and tennis courts. A stone's throw away in an adjoining street, the United States government built "The American School," a cleanly designed structure housing a grade and high school for the children of

American Embassy employees and other diplomats. A sprinkling of American immigrant youngters and the children of Israelis who want their offspring to learn good English also are students there.

The contrast between the rural simplicity of the Israeli village and the American and European exurbanite in the Kfar is disconcerting, but withal quite unexpectedly attractive. Sad, too. Rishpon is severely different by choice. Signi Ali across the highway is still something of a *ma'abara;* many of the housewives there work as servants in the Kfar. A little farther east live Arab farm laborers, and not too much farther east many recent and not so recent Afro-Asian immigrants dwell in an altogether different world, an existence not far above the minimum poverty level. The contrast is almost as marked as that between affluent suburbia and the inner-city wretchedness of Detroit, Chicago, Atlanta, New York and other big American cities.

Shortly after we moved into our new home in the Kfar, amenities we had shipped during our visit home arrived at Haifa Port. Previous experience had made us veterans and we easily maneuvered through the maze of identification and customs procedures to bring our belongings to our new home. With the additional furnishings, Kitty proceeded to make the house livable.

I fell into a regimen of painting and writing well after sundown. Those quiet nights in the Kfar in my *ulpan* (studio) when the soft breezes from the sea overcame the blazing heat of the day were my most pleasant hours in Israel. The magic of the Israel sky at night had a seductive hold on me, especially that first summer of 1969 in the Kfar. I doubt that there is any place on earth where the heavens are so near. I realized the closeness of the ancient Hebrew to the Godhead when he beheld the Israeli sky at night.

Outside the largest window of the ulpan our landlord had thoughtfully planted a lemon tree. By the time we moved in the tree was bearing its second crop of very respectable lemons. I would often stroll out at midnight to pluck a lemon and grandiloquently cut it with my palette knife, then squeeze the juice into a glass of gin and bitters. Another joy of my soirées was listening to the radio. After midnight the Israeli broadcasts shut down and Jordan, Egypt, and Cyprus, and even southern Europe came in clearly, if incoherently. But the music was good. The Voice of America, the Voice of the Soviet Union, the BBC, even Yugoslavia, Turkey, and Romania could be heard. As a jazz buff of long standing, I delighted in hearing many old tunes played from these unlikely sources. For once I was pleased that my language deficiences prevented me from understanding the political propaganda being spewed out between the good music. I did writhe, however, to hear the American programs offered in "basic English," which consisted of news, U.S. version, intoned in very slow accents of flat midwestern slurred tones. Even the British programs were more palatable if only because of the excellent diction of the portentous newscasters, though their unsubtle anti-Israeli slantings disgusted me.

Our house was located on an elevated street called *Hahoresh* (prepared field). It was American ranch style in design, the rooms laid out around a small atrium, open to the sky, which created privacy for the bedrooms and separated them from the large living room that occupied the entire front of the house and opened out into a spacious tree-shaded lawn. The house was built of concrete blocks, some shaped like wooden slats, both the exterior and interior, enhanced by real asymmetrical wood in the ceilings and paneling in the rooms and the windows and doors.

The problem of caring for the garden, lawn, shrubbery and trees was solved by hiring Ovadia, a dignified Arab gardener who was recommended to us by a neighbor for whom he had worked for many years. While the once or twice a month attention our garden received from Ovadia did not make our grounds a show place, we did appreciate Ovadia's dependability and enjoyed his young sons and nephews who often came to help him.

Hahoresh was the first street above the main highway, and a bus to Tel-Aviv stopped opposite our house each hour. The main shopping center at the entrance to the village was a five minute walk from our house. We patronized most of the shops there, especially the fine meat market and gourmet food shop of Albert and Vickie Halfon, who became our good friends over the years. Though the center also contained an American style supermarket, Kitty preferred to buy our food supplies at a little family-owned grocery store, and the green grocers next to it, a five minute walk in the opposite direction toward Rishpon. Amos Romano delivered the groceries, and we came to know him and his family during the ensuing years. Occasionally Amos would sell us crabs and small lobsters, which his fishing captain brother in Ashdod made available to him. (The Romanos didn't eat these delicacies themselves. They aren't kosher.) Amos told Kitty about the fishermen across the highway at Signe Ali. One of her great pleasures was to drive over to the sea early of a morning to buy the choicest of the catch when the fishing boats came in.

Robert soon adjusted to the Kfar-Rishpon school, a modern one story series of attached rooms in an el-shaped pattern surrounding a spacious sports and play area. The rigidity of instruction and classroom discipline and the emphasis on Bible study, too much homework and rote learning often proved galling to Robert and to most of his Anglo classmates. But the teachers were sincere and generally able and the parochial atmosphere of the school, indigenous to all Israeli elementary schools was alleviated by sports — soccer, hand ball, volley ball, basketball, and track. The general keenness of the students made for a high degree of competitive learning even if the dullness of the process and the emphasis on subject grading were irksome. In his four years at the school Robert beame completely proficient in Hebrew. When he entered the fifth grade in the U.S. he discovered that he was much more advanced in arithmetic, reading skills, and world geography than his peers in Ann Arbor. We were glad that we had not sent Robert to the nearby American school where he would have learned little Hebrew and acquired less study discipline in the easy permissive atmosphere prevailing there.

When Sara was two years old she began to go each morning to a nursery school operated in the village community center a stone's throw from our house. During most of the year the youngsters played out of doors, watched over by Rutie, the motherly *ganenet* (kindergarten teacher) whom they all adored. Sarah Sa'adi usually arrived early enough to take little Sara to the *gan* (garden) and to fetch her home at noon. Between Sara and the gan where, of course, only Hebrew was spoken, Sara soon became a little sabra, speaking with a perfect deep throated Yemenite accent. After six months in Ann Arbor she forgot her Hebrew completely.

One of the reasons I wanted to live in the Kfar was because Jules Cuburnek, my old friend and B'nai Brith colleague from Chicago, lived there. Jules came from Chicago to Israel in 1948 to fly for the Israel air force in the War of Independence. After the war, he returned to the United States and did not visit Israel again until 1965. He had never lost his zeal for the country and welcomed the chance to revisit Israel as a delegate to a B'nai Brith convention and to look up his old air force companions. At a reunion party, he met a handsome brunette divorcee, Ruth Senior, and fell in love with her. Jules returned to Chicago, wound up his business interests and returned to Rutie to establish a new life. Soon afterward Jules and Rutie were married and now they live in their pleasant home in the Kfar. They have a little sabra son of their own, and Rutie's two daughters live with them. Soon after they were married Jules' daughter came from the U.S. to visit them. During the visit Karin met an Israeli physical training instructor, married him and they now live in Netanya with their two children.

Jules' Hebrew is rudimentary. His lack of facility with the language is something of an asset in his position as a teacher of English in a vocational high school. He had a teacher's certificate from the University of Pittsburgh, which even in his wildest dreams, he never expected to use.

He has a loving wife, a family, and his golf at Caesarea Country Club. I often picked him up at his school in Netanya to drive to the golf course. With his fierce Jewish nationalism and his pleasant personal life he fancies he has become "the Israeli compleat." Not really. He is more accurately a latter day country squire, Israel based. He lives a good life.

All of the houses on Haganim street are residences. The west side of Hahoresh street, our street below still retains *moshav* characteristics, with chicken farms, and stables, and cultivated fields extending down to the Sea Road. Some of the farming is a myth. The few crops are often unharvested, sown only to maintain a nominal agricultural posture for tax purposes. A few unpretentious houses adjoin the farms, built by former settlers for rental. Several of the small farms, however, are still owned and operated by the original settlers and their middle-age children, unostentiously living their tradition and their faith. They could gain small fortunes if they sold their land, but they are not in the least interested. They are happy that their beloved Kfar has prospered. They welcome newcomers. They value the opportunities for their children to broaden their horizons by meeting and knowing youngsters from abroad. Decorously and with quiet dignity, they sell their surplus eggs and produce to their neighbors. Kitty bought her eggs and vegetables from Miriam, our neighbor across the street.

While the south half of the Kfar still retains much of its original small farm-village look, the north end especially of Hahoresh street, begins determinedly to look like the exclusive suburb the Kfar is. Imposing mansions of ten rooms and more designed by the outstanding architects of Israel, some in collaboration with colleagues from abroad, stand importantly on half-acre plots along the east side of the street. Elaborate landscaping has transformed the raw land into well-groomed estates.

Scattered throughout the north end of the Kfar also are official residences of ambassadors, and homes of captains of industry, executives of the Jewish agency, doctors, lawyers, architects, military attaches, Israeli army officers.

* * *

Because there are so many diverse peoples living in the Kfar, one hears many languages spoken there besides Hebrew — English, German, French. Knowing English is a must in the Kfar as more than a few Israeli monolinguists have discovered to their discomfort. It was to be expected that the rich would come to the Kfar impressed by the status which they believe the address confers — instant upper nobility. These newcomers are not particularly happy there. They have found to their surprise that most of the residents enjoy the Kfar because of its simple physical beauty and the ease with which intense privacy of living can be practiced. There is no feigned neighborliness. The Kfarites subscribe to Robert Frost's tongue in cheek maxim, "Good Fences Make Good Neighbors." Some of the newcomer Israeli residents tell their friends they have found the Kfar to be a snobbish place. They are quite wrong. Rather, they are disconcerted by the discovery that their particular brand of snobbery, the possession of much money, is quite meaningless in the Kfar. They are dismayed to learn that some of the most affluent residents of the Kfar are looked upon as caricatures precisely because of their ostentatious display of their wealth. Understatement is not yet a general virtue in Israel.

In the center of the Kfar the Rassco company built in 1960, Neve Aviv, an expensive old people's home. They don't call it that, of course. They chose rather to use the term fashionable in the United States, because they hoped to attract Americans who can afford to live there. A senior citizens' residence. The place is not at all unpleasant; indeed, it is quite one of the nicest of such grim institutions. A jarring note is a huge flashing neon sign that can be seen by the traffic passing on the highway — "Spend your golden years at *Neve Aviv*" ("Oasis of Spring!"). The building is well-designed and looks like an apartment hotel. It is nicely landscaped. The rooms and public spaces are comfortably appointed, and the management makes a sincere effort to care for and entertain the frail elderly people who live — and die — there. Most of the residents are American; others are German, Swiss, South African.

Many have come to the Oasis of Spring of their own volition, others are parents of Israeli and American children who can afford to pay the rather substantial tariff. The idea of living in comfort in Israel is intriguing to many of the guests who have been Zionists all of their lives. They wander up and down the shaded streets, walk to the shopping center, sit for hours chatting on the bench at the bus stop and in front of the post-office a stone's throw away from the house where we lived. Often they wander off a few blocks and are gently directed home by the children of the Kfar. Almost always they are answered in the language in which they ask directions, generally English, sometimes Yiddish or German. They are particularly pleased by the courteous English or German of the children. It is good that the Israel they know is the Israel of Kfar Shmaryahu. *Lama lo* (Why not)?

Not all the residents of the Kfar live in mansions or fancy villas or are original *moshavniks.* Some are conventionally middle-class, living in the many small two-room attached houses or pensions available to new immigrants and single persons at modest rentals. These accommodations are occupied by employees of the shops and offices in the Kfar and by people who work in nearby communities.

Gilian Kay came from a second-generation South African family with deep Zionist interests. She was a psychology major at the University of Johannesburg and continued her graduate studies at Tel-Aviv University. But her real interest is tennis. She was good enough at the game to achieve national ranking in South Africa. In her middle twenties, she came to Israel some years ago for a change of scenery and to avoid impending spinsterhood. She found plenty of tennis buffs among old acquaintances and an opportunity to teach tennis privately at the Kfar where she lived for a year in a small house with a couple of roommates. She taught my son Robert tennis and good sportsmanship and they became great friends. While continuing her studies at the University of Tel-Aviv she earned her living as a popular tennis coach. Gillian is deep in the Israeli tennis world, where the game has been a popular sport since Mandate times. She ranked high among the woman players in the country and finds Israel pleasant and much freer than South Africa, especially in attitudes towards sex and personal privacy. To other Anglos who are disturbed by Israeli parochialism and chauvinism, she says simply, "You pick and choose your friends and companions. There are plenty of nice people, quite wonderful people here. They're all Jewish, which is also a plus to me. The idiots and uglies you avoid and ignore. It is difficult sometimes, but it can be done. Certainly much easier to stay away from them here than from horrible people in South Africa." She thinks Kfar Shmaryahu is quite the nicest spot on earth. Her students respected her. Some of them, both boys and girls, adored her, even though she was a bit of a martinet about good manners and sportsmanship as well as good tennis.

Our neighbors in the Kfar were certainly among the nicest people we have ever known, and the three years we lived there were pleasant and rewarding, if not fulfilling. It could be argued that the Kfar is not really Israel, or even that it is something of a refuge for escapists. Not entirely so. The Kfar is typical of the peculiarly Israeli contradictions — extremes of lifestyle within a small village, heterogeneous populations that retain their unique quality of life while frankly accepting the melting pot that boils on. However, the frontier syndrome of technologically welding new communities out of very new and raw areas was avoided in the Kfar, mainly due to the preponderance of white collar professionals and the executives who live there. In that sense the Kfar is atypical.

The author, Mrs. Leone Alexander (his first wife), and Edward G. Robinson, 1952.

2. Looking for Involvement

The days and years slipped by sunfilled and pleasant, indolent and peripheral. My urge to paint came in cycles. For weeks on end I did not go near my studio, and then with a burst of energy I would spend night after night sketching with charcoals and painting in acrylic with a palette knife. In packing up to leave Israel in the summer of 1972, I was amazed to discover that I had turned out some 75 paintings and drawings.

In retrospect, I realize that I really did not want during those four years in Israel to routinize my existence with a position of daily responsibility. Rather I preferred to drift along casually, expecting life to encompass me. Decades of work discipline, however, created guilt feelings that made me itch to be "doing something." I abhorred the notion of being "retired," and rejected this description of my status. When friends asked what I did in Israel I usually answered, "Oh, I managed to keep busy doing a lot of things that all added up to pretty much of nothing." The description was not entirely accurate, because I had come to the realization that my fifteen or so previous visits had been only prelude to knowing the country and I accepted every opportunity to travel aound, to meet people, to do whatever cropped up, however bizarre or incidental.

I fatalistically resumed Hebrew studies at Ulpan Akiva, by then fully aware that I would never master the language. I found the Ulpan a convenient alibi for evading the growing gnawing question of the personal validity of our settling in Israel. The plusses were many, and increased as we became acclimated in the Kfar where the language barrier was insignificant.

But the sense of expatriate living persisted. We were dwelling under most pleasant circumstances. We had friends and neighbors with whom we could communicate. We even had a few acquaintances with whom we shared common beliefs, experiences, convictions, enthusiasms and prejudices. But we were in Israel, not of it, and as time went on this sense of apartheid deepened and increased instead of lessening as we had hoped. For Kitty, a social person, this simply confirmed the feelings she had before we emigrated. But for me it was traumatic shock, which I refused to accept. I had never for a moment admitted the possibility that I would not adapt to Israel, would not become integrated into the scene. I was wrong.

I assiduously avoided using any of the contacts developed over the years to secure a place in the Israeli scene, abhorring the notion of protekzia (pull-influence). In the years that I lived in Israel very few of the "Establishment" whom I had known for years were aware of our presence in Israel. As time went on I became desperate enough for involvement to make a few tentative approaches. In every instance I was received with cordiality, even warmth. But I became aware soon enough that all of these good people had their own concerns. Many proferred suggestions and advice, but nothing came of it even though I made it clear that I was volunteering my services and was not looking for a job.

Shimon Peres, who is now the Minister of Defense, was one who did accept my offer of service. I did some editing and writing for him in connection with the Arab "Administered Areas" and I learned a good deal of the workings of the Israeli government in the territories acquired in the Six Day War; I came to respect the scrupulous decency with which the military establishment was handling this almost impossible task.

Label Business

My involvement in a business early in 1968, only a few months after we came to Israel, proved to be a clinical demonstration of the casual American immigrant investment syndrome. A young Canadian friend, Aryeh Cooperstock, had been a comrade of my two older daughters in *Habonim* (the Zionist youth group of the Labor Zionist Organization) during the 1950's; I had kept up a friendship with him over the years. On a trip to Expo '67 in Montreal, my family and I spent some pleasant hours with Aryeh and his young wife Michal. He was deeply committed to Israel.

In the spring of 1968, a few months before we left for Israel, we met the Cooperstocks again in New York where Aryeh was working as a city planner on Mayor Lindsay's staff. Aryeh and Michal were eager to emigrate to Israel if they could find a place for themselves there. Michal had an added incentive to go back. She had grown up in Israel, had served in the army, and had left a young son by a previous marriage with whom she longed to be reunited. Even though her former husband had custody of the boy, she felt she would at least be able to see him from time to time if she lived in Israel.

Aryeh asked me to investigate the possibility of an enterprise that might make it possible for him to earn a living in Israel, even if he could not immediately find an opportunity in city planning, his chosen profession. A wealthy friend of his had for years been obsessed with the idea that there existed a market in the U.S. for Israeli cigarettes and had told Aryeh that he would finance him in an exporting business. I agreed to check the possibility out for Aryeh.

The general counsel for the Israel Tobacco Company turned out to be a good friend of Ovadia Rasiel who called this gentleman. As luck would have it (good or bad), it developed that the principal owner, a Mr. Wicks, was visiting in Israel at the moment. A meeting was set up and I met Wicks at his suite in the Dan Hotel. He was a keen old English gentleman — bluff, hearty, and completely open. We struck it off and he explained the whole Israeli tobacco business as well as the history of the cigarette business throughout the world. He had been the first promoter of the modern cigarette filter and still retained distribution rights to the British cigarette enterprises that he and his family had sold years before.

Wicks had started the Israeli enterprise to establish a Jewish refugee friend of his who had been his agent in Germany before WW II. The business had prospered, but Wicks and his family had poured all the profits back to expand the company. I explained the purpose of my visit, emphasizing that I was interested only in finding a niche for my friend.

Wicks made it paintfully clear that he thought little of exporting Israeli cigarettes to the U.S. He had researched the idea several years before and cordially explained that the sentimental Jewish market could not sustain the business, and that the exporting costs and customs duties were prohibitive. He left it that if Aryeh's friend wanted to spend the money to further research the idea, Wicks would give him every cooperation and would be glad to see Aryeh and his friend in the United States, to which Wicks traveled often. But nothing ever came of it.

Wicks was much more interested in me and my reasons for emigrating to Israel. In a long and pleasant chat, during which we polished off a fifth of Scotch, he quizzed me about my background and my activities for Israel in the U.S. and especially my plans for an occupation. I told him that I was not looking for a business to get into, but that I was hoping for involvement in activities that would make living in Israel fulfilling for me and my family and in which I could utilize my business and legal experience and my American background. During much of the time we were together his Israeli factory manager was with us, answering the telephone and taking care of company business, as Wicks was flying home to London that night. When the manager left the room, Wicks said to me, "I want to say something to you that I don't want my manager to hear. Don't under any circumstances invest any of your funds in any business in Israel and don't obligate yourself personally in any business that you may get into. All of the enterprises in this country are based upon government funds, bank loans, and money generated abroad, especially from your country. I don't know anyone who invested his own money in this country who didn't lose it."

I was astounded to hear this cynical analysis from a man who obviously had been an ardent Zionist for half a century and had created one of the most prosperous businesses in Israel. And I said so. He replied, "Our original investment was very modest, and we made it exactly at the right time. Besides we had a superior manager and partner who knew the business and was hungry. And we haven't taken any of the profits out of the business."

Actually, I did not consider Wick's advice of any importance to me because I had little in the way of funds to invest and no intention of engaging in business. I had just recently retired from a business enterprise in the United States and told Wicks about the fifteen years I had spent in developing the industry of manufacturing and installing permanent plastic traffic lines. I believed it was clear that I did not want to be involved in industry or in my profession of law. Several days later I received a call from Wick's manager. He told me Mr. Wicks had asked him to solicit my interest in a business involving placement of labels on plasic containers by a thermo process not unlike my thermoplastic business in the U.S. I was flabberasted that Mr. Wicks would have made such a suggestion after his lecture, but was intrigued and agreed to talk to the young man, a friend of Mr. Wicks, who was seeking a partner.

The young man turned out to be a clever Englishman who had emigrated to Israel with his family as a boy in the early 1950's. His parents had been friends of the Wicks for many years in London. He was one of the outstanding package designers in Israel. A principal client of his, of course, was the Israel Tobacco Company.

He told me that at an industrial machinery exhibit in the previous spring, an American Company, the Dennison Corporation, had exhibited a machine that impinged labels onto plastic bottles by an automatic heat process. He further explained that the plastic container business in Israel was growing rapidly, and there was a real need for superheated labeling to replace paper labels and the slow, cumbersome, expensive silk-screen process used in Israel. He had prevailed upon the Dennison Corporation to leave the equipment and to grant him an option to represent the company in Israel. "Was I interested?"

I asked Soloman why Mr. Wicks had not shown an interest himself, being a family friend and all, and the investment required being so modest. His reply was logical enough. "Mr. Wicks told me that he had decided to confine all his business interests in Israel to the tobacco industry. As you know, he is an old man and only visits Israel several times a year. He told me I needed an associate who lived in Israel, could assist in developing the business and was experienced with American business enterprises. He thought you would be interested because you have a background in thermoplastics and needed some activity to occupy your time." Logical enough.

And thus against my firm resolution I found myself in 1970 the principal guarantor of loans for a business that after a year and a half had not gotten off the ground. We had a new rented factory in a suburb of Tel Aviv. Our machinery wouldn't work with decent precision despite the experts sent out by Dennison from the States and England. We had one small contract that we couldn't fulfill and several prospective customers my young partner did not want to supply until the equipment produced a steady flow of adequate labels. Since the prospective customers were all Soloman's clients under his other hat as package designer, he couldn't jeopardize his professional standing, nor his bread and butter.

So the shipping problems and the customs problems mounted and multiplied, and the rent and electric bills and wages and interest and principal on the bank loans accumulated, and what had originally appeared a simple and viable enterprise became a nightmare.

The basic elements for a successful industry were present. There was no need for investment in new materials or large inventories. The process was simple and automatic and had long proved successful in the U.S., Europe, and the Orient. Plastic conainers were becoming popular in Israel, especially for pharmaceuticals, cosmetics and food stuffs. The Israeli population was beginning to appreciate sophisticated packaging and labeling.

But the business remained on dead center and I finally opted out. My young partner found others to take over my role and relieve me of my guarantees. I was able to withdraw with a small financial loss and the benefit of rich experience in the pitfalls of starting a new business in Israel. At the end I began to wonder whether Mr. Wicks really had suggested me as a potential partner. I never met Wicks again and I never have bothered to communicate with him to find out if he had in truth changed his mind about the advice given me or had made an exception on behalf of his young friend.

Bloomfield

I have always been interested in the stage and, in fact, played several minor roles in professional productions in Chicago. In late 1969, I was offered a minor part in a movie in Israel and accepted with alacrity. The scenario was based upon the most popular sport of Israel, soccer, which in Hebrew is called *kadoor regel* (football). Richard Harris, the famous Irish-American movie actor and Romy Schneider, the equally prominent German-American actress, were the stars. Most of the action was filmed at Bloomfield Stadium, a large soccer arena in the heart of Jaffa. Soon after the filming started, a controversy arose between the Israeli director and Richard Harris, and Harris decided to direct the movie himself. Unfortunately, Harris' sincere efforts did not compensate for his lack of experience as a director and despite the million dollars expended by the producers, the Israeli Government, and the Israeli and English interests, including Wolf Mankiewicz who wrote the scenario, the movie was a bomb.

I thoroughly enjoyed the experience, witnessing with disbelief the waste, duplication, and utter chaos that, I was told by the actors, cameraman, and make-up people, stand-ins, electricians, prop men, wardrobe mistresses, bookkeepers, and all the other technicians engaged in the effort, was the way all movies are made. The cast and crew were from all over the world. Israelis, Americans, Englishmen, Frenchmen, Germans, Australians, Italians. They worked together easily despite formidable language barriers. A real camaraderie prevailed. Most of the actors were Israelis but were required to speak in English, which did not make for smooth continuity. In the finished film their voices were dubbed. The shooting time, scheduled for six weeks, dragged on for three months.

Almost a year later the movie was finally shown in Israel. I went to see it at a theater in Tel Aviv where it played for only a week. I had truly hoped that it might be a success, particularly because of the great effort of Richard Harris, who I had come to like and respect, and because of the sincerity of all the participants and the enormous (for Israel) amount of money that had been invested. The audience's reaction confirmed my worst fears. They laughed in all the wrong places and obviously did not accept the very Anglo Irish Harris as an Israeli football hero. I winced during the two scenes in which I appeared. Although very brief in the movie, they had consumed hours and days of takes and retakes. I was convinced that I was not cut out to be an Israeli movie actor.

Off-Dizengoff Players

Despite the disaster of "Bloomfield," my interest in the stage remained undiminished. Ora Lichtenstein was a formidable lady with indomitable energy. She and some young Americans decided to form an independent troupe. They solicited my interest in the venture and we organized ourselves into the "Off-Dizengoff Players." Dizengoff Street is Tel Aviv's Rue De La Paix.

The first (and last) venture of the "Off-Dizengoff Players" was a series of three modern one-act plays that enjoyed several performances at a charming little auditorium in the Sholom Aleichem Memorial Center in the northern section of Tel Aviv, and at the Khan Theater in Jerusalem, a fine little theater in a centuries-old Turkish inn that has been exquisitely remodeled by the Tourist Ministry into an entertainment center. I was the business manager of the group. This position involved talking the authorities—particularly the very cooperative Tourist Ministry officials—into subsidizing our venture. They were intrigued by the idea of theater in English as an attraction for American and other English-speaking tourists. speaking tourists.

I also negotiated with printers, arranged for newspaper advertisements and publicity, solicited help from tourist hotels, the Hebrew University people in Jerusalem, the American cultural center among others, placed tickets for sale at ticket agencies, and came to know the endless chores required to produce plays. All of the youngsters in the troupe pitched in with a will to build stage sets, design and sew costumes, transport props. It was a spirited cooperative activity and we were all rewarded by the success of the performances, both from the audience reaction and the better than fair critical acclaim in the press. Most of the American students returned to their universities in the U.S. and "Off-Dizengoff" ended its short-lived career. (In 1974, when I came back to Chicago to live I resumed my interest in theater and producing by organizing a professional company to present chamber theater readings).

Israelis share with fellow Jews the world over the love of entertainment of every variety. The Israel Philharmonic Orchestra, based in a fine modern auditorium built in Tel Aviv in 1958, is one of the best in the world. Its musical director is Zubin Mehta, the charismatic Indian conductor of the Los Angeles Symphony. In recent years the orchestra has helped produce world renowned Israeli musicians, violinists Itzhak Perlman and Pinchas Zukerman, pianist and conductor Daniel Barenboim, and many others. There are several first rate ballet groups, notably the Inbal Dancers and the Bat Sheva Company.

There are numerous theater groups in the cities which perform for the most part Hebrew translations from the English and French of modern and classical plays. Though Israel has yet to produce a great playwright or writer, a substantial output of literature and poetry has already been written and a number of Israelis are considered competent writers by world standards. The late S. Y. Agnon, an older writer in Hebrew who died in 1970, shared the Nobel Prize for literature in 1968.

Interest in serious art, music and literature is confined to a very small percentage of the Israelis, mostly educated older Ashkenazis and their educated children. The popularity of the really tenth rate music and homegrown comedy of Israel attests to the fact that the taste of the Israelis is at this stage at about the level of the Second Avenue Yiddish theater of New York's lower East side before World War II.

Validor

In the early 1950's Erika and Harry Shadmon came to Chicago from Israel to seek medical help for a hip problem that had plagued Erika for years. She had been a kindergarten teacher in Israel. Erika and her husband had an idea to build a camp complex where American and European youngsters could spend summer vacations. The concept was attractive and they persuaded me and a number of others in the U.S. and Canada to undertake the project. Over the next several years the Sharon Youth Hostel, known popularly as "VALIDOR" was built in Herzliya on the Sea, with a big swimming pool and comfortable large rooms for the youngsters. The original plans envisioned a very modest outlay, but by 1960 we had invested several hundred thousand dollars.

For a number of years the camping activities carried on and some hundreds of young teenagers spent their summers at Validor, whose program included touring the country. One of my daughters, Joan, was in the first group in 1959. But the project was a financial failure and the summer tours were abandoned. The operation went heavily in debt. The Shadmons seemed to prosper, though the enterprise did not.

In 1965 I persuaded Teddy Kollek, the mayor of Jerusalem, then the head of the tourist department of Israel, and his associate Meyer deShalit, to buy Validor for a government hotel and restaurant school. Because of a misunderstanding about taxes, the sale, which would have repaid all of the investors' funds, fell through. By the time I emigrated to Israel in 1968, it was painfully clear that the property had to be sold if the investors were to recoup any of their money. Somehow or other, though the hotel was operating successfully, the debts increased and increased. During our first two years in Israel I made a few desultory attempts to find a buyer, and by 1971, decided to launch a determined effort. My fellow investors in Chicago had urged me to once and for all finish the project, since our effort to create relationships between American Jews and young Israelis had disintegrated into a distasteful failure.

During 1971 I visited many government agencies, real estate brokers, lawyers and acquaintances trying to find some group interested in buying the really attractive property located on a high dune a few blocks from the Mediterranean Sea in a village that was fast becoming one of the best known resort areas in Israel. I showed the place to a number of potential investors from the U.S., South Africa, Europe and Canada. All of them were intrigued with the property but its rather dilapidated condition turned them off. One group thought to transform Validor into a medical center. Another investor considered it for a parents home — what is called a "senior citizens" residence in the U.S. The Conservative Synagogue Association of the U.S. toyed with the idea of buying it as a summer camp for their young people.

I spoke with the late Aryeh Pincus, the head of the World Jewish Agency, about the property suggesting that Validor could be used by the Agency as an ulpan. At one stage I thought I had a deal with an Israel Youth Hostel Organization, but those negotiations fell through because they couldn't raise enough capital.

Mr. Pincus had referred the matter to *Tour V'aleh* (Touring and Immigration) a division of the Jewish Agency engaged in hosting prospective young immigrants for a few weeks while they decided whether they wanted to settle in Israel. Tour V'aleh was seriously interested in the place. It exactly fitted their need, but the bureaucratic problems of generating adequate funding were too much for them. However, they did send us a prospective buyer who was interested in running Validor as a hotel and who had agreed that if he bought the place, he would make it available to Tour V'aleh for several years at reasonable rates.

I spent many days and months on this negotiation because I knew that the American investors would be somewhat mollified if the loss they suffered in the sale should be partially compensated by seeing Validor once again utilized for its original purpose — to acquaint young Jews from all over the world with Israel.

Validor finally was bought by the group of German Jews from Frankfort that had been referred by Tour V'aleh. During the negotiations Israel had once again devalued the Israel currency from 3.5 to 4.2 pounds to the dollar. For a while it looked as if this negotiation would fail like all the others. But the Frankforters wanted the place. We worked out a reasonable adjustment on the price and the contract was consummated. The utilization of the place by Tour V'aleh was stipulated as a condition of sale, but the buyers agreed to this only as a pious resolution and not as a binding contract.

The stipulation did afford some comfort to the original owners, a compensation for their very considerable financial loss, although I doubt whether Validor has ever been made available to Tour V'aleh's prospective immigrants. In any event, Validor became a cheerful, bright, and happy resort hotel, much more attractive than it had been for many years. The considerable time I spent during 1971 on the Validor sale was especially rewarding because of the insight I gained about Israel financing and the continuing interest in Israel investment manifested by Jews and Jewish organizations all over the world. Not the least of the compensations was the contact I had with former Eastern European Jews in Germany who in recent years have acquired formidable business interests in Israel, particularly in the hotel and apartment field. These ex-DP camp inmates are proof again of the resilience of Jews over the generations.

Fruit of Light

I mention the Rassco Corporation (Rural and Suburban Settlement Company) many times in these pages. I was involved with this company very early in my Israel activity in the U.S., starting with my acquaintanceship with the late Dr. Herbert Foerder, who was one of its founders in the early 1930's and the managing director of the company during its formative years until he became the Chairman of the Bank Leumi, Israel's largest bank. I had early on encouraged Dr. Foerder to establish the Rassco company in America, to seek American investment capital. Their first investment group in the U.S. originated in Chicago in 1952. For almost a decade the Chicago headquarters of Rassco was located in my law offices there.

I had gathered together a small group of investors to participate in a joint venture with Rassco to build apartment buildings in Ramat Shaul, then an isolated area on the hillside of Mount Carmel south of Haifa, and today a flourishing suburb within the environs of that port city. When I moved to Israel in 1968, I met for the first time Dr. Louis Pinner, a colleague of Dr. Foerder from Germany and our neighbor in Kfar Shmaryahu. Dr. Pinner invited me to join the board of directors of a then Rassco subsidiary called Rassco Plantations, which today is known as Pri-Or (Fruit of Light), an independent citrus company that owns and manages plantations growing oranges, lemons, and grapefruits. He suggested that I could make a contribution as a voice for foreign investors in Israeli citrus groves. In my eagerness for Israeli immersion, I unwisely accepted nomination to the Board of Directors of Pri-Or.

The proceedings of the monthly board meetings were conducted in Hebrew, and all of the voluminous notes and reports were issued in Hebrew. I was lost. I had to call upon all the creative talents and adroitness I could muster not to appear as the idiot compleat at these meetings.

I didn't know what the hell my fellow Directors were talking about most of the time. When someone made a wisecrack, which occurred frequently, I smiled benignly and knowingly. Once in a while I would throw in a word in Hebrew to maintain my balance. I knew full well that everyone on the board understood and spoke English, but I had to use my native tongue sparingly because I was supposed to be something of an Israeli. I am certain that most of the members of the board were delighted to sense my constant agony. It was a subtle way to get even with all cocky Americans who, as they too well knew, had provided most of the funds which made their company possible, even though I myself was not one of them.

I carried on with this charade for almost two years. Dr. Pinner was my neighbor in the Kfar, and after most of the meetings I drove him home. He would patiently in his very good English explain to me what had transpired at the meetings though he politely insisted that I had understood most of what had gone on. If so, it had to be through a process of osmosis. My kind friend was being more than charitable. Interestingly enough, Dr. Pinner is more fluent in English, *Yekke* that he is, than in Hebrew, which he has known since his arrival in Palestine in 1923. I was willing to accept his judgment that the board members thought I was a quiet, thoughtful man who listened to the proceedings and did not, as a freshman member, try to interpose dubious judgments.

Top: From left: unidentified man, Mayor Abba Hushi of Haifa, the author, and Julius Ginsberg, Labor Zionist leader of Chicago.
Bottom: Franklin D. Roosevelt, Jr., the author, and unidentified man, Detroit, 1954.

3. The Quality of the Scene

Ben-Gurion's Zionist basic for immigration is today as unfashionable in Israel as was the Grand Old Man himself in his last years. The Israelis long since have stopped believing that Western Jews are threatened by anti-Semitism. Israelis however, have found other rationalizations for suggesting that the Jews should come to Israel to live, based on the general quality of life in America and the physical danger to life and limb for big-city dwellers.

Two complementary myths have been added to Israeli folklore. America is a jungle and Israel is an idyllic paradise. The jungle book theory goes something like this: Hordes of Blacks roam the streets of the big cities, especially New York, Boston, Chicago, Los Angeles. They kill, rape, maim, rob. They set buildings on fire, they rob stores and banks. They steal automobiles and kidnap women and children. It is not safe to ride in a cab; to walk on any street at night; to go to the movies, a concert, a restaurant. Americans live in constant fear. They triple-lock their doors and never open them to strangers. Nor is the violence attributed only to the Blacks. There are hoodlums, radical youth, dope fiends in the jungle raising general hell and making life unsafe for law-abiding citizens. All of this has turned the United States into a kind of democratic police state. It is not claimed now that this horrendous situation is directed at Jews, *per se*. However, the Israelis know that the majority of the six million Jews of America live in the big cities, and thus many of them are at the receiving end of the terror. When Israelis are told by American visitors and even by Israelis who have visited the United States that this picture of America is distorted and greatly exaggerated, they simply don't believe it. They prefer to hold on to the jungle myth, because it comforts their own egos, and assuages their subconscious envy of the richer, more luxurious life of American Jews.

In contrast to this grim picture is the story Israelis tell to regale American visitors and new immigrants. With variations of emphasis it goes something like this: Israel is safe. Any woman can walk any place in the country at any time of the day or night and with perfect confidence. There is little crime, certainly as compared to the United States, and because the police are efficient and incorruptible most criminals are quickly apprehended. The Israelis are people who respect law and order. Their children are taught respect for authority.

In recent years an increase of crime, especially in Tel-Aviv and the larger cities, has made it more and more difficult to keep this picture in focus. Bank hold-ups and armed robbery, auto theft, burglary, mugging, arson, strong-arming, rape, blackmail, extortion have become commonplace. The automobile and easy access to firearms (to some extent the result of the large numbers of Israeli youth who serve in the armed forces, remaining for years thereafter in the reserves), have increased the incidence of crime alarmingly. Small-scale mafia-patterned organized crime does exist in Tel-Aviv, and even in Jerusalem. During the shooting weeks of the Yom Kippur War, crime decreased substantially only to reach and even exceed pre-war levels in a few short months.

There is forced and voluntary prostitution complete with pimps on all the main highways and in the slums of Tel-Aviv, Jaffa, and elsewhere. The ladies are called "The Highway Queens." (There is precedent in the Bible for this enterprise. The widow Tamar seduced her father-in-law, Jacob's son Judah, masquerading on the road as a prostitute. From this union was born Zerah, ancestor of King David and of Jesus Christ.)

One of the less attractive new Israeli exports is several hundred young prostitutes who fly to Germany each year. This phenomenon developed soon after the expansion of air travel between Israel and West Germany. Some of the affluent tourists coming from there, both Jews and non Jews, were greatly attracted to the teenage Israeli girls, mostly from poor homes, who in recent years have flocked to the bright lights of Tel Aviv and Jerusalem. They paid these girls five and ten times more than the five or six dollars they were getting from the locals and which they had to share with their pimps. The Germans, some of whom themselves were in the prostitution business in Frankfort, Munich and Berlin, also persuaded some of the more attractive ones that they could fare much better in the free spending German cities. When the first Israeli girls returning on visits, told their sisters of the money to be made in Germany, the trickle became a steady flow. Most of these poor young girls go to the continent to escape their pimps who exploit them viciously.

The Israelis are distressed and concerned about the increase of crime. They find it bewildering and especially embarrassing to admit its existence to fellow Jews from abroad. Visiting Jews are eager to believe that crime is minimal in Israel. Many Jews share a common myth that few Jews drink whiskey (a notion that persists even in the United States). They also believe few Jews are criminals, that Jews are not prostitutes and pimps, Jews aren't gangsters (well, a few in the United States), ergo crime can't be much of a problem in Israel. Unfortunately, despite Jewish chauvinism to the contrary, crime is a serious problem in Israel.

The nonsense that Israel is an idyllic paradise is purely for export, because it can't be swallowed locally by new immigrants, and only in small gulps by tourists. The evidence of one's eyes, ears and nose is too strong to the contrary. The land is beautiful, breathtaking. The climate is magnificent, but the "blessings" of modern technology, science, and industry are rapidly despoiling the land. Belching smoke into the air and discharging wastes into the lakes and rivers and seas is still permitted. The same clash of interests between industrial developers and environmentalists prevails in Israel as in other industrial countries. Enlightened public opinion and concerned officials are not as yet a politically effective force to prevent galloping and probably irrevocable destruction.

The Israelis discovered the automobile about 1960. True, there were many automobiles and trucks and motor-propelled vehicles in Palestine in the early days of the State. But in recent years new well-paved highways have been built the length and breadth of the land. Growing prosperity, the convenience and attraction of mobility, and the status importance of the family car have converted the former Israeli pedestrian into a rider — worse, into a driver. And what a driver!

The authorities have tried to adopt advanced traffic safety devices and traffic laws. The courts are assiduous in convicting offenders. The requirements for obtaining driver's licenses and in maintaining brakes, lights, windshield wipers, are exemplary. But the carnage on the city streets and on the highways continues unabated. Traffic deaths and injuries, property destruction, loss of work hours, all have combined to make the traffic problem a major concern of government. Motor vehicles spew poisonous exhaust fumes all over the land. In the cities cars are parked bumper to bumper in every street. Driving in mid-town Tel-Aviv and Jerusalem is as vexing a misadventure, as tortuous a chore as in New York or Paris or Tokyo.

The fact that too many Israelis are poor drivers, impolite, and reckless, doesn't help the traffic problem. It is quite understandable, if not forgivable, that the Israelis have taken to the motor vehicle as a dangerous toy instead of a means of transportation. Americans have grown up with cars for generations. The automobile age came upon Israel full grown. The streets, even in comparatively new cities like Tel-Aviv, were not designed to be choked with thousands of automobiles. The volatile Israeli temperament has been exacerbated by years of living under uneasy military truce conditions and five shooting wars. The concept of yielding the right of way is alien to an independent character molded by 25 years of strife. Little wonder the Israelis have short fuses. It doesn't take much for them to whack the automobile in front of them, run a red light, sideswipe a slower driver. Proportionately, more pedestrians are run down by motor vehicles in Israel than in any place in the world; accident insurance rates are predictably the highest, and increase every year.

How does one measure the quality of life? The electronic world measures quality by statistics. Israel scores high in this test. In 25 short years Israel changed from a rural agricultural country into a modern industrial nation, complete with all the devices and credentials. Imagine, women used to wash the laundry in brooks, the Arab ladies pounding the dirt out with stones, the Jewish ladies using brushes and scrub boards in laundry buckets. Many of the homes were lighted by candles, kerosene lamps, gas fixtures. The diet consisted mostly of food grown by the family on the farms or bought in a primitive neighborhood store. Now it is packaged, homogenized, additive preserved, varied, and purchased in a large, well-appointed supermarket. The material list is endless. The reader need but look at all the products in any shopping center in the United States. If he has the price, the Israeli can buy the same things made in Israel (or imported from the United States, Germany, Japan, France, Hungary, Romania, England). Twenty years ago there were more bookstores in Tel-Aviv per capita than in any city in the world. There still are. Twenty years ago you had to scour the city to buy a bottle of Scotch whiskey. Now you can buy Scotch whiskey in every store and kiosk next to all the bookstores.

If the quality of life is measured in terms of television sets, radios, tape recorders, record players, electric washing machines, hot water, carpeting, automatic heaters, motor scooters, well-cut clothing, furs, jewelry, water beds and foam rubber mattresses, mechanical toys, automobiles and even private airplanes, Israel has made it. Just as in the United States however, the price for so much sophisticated packaging and creature comforts has been too high. And the quality is questionable. The extremes of prosperity and poverty perhaps are not polar but the gap is widening and the concomitant bitterness grows.

Outside of Israel, people know little about the many difficult problems of public transportation, housing, personal debt, welfare, child care, high taxes. Israel's cost of living in terms of net take home pay measured against the price of goods and services probably is the highest in the world. To know this is to begin to understand the resentment against the prosperous new immigrants, whose arrival with pockets full of money raises the cost of everything for the native Israeli — or so he believes. No wonder most Israelis really don't want any more immigrants, no matter what they or the government say to the contrary.

Israel allegedly is a socialist state; most all public services are owned or controlled by the government — radio, telephone, the postal system; the electric company, the airlines, passenger and freight rail facilities. Ironically, the bus companies, which provide 95 percent of public transportation in Israel, are not publicly owned. They are the property of two major co-operatives, Egged and Dan, both founded during Mandate times. It is intriguing to learn that an Israeli bus driver (that is, if he is a member of the co-op) is a partner of the bus company. It isn't that intriguing for the passenger who gets squeezed into the foul-smelling bus, or gets passed up waiting for it because there is no more room. The powerful position of the bus co-operatives in the Histadrut and the labor parties explains the reluctance of the government to deal squarely with the situation. Fares are kept down by government subsidies to make up deficits caused by high salaries and flagrantly inefficient bureaucracy. The socialist public spirit that brought the bus co-ops into being a half century ago has long since evaporated. Morale of service has been replaced by morale of high income. The public is the victim, as usual. The convolution and intricacies of party ties and political clout keep the myth alive; *Chaver Egged* (Member of Egged Cooperative) remains among the sacrosanct shibboleths, too sacred to be tampered with. As in the United States, England, and in all the democracies, labor in Israel has become a conservative self-serving segment of acquisitive society.

The Israeli lives for the most part in his own house or flat, which nominally he owns. There is very little rental housing available in Israel, and there is little likelihood that there will be in the future. As with almost every life situation there, the reasons are immediately historical. When the nation was young, most people lived in a rural environment; housing was built and owned by a kibbutz, or by an individual farmer or tradesman, often financed by his relatives or Jewish organizations abroad. Since the beginning of the State and the growth of new urban areas, the majority of the Israelis live in flats in housing developments, or in large apartment houses built in the cities during the 50's and 60's. These are four and five-story walk-ups, adequate but unimaginative, drab, but certainly not comparable to the wretched tenements in the inner cities of the United States. Up until a decade ago apartments were relatively inexpensive and somehow or other the money was found to buy them. Only thirty or forty percent of the purchase price was financed by mortgages. The husband and wife worked. The older children worked. The mortgage was paid off.

For new immigrants during this period, the government and the Jewish Agency — working with contracting, financing, and technical subsidiaries of the Histadrut — built flats and made them available to the newcomers on liberal, actually charitable, terms. As the newcomers became established, they were able to buy their flats and finally pay off their loans. Housing assistance for immigrants still follows this benevolent pattern. Despite the shrillness of the cries of some of the new Russian immigrants, they are ensconced in flats that they could only dream of in Mother Russia.

In Israel there was created a peculiarly Jewish device that worked very well for twenty years, but later brought on unforeseeable difficulties yet to be resolved. Key money. Flats, stores, workshops, whose owners did not need to occupy them, were made available. Those who were able raised some money and "bought the key." The key money averaged approximately a fourth of the value of the flat or shop. This gave them the right to occupancy indefinitely upon the payment of low rental, which with inflation became nominal rental. Their right to permanent occupancy became fixed by law. As a result these occupants became life tenants and their occupancy rights continued after death for members of the immediate family. The unpopularity of rental housing and renting of properties can be traced directly to the institution of "key money."

What about Israelis who are not new immigrants, who are not prosperous, who are young soldiers just released from the armed forces and wnat to get married and settle down in their own homes, who don't have rich relatives in Israel or abroad, whose bride's parents can't help, who don't occupy a key money flat, whose parents have no room for them, or who don't want to double up into crowded quarters. What of them? It's tough. So they aren't about to urge new immigrants to come to Israel. They don't even pretend to believe that immigration is a good idea. Sometimes, especially since the Yom Kippur War, they even flirt with the idea of emigration.

Organizations have been formed to pressure the government to provide housing for young marrieds. Protest groups have sprung up all over the country, in Tel-Aviv, Jerusalem, Haifa. Petitions are filed. Delegations visit the Prime Minister, the Minister of the Treasury, whomever. Housing is of such importance, or rather the lack of it, that Israel has a Ministry of Housing, that also is importuned by the protesters. These manifestations of anger, and despair have accomplished little more than to emphasize the depth of the problem and the direction of possible solutions.

Housing was being built at a furious pace until 1974 — when the economic crunch and galloping inflation slowed it down. Thousands of units almost completed, just being started, half-finished, can be seen all over the country, but principally in and around Jerusalem and Tel-Aviv. Many of them are sold before they are finished or are quickly bought when they are ready to be occupied. Who buys them? Affluent Israelis, and others who have access to equity funds and loans through bank connections, business associates or employers, or can borrow from relatives in Israel and abroad. Many of these apartments are bought by new immigrants who combine their own funds with liberal long term, low interest mortgages made available by guarantees of the Jewish Agency. In recent years, expensive luxury units in apartment buildings and hotels on the Mediterranean shore and in Jerusalem have been bought by wealthy Americans and Jews in other countries as a place to spend a few weeks a year visiting Israel. "Have a home away from home — buy a foothold in Israel." read the advertisements!

A running debate has been carried on for years concerning the morality and economic good sense of building luxury units while the poor and young Israeli citizens need housing so urgently. It is argued that needed skilled labor, which in the building trades was until the middle 1970's very much in short supply, is diverted to this construction. Also such construction siphons off materials, generally increases construction costs, and promotes inflation. The argument is intensified by the fact that some of the corporate developers of these units and many of the contracting firms are partially or mainly owned by the government or by Histadrut subsidiary corporations. The largest single builder of housing in Israel, both low cost and luxury, is *Shikun Ovdim*, freely translated as Workers' Housing, a Histadrut subsidiary.

The arguments for building luxury housing are also valid and persuasive. Most of the hard currency financing for this construction comes from overseas. Many of the materials, especially for the interiors, are imported. The pump-priming provided by United States dollars invested in these enterprises makes it possible to acquire much needed architectural, engineering, and construction know-how, to train Israeli workers (including many Israeli Arabs and Arabs from the Administered Areas and young men just out of the armed forces) on-the-job and with pay. Funds from abroad also are made available to Israeli banks and loan companies for mortgages. The housing branch of Histadrut claims that the profit it makes on a luxury flat, paid for in foreign currency, enables it to build a worker's flat for an Israeli below cost. Perhaps so. In any event, the debate rages on.

Meanwhile many young people, and their older brothers and sisters and parents and young children, remain doubled up in tiny flats, houses, or shacks. Many of the living quarters had years ago been put up as "temporary housing" for immigrants. Almost all of them were jerry built, long before modern plumbing, electricity, heating, or planning were introduced generally into Israel. The occupants improvise and plan and hope. The shantytown appearance of some areas of Tel-Aviv, the result of little or no planning and even less zoning enforcement, is a constant shock to visitors who wander a few blocks away from the seashore hotels.

The bottleneck that continues to restrict the average Israeli looking for decent housing is the lack of financing. He simply cannot get a big enough mortgage. A new immigrant can obtain an 80 percent low-interest mortgage. An Israeli with a good job and two other members of his family working may wangle a 40 percent loan at best, and pay 15 percent or more annual interest. Where does he get the other 60 percent? Most often he doesn't, so he stays where he is. The problem of mortgage financing for Israelis has plagued the bankers, economists, and politicos for years — with no solution in sight. No Israeli ever has much ready cash on hand. Even if he has a bank account with a balance in it, he is usually in debt. The legerdemain of deficit financing operates — buy now, pay later — at the highest levels of defense, industry and in government budgeting. Stalling creditors is an Israeli art. In fact, overdraft checks are almost automatically honored by the banks, with interest charges, of course. A substantial part of daily routine business operates on the overdraft system, not unlike the American bank credit card — without the card.

The Israeli rarely knows what a tremendous percentage of his income is eaten up by interest and finance charges. He will probably remain in debt all his life, but he does have a television set, a new living-room suite, his wife has a winter coat, the family has an automobile. But he can't buy a house or a flat on credit. Many contractors have gone bankrupt by extending credit and hoping to be paid. Contractors, architects, subcontractors, materials suppliers insist that they be paid in advance and as the work progresses. When payments are not made, they discontinue the work. Throughout Israel one can see partially completed houses, apartment buildings, factories and workshops, hotels, gasoline stations, office buildings. Some of them remain unfinished for years. Eventually they are completed, not always by the original promoters.

The advent of Western civilization has brought the doubtful blessing of public welfare to Israel, American style. A truism of Jewish conscience has always been that the Jewish community looks after its widowed and orphaned, the maimed, the aged, the mentally retarded, the deaf, the halt, and the blind, as a communal Jewish responsibility. Jewish families and relatives have always looked after their own, privately or through their synagogue and Jewish community organizations. This tradition, however, has become attenuated in Israel. The Welfare Ministry of the government in Israel has assumed a primary responsibility to care for the unfortunate and the poor. That is not to say that the Jewish tradition of caring for the dependents of the tribe is not still practiced extensively in Israel in the Ashkenazi, Sephardic and Afro-Asian communities. However, the magnitude of the problem of taking care of thousands of refugees and newcomers and thousands of children required substantial public aid from the government. It is a mark of the coming of age of Israel as a nation that welfare and child care is a function headed by a minister with cabinet rank.

Welfare problems arose with the earliest immigration after 1948 and grew as immigration increased. Many thousands of poor, sick, maimed, elderly and children came from Europe, Africa, and the Arab countries. Implicit in the "Law of Return" was the Biblical and public requirement to look after the "returnees" once they arrived on Israel's shores. Many of them had no relatives or friends to turn to. The ethnic communities were not organized to assume these responsibilities. The members of these communities themselves had all they could do to sustain themselves and their families. Thus the welfare apparatus grew into a major branch of government. Its funding requires millions of Israeli pounds annually. Inevitably this activity has become a bureaucracy, with all the concomitant impersonal rigidity and red tape marking such bureaucracies in all countries. Israel is fortunate in being bolstered in its welfare and public assistance functions by large Jewish organizations abroad that provide funds, expertise, and personnel in every area of these activities.

For a generation or more the Israelis have also assumed a generous share of the burden of the assistance required in specialized welfare areas, such as aid to the blind, deaf and crippled; child care; training for victims of the crippling diseases; whatever needs the less fortunate have. Israeli organizations work cooperatively and effectively with counterpart Jewish organizations abroad in the area of welfare and medical philanthropy. The common goals of the organizations and the government departments have tended to minimize the rivalries, duplication, tugging and pulling, honors seeking, and self-aggrandizement, which mar so many other fields of activity in philanthropic circles.

The Israelis are not afraid that western immigration will add to the welfare problem or will require additional taxes to help indigent newcomers and their children. Nor does one hear any suggestion that the Soviet Jews should be discouraged from coming to Israel because they will add to the welfare burden, although they do and will. The resentment against favoring the immigrants in housing accommodations does not extend to welfare gripes. Indeed, the fact that the Israelis know full well that there are no indigent Anglo new immigrants from western countries offers another clue to the real if unspoken resentment. Simply — the Israelis accept the Russian immigrants because they consider them refugees and they must come. *Ain breirah* (no choice). And if this will create additions to the already heavy welfare budget — also *ain breirah.* The Anglos and Westerners aren't refugees. They don't have to come and so why should they? Many Israelis feel that there are enough Israelis already and the population will continue to grow with newcomers from the Soviet Union and the other Jews who will come because they must.

"Protekzia" is a modern Israeli term for a peculiarly Israeli phenomenon. Protekzia is complex and cannot be accurately defined by any one English synonym. The closest words probably are influence or pull "not what you know, but who you know". It sometimes involves bribery, but rarely. It can mean currying favor, political clout, subtle blackmail, nepotism, the evils of bureaucracy, obtuseness, a pretty face, old school ties, benign neglect. In Israel it sometimes works adversely, negatively. The directive of a department head to a clerk to do something special outside of the regular routine or in a hurry for a friend or relative of the department head can be disastrous for the friend or relative, if the clerk should happen to resent the directive and sabotage the order.

The institution of tenure, confined in the United States mainly to academic circles, exists in Israel in every field of social, political, and economic activity. Thus, the power of executives and administrators is circumscribed by the set-in concrete position of many job holders in the public and private sectors. And the reaction of bureaucrats often range from indifference to hostility, when they are confronted with *protekzia* in which they have no personal interest. This is well understood and orders the subtlety with which *protekzia* is practiced. The maddening and studied "I don't know what you want" of the Middle East is a Levantine ingredient that can deflect efforts to exercise *protekzia* American-style. The Afro-Asians and Oriental Sephardic Jews, who now constitute a majority of the Israeli population, have added their soupçons to the potpourri in the practice of *protekzia.* The politico-clerical religious establishment are among the most assiduous practitioners of the art. So are the kibbutznikim, despite their generally valid moral postures.

Protekzia involves ethnic, tribal, familial, personal, political, religious, material, erotic, corruptive elements. The practice of it more often than not also involves elements of rough justice, gentleness, compassion, pity, and intuitive understanding of misfortune. In short, it is everything that Israel is, in all its glorious contradictions. It is indigenously Israeli.

A few random examples. Our label company had a bank loan overdue. I asked the president of the bank whom I had known for years, to recommend an extension to the loan department. The president called the loan officer and asked him to see what he could do to extend the loan. The loan officer courteously advised me that the loan must be paid. When I was in the president's office I discovered that his secretary was an old acquaintance whom I had met in Chicago when she worked in the Israel consulate. Not wanting to disturb her busy boss I called her for advice. She promptly called the loan officer unbeknownst to her boss and the loan was extended. Did she tell the loan officer that her boss wanted the loan extended? Nothing of the sort. She told the loan officer that I was a friend of hers and she could vouch for me.

A young immigrant friend needed his temporary resident certificate renewed by the Ministry of the Interior so that he could continue to work. Ordinarily this takes a tortuous two days and requires that the immigrant come to the office at 7:30 in the morning (the Israeli work day starts very early, especially in the hot summer months). My friend feared he would lose his job if he took time off. At my request, a lawyer friend called a cousin who is an official in the office of the Ministry. Early one morning the immigrant met the cousin who took him into the office handling renewals, said a few fast words in Hebrew to a colleague there, and in a few minutes the documents were filled out and stamped and my friend went to work.

The son of one of our neighbors joined a kibbutz with his young Christian wife to whom he was married by a reform rabbi in the United States. The wife had converted to Judaism after diligent and serious study. She is pregnant and the baby is due in a month. The husband is informed that there may be a serious question concerning the "Jewishness" of the child by Israeli legal and orthodox religious definition. Conversion takes four months of assiduous study and the wife will be required to undergo searching examination by a rabbinical board as to her knowledge of the Bible and rules of conduct, religious practice, and as to her sincerity. The young couple are in a state of panic. A fellow member of the kibbutz offers to call a friend of his whose brother is a rabbi in Tel-Aviv. The young rabbi suggests that they see a friend of his, a religious lawyer of some prominence in religious political circles. He will make the appointment. The young couple sees the lawyer. He is very pleasant and encouraging. He knows a rabbi who speaks excellent English and specializes in conversions. He can see how sincere and intelligent the young bride is. He calls the rabbi who undertakes the tutoring for a fee of one thousand pounds (about $235.00 then). The bride has three one-half hour sessions with the rabbi, during the course of the next week. He is a good teacher, she is an apt pupil. The following week teacher and pupil appear before a board of three rabbinical sages. The session lasts an hour. The young lady is put at her ease and the examiners are sympathetic and understanding. The conversion is completed and certified. A Jew will be born. Strange and wonderful are the ways of the Lord.

Education in Israel

From the long period of the British mandate, Israel has inherited many British institutions and customs. One of them is the basic secular education system in a modified form. The British almost sadistically weed out their less affluent youngsters, foreclosing their chance to go to university before they reach secondary school age. The Israelis give their youngsters more time to face the executioner. Until very recently only a handful of high school youngsters had any plans or hopes to go on to the university. For most families the tuition is prohibitively high, and the competition for the available places is grueling and frightening. The *Bagroot* (matriculation) requirement is only a preliminary step. All able bodied boys go into the armed forces on reaching their 18th birthday whether they are in school or not. Even now, a small minority finishes high school, which only in recent years has been public and free for a year or two; before the end of the 1970's free public high school hopefully will be available throughout Israel. The whole higher educational system is rapidly approaching the standards of the western countries. In no small measure, this is being achieved by the extraordinary generosity of the Jewish communities of the United States, Europe, and South America. Millions of dollars have been donated to build high schools and universities and to provide funds to maintain them and to train teachers.

The number of youngsters who make the universities or the Technion in Haifa after army service however, remains distressingly small — less than 5 percent. The percentage from the Afro-Asian and Sephardic population is starkly less. The reasons for this are obvious enough. Given their large families and low income, it is generally out of the question for Sephardic youngsters even to attend high school. Then there is the difference between the Ashkenazi and Eastern attitude towards formal education. In North Africa and the Arab countries the Jews in recent centuries did not have the opportunity to develop traditions for education. In those countries only a handful of the rich aristocracy were educated. And only the males. Little wonder then that in Israel the Sephardic parent says, "We need bread in the house, go to work, my child," while in the Ashkenazi family the parent says, "Even if there is no bread in the house, you'll go to school, my child." This situation is rapidly changing and within another generation it is likely that whatever differences between the ethnic communities remain, respect and opportunities for education will be universal amongst all Israelis.

Many separate forces at work in Israel will in a few years combine to blur the disparities that now exist. The influence of three years in the armed forces is incalculable. Youngsters are thrown together in an atmosphere of absolute equality. Any lingering prejudices of color and ethnic background quickly disappear. What remains is respect for integrity, courage, humor, literacy, ambition, energy and a pervasive fundamental camaraderie. However they went in, most of them come out literate and all of them are Israeli.

As the pace of sophisticated technology accelerates the essentiality of education increases. Israel now provides eight years of universal free education, and school attendance is compulsory until age fourteen. With the concerned generosity of the Jews of the Diaspora, the Ministry of Education may achieve a goal of twelve years of free compulsory education by the end of the decade. Public opinion is solidly behind the principle of universal free education. Only the conviction of the need for a strong defense establishment unites the Israeli population more.

Some older Oriental Jews have even changed their attitudes towards schooling for girls. Their children and neighbors have educated them. Many of these children are now adults and parents themselves. The new generation of Oriental adults remember with vivid bitterness the indifference and prejudices of their parents. Like Jews everywhere, they intend to see to it that their children get the education they didn't. Unlike their parents, they will make personal sacrifices to send their kids to school.

Manifestly, the availability of college and university education moves at a slow pace and there is no likelihood of a proliferation of colleges and universities. Israel hardly needs the empty symbolism that most American college degrees now represent. There is, however, a steady, even dramatic progression of growth of colleges, universities and institutions of higher learning in Israel. Only fifteen years ago it was Hebrew University in Jerusalem, and Technion in Haifa, and that was it. Today it is also Tel-Aviv University, University of the Negev in Be'er Sheva (now named Ben-Gurion University), Bezalel in Jerusalem, University of Haifa, Bar-Ilan in Ramat Gan. Several other municipal and private colleges and technical schools are in the making.

A few years ago only a handful of Sephardic young men and women were part of the university student body. Today there are thousands of them, though their number still remains less than their proportion in the population. The Sephardics and Afro-Asians now constitute more than 60 percent of the total Israeli Jewish population, and more than 65 percent of the children in the early grades of the public schools. At the eighth grade level the percentage drops to slightly less than 50 percent. In the early grades of high school the school population is approximately 40 percent Oriental and 60 percent Ashkenazi. The high school graduate statistic in 1972 was 70 percent Ashkenazi, 30 percent Sephardic. Sadly, the number of eighteen-year olds who pass their *bagrut* exams is considerably smaller than the number who finish high school. And the number of applicants to all of the institutions of higher learning are many times greater than the number who are accepted.

Most Israeli university students are politically conservative. They are not rebels. There have never been any student riots in the Israeli universities. There have been demonstrations concerning academic affairs, though, at Hebrew University, and in recent years an active liberal movement has made a substantial impact at Haifa University. In some ways the passivity and unquestioning acceptance of educational authority in the universities may be compared to the dogmatic traditions of the orthodox religious *yeshivot.* In America and Europe, even in South America, many Jewish students are leaders and participants in the foment against blind acceptance of tradition and the "Establishment." Rarely in Israel. It is predictable that as a result of the Yom Kippur War and the schisms it revealed, there will be much more student activism. The instinct for independence of thought and action may have been dormant in the Israeli student, but it certainly existed below the surface. The growing numbers of Jewish and other students from abroad may also stimulate the Israel campuses to more joyfulness and gaiety.

4. Religion in Israel

The role of religion in Israel is confusing and confused. Nothing more vividly demonstrates the contradictions of Israel today than this facet of Israeli life. Israel is not a theocratic state, though political clericalism is a significant force in government and society. The country has always been ruled by a socialist labor oriented government, yet that government sometimes is abject in its obeisance to the Orthodox hierarchy. Clericalism does exist and every Israeli is affected by its pervasiveness, yet less than 20 percent of the Jewish population are committed Orthodox Jews.

The fact that there is a Ministry of Religion, headed by a minister of cabinet rank, attests to the official importance of religious Judaism. In practice the Ministry is overshadowed and dominated by a well organized chain of command rabbinate, headed by a chief Ashkenazi rabbi and a chief Sephardic rabbi. The insistence of the Sephardic religious communities on their own chief rabbi is telling evidence of the ethnic schism that still obtains in Israel. Important phases of personal law and marriage, divorce, adoption, alimony, child support, inheritance are under the jurisdiction of rabbinical courts, though the majority of the Israelis are non-observant Jews opposed to the legal status of religion, which touches their lives and invades their freedoms at every turn. Even so, the Israelis for the most part accept the religious establishment fatalistically and shrug, "It's a Jewish country after all, and so it must be."

The only citizens and residents of Israel who are free of political and legal restraints in the practice (or non-practice) of their religion are the non Jews — the Moslems and the Christians. Thus far, the Orthodox power structure has successfully prevented Reform Judaism and even Conservative Judaism from gaining a real foot-hold in the country and it has been protected in its medieval obscurantism by the ruling political establishment.

The question "Who is a Jew," which in Israel is much more than a philosophical exercise because important legal and personal rights are involved, is still determined by the religious establishment. Ridiculous and demeaning legal fictions are required for non-believers to maintain simple individual dignity.

The Orthodox religious establishments continue to be genuinely committed to selective Western immigration. They want their people to come to the Holyland even if it means emptying out all of Williamsburg. From their religious and ethnic point of view they are correct and consistent. Their Israel has not changed. It remains the Holy Land, peopled only with a minority of believers. The most extreme of them, the Neturei Karta, do not recognize the existence of the temporal state; they await only the coming of the Messiah. All of the religious Jews in Israel want to increase their numerical strength; the more optimistic believe that one day they will be able to control the country politically through the ballot box. They argue and believe that the only real justification for a Jewish state is Orthodox Judaism. To many of them the non-believing Israeli is a Goy.

There has been no rush of Orthodox American Jews to make the ultimate pilgrimage. This is not as paradoxical as it may seem. The extremely Orthodox in Israel feel that they live on a sort of island surrounded by a sea of non-believers, more despicable than Moslems or Christians — Jewish Goyim. Despite the almost provocative tenderness with which they are treated by the Establishment because of their exaggerated political strength at home and abroad, they don't have it all their own way. Buses do run on Shabbat (the Sabbath) in Haifa. Night clubs, restaurants and theaters are open in most of the country on Friday night, even in Jerusalem. The religious establishment tried to prevent television on Friday night but after a bitter campaign, it lost. And so on. In Williamsburg, the Orthodox Jews know they are in Galut (exile). But at least within that obvious ghetto there exists a Jewish religious community much more pristine than in Jerusalem — except in *Mea Shearim* (the orthodox section of Jerusalem near the old city). In Williamsburg they live as their ancestors did in medieval Russia and Poland — *sans pogroms.* They are not likely to leave for Israel, and one day it may be that Williamsburg not Jerusalem will be the Mecca of Orthodox Judaism, to mix holy metaphors.

The Orthodox Jews have developed a sort of drab talent for turning their little residential enclaves into instant Eastern European *shtetls.* One sees these ugly and barren shikunim (housing developments) that look like movie sets for "Fiddler on the Roof," everywhere — complete with dirty streets, little greenery or decoration, beautiful big-eyed urchins with side-curls (payot), kerchiefed pale-faced women in voluminous skirts, caftaned bearded men, wearing shtremele (round fur-trimmed hats) or black fedoras with narrow brims. They come complete with yeshiva (religious seminary), chedder (Hebrew school), shule (synagogue), and mikveh (ritual bath) — a sort of perverse victory of the Word over the desert.

The deeply committed Orthodox immigrant from America or Europe finds it easy to adjust to Israel. He is the most successful immigrant of all. He has created an environment identical to his familiar surroundings and life back home. Even the physical atmosphere is pretty much the same. Communication is easy. Most Orthodox in Israel speak Yiddish in daily commerce; Hebrew is the holy tongue, reserved for the Bible. In fact, most Israeli Orthodox know secular Hebrew and use it more than they are willing to admit. The newcomers, of course, know Biblical Hebrew and in course of time learn to use it secularly.

Among the Orthodox immigrants are some hundreds of converts to Orthodoxy from the United States who are even holier than Caesar's wife. They are young people from largely assimilated backgrounds whose parents' Judaism didn't go beyond membership in Hadassah or B'nai Brith or their local Zionist chapter. Some of them come from socialist labor homes. The less exposure they had at home to religious Judaism, the more deeply Orthodox they become in Israel. Like all converts they are the most ardent of all and easily fit into the parochial life of the religious Jews in Israel. They exemplify the old gag about the Jewish boy in America who, to the horror and misgivings of his parents, brought home a Christian bride who readily agreed to conversion. After a few months the new daughter-in-law refused to eat at her in-laws' home because they weren't kosher enough.

"Elefantville"

Early in his career a young American hassidic rabbi, Mordechai Elefant, from the Williamsburg area of Brooklyn recognized the possibilities for a career in burgeoning Israel. The options implicit for an American of his religious background, training, and education, and with an understanding of the Israeli and American scenes were almost limitless. He has not failed to exercise most of these options, many created by his own drive and imagination, and he will probably continue to do so if he does not come a cropper. It is not likely that he will. He may be elephantine, but he is very light on his feet.

The good Rabbi was born and raised in Brooklyn in a family of hassidic scholars, some of them rabbis, some business people. His family came from Hungary between World War I and World War II to join the thousands of Jews who during the past half century have created on the shores of the East River one of the largest ghettos of Orthodox Jews in all of history. Like most of the youngsters of his background, he attended secular grade school and then a religious high school, studying all the while each day the Bible and the Talmud and all the holy and religious tomes and literature necessary to become *a chacham* (wise man), a propensity for which he had exhibited as a little child. It was early accepted in his family that he would become a rabbi and he attended a Williamsburg yeshivah, graduating with distinction, receiving *smichut* (ordination) at the age of 21.

Soon after he traveled to Israel on a visit, and immediately realized that his future lay there in the promised land. Though hardly a modernist, he knew that to capture the imagination and loyalty of the younger generation of American and Israeli Jews and to establish their commitment, Orthodox Judaism had to create some relevancy to the world of today. Furthermore, he early became aware of the reverence and nostalgic respect that Orthodox Judaism invoked in American Jews, whether they were observant or not. He also discovered the respect for Jewish Orthodoxy among many American non-Jews. This romanticism associated the victories of the Israeli armed forces in the War of Independence with the Jewish religion; many American *Goyim* believed that the Jews had engaged in and won some kind of a modern crusade against the infidels. Little did the Christians (and many Jews as well) realize that many of the religious youngsters in Israel, the *yeshivah bacherim* (seminary students), rarely served in the defense forces. Most opted out of the army on religious grounds, although they certainly had not learned their pacifism from the Old Testament, probably the first military manual in history.

Elefant recognized the rich veins of gold in all these unexplored mines of America. He determined that his mission in life would be to research the literature of the Bible and the Commentaries and to relate them to Israel and the Jewish communities in the United States and elsewhere; to use these studies to build a path over which the modern children of Zion would become pilgrims to Israel and would help build the new State for the greater glory of man and the Ineffable One — *Baruch HaShem*.

In the middle 1950's Elefant established an institution with the imposing title of the "Israel Torah Research Institute" (ITRI), an American educational corporation. Soon afterward he established a counterpart in

Romema, a section in the northwest part of the new city of Jerusalem that before 1948 had been an Arab enclave. He was by then married to a pretty buxom daughter of an Orthodox Jewish family. Goldie was bright, personable, and devoted to her brilliant young Rabbi. She has not only been an understanding wife, but a resourceful assistant in his work. At the beginning of the enterprise, Goldie looked after administrative details in the offices of the Institute in New York. Later when they established the Institute in Romema and emigrated to Israel, she kept the home fires burning, while her indefatigable and peripatetic husband traveled the United States, Canada and Mexico, and back and forth to Europe and Israel to raise funds for his institution.

Within a few short years, ITRI in Jerusalem became a recognized Bible school and a seminary preparing students for the rabbinate. Rabbi Elefant had acquired a complex of buildings for classrooms and dormitories, a faculty of serious scholars, and a student body of several score young men from all over the United States. Interestingly, most of Rabbi Elefant's students are not from the hassidic community of Williamsburg. His institution was and still is considered too advanced and modern and untraditional for Williamsburg. The young rabbi, though recognized as a talented scholar and a descendant of a respected family, was not a member of the hierarchy hassidic establishment. He was not a descendant of one of the dynastic hassidic families that have controlled and handed down the leadership prerogatives of yeshivot, religious communities, schools, and synagogues in Europe in the 18th and 19th centuries, and thereafter in the United States and in Israel from generation to generation. Elefant is busily engaged in establishing his own empire and his own dynasty. He proselytizes his students and followers from all the Americas. Some of his students come from non-observant and assimilated Jewish families, and often these youngsters become the most devout and assiduous hassidim.

Likewise, Elefant has sought and found funds from non-hassidic donors and for the most part, from non-strictly observant Jews and from casually observant Christians. He has a brash and open approach that has been seductively successful with the most diverse kinds of people of every strata of education and sophistication. Unlike his American evangelistic counterparts, he has eschewed large meetings. His style is not the filling of collection boxes with small contributions from thousands of donors through mass carnival type exhortations. He works independently from the major agencies for Israel fund raising and he has developed a formidable list of donors on a very personal basis. His evangelism is altogether private and unique.

Rabbi Elefant knows that the interest to help Israel is strongly motivated by religious impulses among self-made American Jewish businessmen, politicians, and public figures. He concentrated on the type of men and women who are active in Israel bond drives and the United Jewish Appeal. Many of these had discovered their interest in Israel rather late, after achieving economic success from very humble beginnings. They had attended *cheder* as boys, generally in the Jewish ghettos of the big cities of the Americas and Europe. They had been *bar-mitzvahed* and thereafter dropped their religious affiliation, only to come back to temples and synagogues as the president or chief donor, just another step toward the prestige they sought to attain in their community. The nostalgic memory of their early childhood religious training provided a Pavlovian response to Rabbi Elefant's kind of appeal.

Elefant succeeds in convincing his clients of the necessity to maintain Orthodoxy in a traditional way and to accept the relevance of his Institute for Israel and the importance of maintaining a continuing religious connection between Israel and the Diaspora within a more realistic and less exotic atmosphere than Williamsburg or *Mea Shearim*.

He teaches many of his donors the dialectics of the Talmud and acquaints them with wise observations of the great sages. He fascinates them with his combination of profound and detailed knowledge of Judaism and his breezy awareness of the twisted ways of modern business. He does not preach or criticize. He corroborates the respectability of wealth, however acquired; it is a comfort to his donors to know that he approves the dictum that the president of the synagogue should be the wealthiest member of the congregation, and not the most learned or the most compassionate. His minimal requirement for them is that they should be charitable, especially in their contributions to ITRI.

Elefant has been sent to many sophisticated and wealthy non-Jews by their Jewish *batlonim* (men of substance) friends and business associates. These Christians, too, have found this strange, self-confident, rumpled Old Testament character to be intriguing, refreshing, and persuasive. Particularly, they have been taken by his boldness and brass. He can walk into the most decorous plushy office, bearded, huge, and very Jewish with his loud Brooklyn accent, so self-assured that the cleverest *shikse* (non-Jewish girl) receptionist quails and rings the boss on the intercom, whether the good Rabbi has an appointment or not. More often than not he does have an appointment, made for him by a judge or a department head, or an important contractor, or even an occasional Catholic bishop. Rarely does he walk out without a sizeable check, or a packet of Israel bonds.

By 1967 the ITRI establishment in Romema had grown into a sizeable section of buildings, old and new, including classrooms, dormitories, and a lovely old Arab stone house converted into headquarters for the Rabbi, Goldie and their personal menage. The buildings contained offices, a study, a library, and spacious living quarters. With substantial contributions from abroad, the Institute embarked upon an ambitious program of building new dormitories and apartment houses to be rented or sold to married students and friends and relatives of students who had the means and the desire to live in Jerusalem in a home of their own in a congenial religious atmosphere. The Rabbi had become an accomplished finance expert, adding the exposure and know-how obtained from his American business friends and supporters to his own formidable capacity to absorb and relate knowledge — religious, business, and secular. With its growing and continued success, the Institute became eligible to borrow mortgage funds from Israel banks and lending institutions. The Rabbi also promoted and arranged joint housing projects in the Romema area with American friends and business advisers.

The Six-Day War had resulted in the return of the old city of Jerusalem to the State of Israel. The Jews of the world rejoiced in the symbolic restoration of the Temple and the actual reacquisition of the Western Wall and the ancient Jewish quarter surrounding it in the old city, though much of the area had been destroyed and desecrated by the careless and malicious Jordanian occupation during almost two decades. A frenzied activity ensued by religious institutions and devout individuals to rebuild the yeshivot and synagogues and living quarters within the walls. Some of the original inhabitants were still alive. They and their heirs and descendants and claimants of the once thriving institutions set about asserting their claims. The problems of disentangling the conflicting and hopelessly convoluted legal rights and titles of the Jews and Arabs, mostly Palestinians, and the Armenians and Greeks and Copts and the other Christian sects, will go on for years and will provide business for many religious and secular lawyers, and cause interminable headaches for the government. This is so no matter what arrangements finally are worked out to provide jurisdiction over the holy places and properties bordering them.

Rabbi Elefant and his colleagues and students of ITRI were as joyous and excited as all of the Orthodox community in the opening of the gates of the Old City and the opportunity once again for Jews to pray at the ancient Wall. Very astutely, however, he eschewed any effort to join the scramble to gain a foothold for ITRI within the sacred walls. He did, however, recognize with early prescience that the area in Southeast Jerusalem between the old city and Bethlehem would become accessible to Jewish settlement after the Six-Day War. One section on the outskirts of East Jerusalem, known as Beit Safafa, had remained an uneasy no-man's land. The German colony had built there a hospital enclave at the turn of the century in a gentle valley, consisting of a cluster of sturdy, handsome one- and two-story Jerusalem stone buildings. During the British occupation, the Mandatory Power had used the buildings for a hospital and a variety of public uses. The buildings fell into disuse during the Jordanian occupation as they were too close to Jewish Jerusalem. A short way further southward towards Bethlehem on the slopes and summits of little hills, wealthy Arabs had continued to live in their substantial and modern stone villas, and had even built new ones between 1948 and 1967. Most of the occupants left these homes during the frightening six days of 1967 and few returned.

Soon after the Six-Day War, the Israel government Land Authority took over the part of Beit Safafa that had lain deserted and from which the Jordanians and Palestinian Arabs had fled — some 70 dunams and the buildings of the German-British hospital unoccupied for 20 years. They were in excellent condition and the authorities set about cleaning and refurbishing them, with the assistance of the Jewish Agency. It was planned to turn them over to the Agency to be used for new immigrants. No specific plan for their use had been developed, and like much of the newly acquired land and property in Jerusalem retaken during the War, conflicting claims and jockeying for acquisition swirled about in the federal government offices, the Jerusalem municipality, and the bureau created by the Defense Ministry to handle the Administered Areas.

The Ministry of Welfare had for a long time eyed the attractive enclave with a covetous eye. They argued with great persuasion that the buildings could be used by them for poor, elderly, and sick welfare clients, and they pointed out that it was unfair to turn over the buildings and land to the Jewish Agency for the use of new immigrants.

The Defense Ministry officials administering the newly acquired territories were opposed to the claims of the Welfare Ministry, mainly because that Ministry was dominated by the Orthodox religious parties with which the Defense Ministry had always had an ongoing antipathetic relationship. The Jerusalem municipality, under the talented leadership of Mayor Teddy Kollek, also was not keen on seeing the area fall into the hands of the religious parties and become an extension of the elderly religious ghetto within the old city walls. The Jewish Agency was caught in the middle. They had no specific plans for using the premises, and they didn't want to become involved in the internecine battles between the Israeli Ministries and the Municipality.

Enter Rabbi Elefant with the solution. Turn over the area to ITRI, and all the problems and conflicts would be solved. He blithely pointed out that the possible uses advanced by the various claimants would be satisfied by permitting ITRI to relocate its schools and yeshivot and establish dormitories and estates there. The students studying in the educational institutions and living in the existing dormitories and the other facilities ITRI proposed to build would, of course, be Orthodox Jews and practically all of them would be new immigrants from the Western countries. Furthermore, others who would come to settle in Beit Safafa would be observant Jews, many of them elderly, and also, of course, new immigrants.

The credentials of ITRI combined with Rabbi Elefant's persuasive logic intrigued the officials. The performance of the Institute, demonstrated by its impressive establishment in Romema, could not be gainsaid. Rabbi Elefant's connections with powerful supporters in America and Europe impressed the Agency and their principal representative General (Res) Uzi Narkiss, who was the Director of immigration affairs for the Jewish Agency.

Privately, the astute Rabbi hammered away at the most telling point of all. The basic conflict between the religious establishment and the secular authorities was fundamental and irreconcilable. Manifestations of it flared in Jerusalem after the Six-Day War. Only nebulous and uneasy accommodations were achieved to maintain some kind of face to present to the supporters and benefactors of both sectors within the Jewish communities abroad. Elefant offered a Kissinger-type solution. His Orthodox religious posture was impeccable; but he was not a part of the religious establishment. On the contrary, his ITRI was almost as resented by the established Orthodoxy as were the Christian and Moslem institutions in Jerusalem. And the secular authorities knew they could deal with him. He was flexible and understanding. ITRI seemed to be God-sent.

ITRI wound up getting the buildings and the land adjoining them, but not without a final last-ditch battle by the Welfare Department. For many months during 1968 and 1969 ITRI had quietly proceeded to move into the buildings and physically take possession. The Welfare Department had also received some quasi-legal approval to take over the buildings and one day in early 1970 they decided on a frontal attack to assert their rights. They marshalled several score of employees and deployed a caravan of trucks and jeeps laden with furniture, furnishings, and supplies to capture Beit Safafa. Rabbi Elefant in his study in Romema had been alerted by his people. Like the Old Testament general and tactician that he is, Elefant dispatched within an hour his entire student body, faculty, and employees with orders to defend their property and to repulse the intruders — with force, if necessary.

I was visiting with Elefant when the call came in, and he commandeered me to drive him to the scene of the battle. When the Welfare Department contingent arrived at the gates, they were met by a determined army of yeshiva *bachurim* armed with sticks and stones and the ineffable righteousness of God and their leader. The caravan slowed down, hesitated, and finally stopped outside the gates. Strong words and a few rocks were hurled. The police arrived to prevent bloodshed and a pitched battle was narrowly averted. Elefant won the battle of Beit Safafa and from then on ITRI was in undisputed possession of the buildings and the surrounding area. The titles and the contracts remain in dispute, and probably will stay that way for years, but possession is more than nine points of the law in Israel.

In the meantime Rabbi Elefant continues to build his empire in Beit Safafa and Romema with equanimity, skill, and vision. He writes his Bible commentaries in spare hours as he plans and builds his dormitories and apartment houses and school buildings, and keeps a practiced weather eye out for other propositions materially to enhance ITRI, perhaps with hotels and rest homes and whatever. He need not travel as frequently as in past years to the United States and to Europe to solicit funds. His friends and supporters and business partners now come to him in Beit Safafa. As the lovely hills east of ITRI fill with newcomers occupying the existing villas, new houses are being built in the gentle valleys, on the hillsides, and on the summits. Within a short time the eastern boundary of Jerusalem and the western edges of Bethlehem will surely conjoin, built up with pleasant housing estates, hotels, people. The unique hassidic flavor of Elefant's accommodating orthodoxy will color the style of the expansion of Beit Safafa in the future. No Williamsburg will it be, however, and certainly no ghetto and no Mea Shearim. Elefant can be relied on to see to that.

5. Hebrew

The language barrier is the single most formidable obstacle to successful settlement in Israel, and the factor most played down in official *aliyah* circles. In fact, the ease of learning Hebrew, the effectiveness of the *ulpan* "pressure-cooker" approach to a pragmatic facility with the language is mostly myth.

Little of the difficulty of learning Hebrew surfaces to the top of the List of What Every Prospective Immigrant should know. The matter is airily passed off as an adjustment that will be made successfully by intensive study at an ulpan. The Jewish Agency, the Ministry of Absorption (*Klitah*), the Ministry of Education, the *kibbutzim* and *moshavim*, private agencies and institutions have created scores of *ulpanim* throughout the country to teach Hebrew to new immigrants and improve the Hebrew of older residents. Much research, serious thought and skill have been expended in these efforts. Most of them used advanced teaching methods and audio-visual aids. A whole library of textbooks and bilingual dictionaries, Hebrew-English, Hebrew-French, Hebrew-Whatever (perhaps even Hebrew-Swahili one day) have been published. The teaching skills and dedication of the instructors are first rate.

Unquestionably, the teaching of Hebrew occupies a higher priority and conern in Israel than in any other country in the world. Even Berlitz schools teach Hebrew in Israel! But withal the results are not too successful. When the lid of the cooker is taken off, the roast is underdone at best and often not even digestible. Why? The alphabet is wholly unfamiliar to new immigrants, not written in script, and reads from right to left. The pronunciation is strange and frustrating to the tongue and to the ear.

Anglos, traditionally monolingual, have the roughest time of all. They often find that they can cope with the reading and writing but they flounder helplessly in trying to carry on an ordinary conversation, in listening to the radio, or in watching television.

Older immigrants have become philosophical about these difficulties. Many of them learn a smattering of the language and let it make do without suffering much psychological damage. It is a common experience for a new immigrant proudly or anxiously trying out his new *ulpan Ivrit* (Hebrew) to be asked by a shopkeeper with a sly grin, in passable English, if he wouldn't be more comfortable in English, Yiddish, or German or French or Spanish.

New immigrants tend to avoid encounters requiring the use of Hebrew. Thus, a language ghettoization develops. English-speaking immigrants seek out and stay within their own language circles. To a lesser extent, so do French and Spanish-speaking peoples, and more recently arrived Eastern European immigrants. The younger *Yekkes* (German Jews) who came on *aliyah* during the 1930's have learned Hebrew well, albeit their accents are execrable; this doesn't bother them any more than did the Teutonic English of Bruno Bettleheim and Otto Preminger on the American scene. The older German Jews encountered the same difficulties, but they didn't bother much to learn Hebrew. There are German Jews in Israel who have lived there for thirty years and speak only German, completely adjusted and disdaining Hebrew with a *sang froid* of which only the *Yekke* are capable. They remind one of the older Jewish "greenhorns" in the United States at the turn of the century who lived out their lives in the Goldine Medineh (golden land) speaking only Yiddish. If their grandchildren couldn't converse with *Bobbe* (grandma) and *Zaydeh* (grandpa) — too bad for them! Similar situations are not unusual today in Israel among all the Ashkenazic ethnic groups. However, Yiddish has become fashionable and intriguing in Israel in recent years and many a sabra, unlike his American counterpart in an earlier period, takes pride and delight in knowing a smattering of Yiddish.

The Sephardic and Afro-Asian immigrants in Israel have encountered adjustment and absorption difficulties that will continue for at least another generation or longer. Fortunately they have learned to speak Hebrew very quickly, often in impeccable and authentic accents. Many of them knew Arabic, which has a close affinity with Hebrew in vocabulary and pronunciation — and some of them even knew liturgical Hebrew. Others had a working knowledge of *Ladino,* a jargon Spanish-Hebrew spoken for centuries in North Africa and among the Sephardic Jews of Turkey and the Balkans. The Yemenites have known Hebrew since the earliest days of the Dispersion. In Israel, almost all of the

Sephardics and "Orientals" consort with their fellow ethnics even though they soon learned Hebrew within their expanded family clan groups. However, very few of those who came as immigrant adults can read or write. Their children, products of Israel's compulsory education system, are all literate.

It is too early to know how significant the language problems will be with the increasing Soviet immigration that began in the 1970's. It seems the language barrier will be more successfully overcome by the Russians than it was by the Anglos and the Europeans. Interestingly enough, they seem to have an affinity for the language. Furthermore, many Russian Jews who secretly hoped to come to Israel during the 1960's — and their numbers swelled after the 1967 war — studied Hebrew assiduously in the U.S.S.R., despite official disapproval and a heartbreaking lack of textbooks, dictionaries, and learning materials. Particularly adept at picking up Hebrew quickly in Israel have been the religious Jews from the Soviet Union, mostly Georgians, who had studied Biblical Hebrew since early childhood.

Ulpans

Some immigrants to Israel find temporary encouragement for their hopes and aspirations in the resident ulpans, where they attempt with varying success to learn Hebrew quickly. In the process they are introduced to the fact of Israel (if not the facts) in company with others who have come with similar aspirations. Since it exudes a homogeneity of hope and companionship, the ulpan helps newcomers cushion the shock of the impact experienced by those who move into the maelstrom of Israeli life immediately upon their arrival. The ulpans are sort of a halfway house or nursery school for adults. They introduce newcomers to Israel under favorable circumstances; the ulpan immigrants see their new homeland sideways, with the handsome profile turned towards them.

A good deal of flag-waving jingoism is included with the language lessons; every effort is made not only to instill instant Hebrew but instant patriotism. It is assumed that the immigrant believes that Israel is the best of all possible worlds. This unremitting approach is not uniformly successful, and many of the students react negatively and are turned off. Subtlety is no more a virtue in Israel's ulpans than it is generally in the Israeli mainstream.

The faculty of the ulpans are dedicated teachers, the best in the Israeli educational system. They enjoy the challenge of teaching a difficult language to students who probably have not been exposed to pedagogical disciplines for a generation or more. Many of these students are simultaneously facing emotional problems of adjustment in a strange bewildering atmosphere. A real measure of success is achieved, though not nearly as great as indicated by the statistics put out by the Israeli authorities. Some of the teachers work in the ulpans for the adventure of coming into contact with people from other lands. Despite their genuine Israeli patriotism, some of the younger and more attractive instructors occasionally marry an immigrant student and take off for other climes.

The ulpan experience results in friendships that become close and lasting. Many a resident of Israel (like myself) counts amongst his best friends and associates fellow students at the ulpan. The nostalgia of those months of pleasant togetherness draws former students back for frequent visits. For some, the euphoria absorbed in the ulpan makes the later harsh reality of Israel living unendurable. The contrast between the friendliness encountered in the ulpan and the pervasive unfriendliness and indifference they afterward meet up with in the general population sometimes embitters them. They complain that they should have been better prepared at the ulpan for what they could expect in the real world of Israel. These complaints are unjust. Everything that exists in that contradictory little land is part of the real world of Israel, the pleasantness of the ulpan life included. For those who do not remain in Israel, the sojourn in the ulpan serves at least as a pleasant memory of a land they never knew.

Ulpan Akiva which I attended off and on during my first year in Israel is the oldest and most famous ulpan in Israel. For many years it operated in a cluster of rented houses and a converted pension in what had once been an orange grove. Now it is located a few kilometers farther north of Netanya near the sea in a group of modern buildings and dormitories in a bucolic moshav setting. The place is complete with swimming pool, dining room, and more than adequate dormitories, lounges, and public spaces. It has the appearance of a resort hotel, which in a way it is. Ulpan Akiva is presided over by its high priestess Shulamit Katznelson, who founded it in the 1950's and who has been its principal and guiding spirit ever since. She is in turn tough, gay, sentimental, easy-going, romantic, realistic, disorganized. She drives her staff hard and in turn permits them to drive her equally hard. She is a third generation *Yerushalmit* (Jerusalem woman), daughter of a distinguished family of scholars and professionals. Her brother Shmuel Tamir is one of Israel's leading lawyers, and as a leader of the opposition Likud Party in the Knesset he is an eloquent right-wing nationalist goad to the ruling coalition. Shulamit's pedagogical professionalism is the result of her sound education in Israel and her years of study at the University of Michigan. Her commitment to Ulpan Akiva is single-minded and complete. It is her cause and her life.

The weaknesses and strengths, successes and failures of Ulpan Akiva directly reflect her contradictory complex character and personality.

The Israeli ulpans are not only ecumenical, they are kaleidoscopic. The students are Christians, Orthodox and Reform Jews, agnostics, rabbis, atheists, priests, nuns, ministers, homosexuals, prostitutes, celibates, vegetarians, Moslems, Buddhists, swingers, old people, youngsters, rustics, sophisticates, grandchildren of Hassidic rabbis and grandchildren of German Nazis. They come from forty different countries and speak 25 different languages. And the mix works. The common goal is to acquire a knowledge of Hebrew and this commonality creates an instant bond. Nowhere is the superficiality of the classic list of alleged barriers between peoples better illustrated. The most unlikely friendships are created there. A half dozen young Greek Jews from wealthy educated families came to the ulpan one summer. They had all been students at an expensive predominately Jewish private school in Athens. They were quick learners, despite their casual habit of missing classes and homework to take off for Tel-Aviv for the discotheques. At the ulpan their best friend was a quiet little elderly nun from Bavaria in Germany, She was tolerant, calm, and fey. The volatile blackeyed Sephardic aristocrats from Greece fascinated her. And she in turn, they asserted when teased by their peers, was better female company than the little nubiles who set their caps for them in and out of the ulpan.

A phenomenon that the ulpan experience reveals is the ease with which friendships develop based upon communion of spirit. Empathy has full rein in the give and take of the daily ulpan routine; differences of age, language, nationality, religious persuasion, class, wealth, offer little impediment. In some situations the lack of a common language that forces classmates to communicate in pidgin Hebrew creates warm friendships.

Rabbis do not necessarily consort with rabbis, nor priests with priests, nor, emphatically, Americans with Americans. An exception are the French who tend to seek each other out, probably one suspects because they are monolingual like Americans, and prefer to speak in their own beautiful and expressive language. Israeli ulpans present fertile clinical laboratories for behavioral psychologists.

Françoise was a beautiful statuesque blond daughter of a wealthy assimilated Jewish family in Paris. When her leg was amputated after an automobile accident, life lost meaning for her. She came to Israel to try to find herself. (She didn't try very hard.) At the ulpan she met a compatriot, a precocious sex-pot of a Lolita who had been sent to Israel by her proper respectable Sephardic Jewish family to see if the inspiration of the Holy Land might have a salutory effect upon her delinquency. Together, Françoise and the Lolita spent the summer ducking classes and casually practicing bi-sexual prostitution. They returned to France before the semester ended, both by invitation and desire. They were even more misfit in Israel than in France, but it had not been an unpleasant summer for them.

Father Pierre, a young priest from the provinces of France, doffed his clerical garb, put on a sport shirt and levis and became plain Peter at the Ulpan. In the year he spent there he also became the most brilliant student in the history of the school. There he met Bertha, a vivacious plain looking young Jewish girl from Rhodesia. She was talented, musical and sexy. They became inseparable companions, then husband and wife. They considered staying in Israel, but finally decided to try France. Peter wanted to continue in the priesthood and hoped that his church would permit him to do so. Peter and Bertha vowed they would return to Israel one day to live.

Father Jean was a French Canadian priest from Quebec. Studying and researching and teaching at the Canadian Catholic College in Rome provided an opportunity to spend a summer in the Holy Land. In Israel, rather than tour, he chose to brush up his Hebrew at Ulpan Akiva. He, too, took off his priest's collar but remained a shy padre. He enjoyed the summer immensely, was the most dedicated if not the best student in our class, and was beloved by all of his fellow students, even the several very Orthodox Jews to whom a Catholic priest was a strange and fearsome creature indeed. He quite simply said to his friends when he left, "I hope and pray that you may find peace and contentment in this land. It is the land of the Jews, it is your land. I will pray for your aliyah."

"Abraham" adopted his Hebrew name the day he came to the ulpan. A blond, pug-nosed Californian, he was in appearance, accent, and attitude pure WASP. He came to the school to learn Hebrew, which he needed in the research position he was about to take up at the Weitzmann Institute as a chemist and physicist. He learned a lot of Hebrew at the ulpan and welcomed the interlude before he went to Rehovot. It amused him that most of the people at the ulpan, even his fellow American students, doubted that he was a Jew. He was. He had even been bar-mitzvahed.

After a year at the ulpan I concluded, in the fall of 1969, that I could not master the language and that the academic somewhat hothouse approach to Hebrew in the ulpan was becoming counter-productive. I resolved rather that I would continue to learn spoken Hebrew just through routine daily life, and to improve my knowledge by soliciting corrections *b'rechov* (in the street). By then I was aware that the Israeli penchant for explaining to the new immigrant the correct word and the right pronunciation, was endemic.

I studied for a couple of months with an earnest housewife teacher who had lived in the States for several years and had a sincere instructional mission. The emphasis was on grammar and the class was too advanced for me. Hebrew *dikkduk* (grammar) for me was irrevocably a lost cause, as it is to many an immigrant.

The battle of the language raged in Palestine and in the Diaspora for years. Would Hebrew or Yiddish — or perhaps even German or English — be the language of the future state? The controversy was won by the Hebraists long before the Balfour Declaration. If the debate were to take place in Israel today, with its millions of people speaking some 50 different tongues some suspect that it would be otherwise. One of the number of unending paradoxes is that those who chose Hebrew were not observant religious Jews. The religious Jew believed, and still does, that Hebrew is the sacred tongue and should not be desecrated as the language of the market place. One still hears mainly Yiddish spoken in Mea Shearim, the religious ghetto quarter of Jewish Jerusalem.

It is likely that English would be selected if they had it to do over again, or Hebrew would be converted to the western alphabet so that it could be read and written phonetically by newcomers at home at least with the ABC's. The truth of the matter is that Israelis have painted themselves into a corner. They are using a language dormant for thousands of years and never properly used and understood by its religious adherents who read the Bible and pray to their God in His language. Hebrew is used only in Israel and in no place else in the world. It is characteristic Jewish romantic *chutzpah* to expect that this language will ever be used by Jews or others outside of Israel.

Every Israeli who aspires to become educated strives mightily to learn English, French, German, Spanish — especially English. It is too late to expect that at this late date, English could be adopted as an equal second language. To suggest this in Israel now is virtually blasphemy. It is also considered by many people privately, and quite honestly, heresy, yet it is an open secret that Golda Meir has an effective vocabulary in Hebrew of only a few thousand words and utters them in an American-Yiddish accent that makes many sabras laugh or shudder. It is also a well-known fact (rarely mentioned) that some of the cabinet members and half of the Knesset speak in similar "broken Hebrew."

Modern Hebrew, less than 100 years old, is already a richly expressive language. It is being constantly enriched by Yiddish, Arabic, French, and especially English. Most scientific, technological, political, and medical terms are straight adaptations from English, pronounced of course in Hebrew accents. The language is also constantly being added to from the jargon of the streets, which consists of expressions developed from straight Hebrew and translations of slang idioms from other languages, plus an infinite variety of combinations of other languages interspersed with Hebrew, all of which results in weirdly beautiful and expressive phrases.

Col. Jacob Avrey, Illinois Democratic committeeman, the author, Abba Eban (then Israeli ambassador to the UN), and Mayor Kennelly, at City Hall in Chicago, 1953.

6. Communities and Communes

Israel is now an urban country. Many more than half the people of Israel are urban dwellers who do not live in Tel-Aviv or Jerusalem. The first five Jewish settlements established in modern Palestine were set up in the 1880's through the philanthropy of Baron Edmonde de Rothschild, a member of the French branch of that international banking family. For many years after their founding, these settlements were the centers of the new Jewish Palestine — raw, rural, labor-oriented, the market towns of a purely agricultural society. In these villages the Arab farmers and shepherds moved freely among the Jewish villagers. There was little or no tension or rivalry between the Arabs and the Jews in those days. After 1948 these older communities developed quite like the newer towns created just before and after the State was founded and today they are disconcertingly similar.

The influx of new immigrants that has doubled and tripled the population, the accompanying spurt of housing construction, the businesses and industries established as the communities grew have blanketed all of them with a sameness of style. Most significant of all is the fact that the great majority of new settlers are Sephardic and Afro-Asian Jews whose life styles have impressed a new cast on the old molds. There may be in older and newer towns percentage variations in the number of immigrants from Europe, Arabia, and Africa, but these differences do not measurably alter the picture. The consolidation and integration of the population proceeds apace in all the communities.

Nothing better illustrates the difference between Jewish Palestine and its metamorphosis into modern Israel than the startling sameness of most of the urban centers, whatever their origins. *Ramle* — 15 miles southeast of Tel-Aviv on the road to Jerusalem, was a devastated abandoned Arab village in 1948. In the 1970's it isn't that different from Petach Tikva, or Ashdod for that matter, except that many of the buildings in Ramle are still old Arab structures. Petach Tikva started as a tiny farm village in the 1880's and all the buildings in Ashdod have been built since 1955. The origins of Petach Tikva — one of the Rothschild towns — stem from the *Bilu* (first modern settlers from Eastern Europe), but its residents today are very similar in the way they look, what they do, how they think, and in their prejudices, enthusiasms, superstitions. And the residents of Petach Tikvah today are not very different from the people of Ashdod. The differences are fast becoming blurred; all the towns are peopled by Israelis in the making. The children definitely become the same as they go through the Israel version of Dr. Seuss's "Sneetches" machine — some with stars on their bellies, some without, and eventually all coming out of the star-changing apparatus looking and acting and feeling the same. (The stars finally become only paper decorations that can be bought in any 10 piastre store.)

Netanya

The early history of Netanya — inseparable from its founder — illustrates the influence of the dynamics of individual personalities on the creation of Jewish Palestine. Its history since the birth of Israel in 1948 exemplifies the pattern of development of all of Israel's urban communities after the arrival of the new immigrants.

In the late 1920's, a short, blue-eyed, blond dynamo of a young man from Petach Tikvah decided to father a new city. He was the grandson of original Lituanian Jewish settlers brought to Palestine by the Rothschild's PICA (Palestine Colonization Association) in the 1880's. In the years that followed, the Dankner family became prosperous citrus farmers and wealthy landowners in the Petach Tikvah area. A clue to the young man's driving ambition (and his vision too) is the fact that he changed his name from the already prestigious patronym Dankner, to Ben-Ami, "Son of My People," and he changed his first name to Oved — "Worker." Somehow or other, he found funds and associates to buy from absentee Arab owners a large stretch of dune land along the Mediterranean, some forty kilometres north of Tel-Aviv on a high cliff overlooking the sea. He obviously had a long view. He knew that there were Jews in America and Europe who were not socialists, and who were not involved with an egalitarian dream, and who would be intrigued with a post Rothschildean padronism.

Ben-Ami journeyed to America to seek out Nathan Straus, the famous American Jewish philanthropist. With characteristic *chutzpah,* he went directly to the non-Zionist German banker. He did not seek money. What he sought was the prestige of the Straus name. Nathan Straus was enchanted by this bold little visionary and agreed to accept the "honor" of permitting his name to be attached to the project, with the stern proviso that no financial commitment was involved. Ben-Ami got what he wanted, the *hechshure* (stamp) of approval. With quiet fanfare the town was launched — a provisional wooden hut or two and a few canvas tents. A generation ahead of the times, Oved Ben-Ami hired a cameraman to take Mack Sennett-like movies of the historical occasion.

The town grew very slowly. It was simply a little market center for Arab and Jewish farmers and perhaps a place for the orange grove owners in the area to consider building their homes. The great depression in the United States and Europe soon followed, drying up his hopes of Diaspora backing. But Ben-Ami persisted. He persuaded some of the members of the large Dankner clan and their friends, relatives, and associates to build houses on the cliff above the sea. He, himself, built a formidable mansion far south of the village (where it stood in almost ridiculous loneliness for many years, as the sand swirled about it). Today, after 40 years, the mansion is located in the center of the city. It remains one of the most impressive houses in the country, dramatic testimony of the perspicacity of this stubborn, extraordinary man.

As the ugly news of Hitler's vendetta against the Jews trickled into Palestine, Ben-Ami sensed the opportunity to divert the impending Jewish disaster to the benefit of his driving dream. He flew to Belgium, Holland, Switzerland and importuned the wealthy Jewish diamond merchants to come to Netanya and to reestablish their diamond cutting industry there. He offered to build factories and shops for them, to find them apprentices to train; to help them build homes; to give them freedom from taxes. He warned them of their inevitable fate and the holocaust that lay ahead. He offered them the safety of a Jewish land where they could prosper in peace and in freedom. He was persuasive. The wiser of them, and the luckier of them, accepted his invitation — unfortunately, only a minority of those who might have come. (Thus was created the beginnings of an industry that has been for years one of Israel's principal hard currency earners. The impressive multi-storied diamond center on the border between Ramat Gan and Tel-Aviv, which houses the largest diamond exchange in the world, affords visible testimony to Ben-Ami's foresight.)

With the advent of the diamond industry, the future of Netanya was assured. Other industries from abroad were established, most of them enticed by Oved Ben-Ami, who had been the town's mayor since its establishment, with the exception of one term when he was defeated by the labor parties. (He made political peace after this defeat in 1961 and continued to rule in a coalition government until he was once again defeated in the December 1973 election.)

After Independence, Netanya also developed into a resort area. It has become a favorite winter resort of tourists from Denmark, Norway, Sweden, and Germany, seeking to escape European winter rigors on its pleasant beaches. Over 50 small, moderately priced hotels cater to them and to many Israeli vacationers from the agricultural settlements and *kibbutzim.* The permanent population of the city is well over 40,000 and at the height of the season more than 100,000 people live there. Its bright main street is alive with shops, restaurants, discotheques, and its beaches are filled with bathers — the atmosphere is convivial, carnival — a sort of Coney Island, Israeli style.

Modern Israel is proof that people determine the character and even the appearance of a place; that a ghetto is not architecturally determined, but subjectively structured by its inhabitants. Watts in Los Angeles has the appearance of a pleasant residential section of a California city. But it is a Black ghetto nevertheless. In the heart of Chicago's huge south side, many buildings stand sturdy on streets tree-lined and spacious — the area is a ghetto nonetheless, the flats filled with angry, despairing, sick, hungry people, and the streets littered with trash. The only ghettoes in Israel — despite the hundreds of towns and cities and even sections of the countryside where filth and rubbish, ramshackle and make-shift are all too obvious to the eye and the nose — are the deeply religious enclaves where life is turned inward by choice. The inhabitants of these religious communities live in a medieval eastern European style because they want to live that way. There is one such little Orthodox community in the heart of Netanya. I wandered into this section when I was a student at Ulpan Akiva, which it adjoined. I could not believe I was in a modern Israeli city. I wondered how this little corner in the center of what was an orange grove in the countryside a short thirty years ago, could have been transformed into a drab dirty little Polish *shtetl.* The effect is surrealist. It is the handiwork of the people who live there — sad, muted, withdrawn.

What Ben-Ami did not foresee and what gives Netanya its current character, is the influx of new immigrants after 1948; this will determine Netanya's future as one of Israel's larger cities. "Ben-Ami proposes and God disposes." Despite the foresight, careful planning, and unremitting energy that created it, Netanya has become a typical Israeli city with a majority Sephardic, Afro-Asian Israeli population. This development did not displease Ben-Ami: He accepts the fact that whatever Netanya will be in the future has long since gone beyond his control and direction.

After the Six-Day War, Ben-Ami helped to organize and became the president of a "Committee for a Greater Israel." He is one of Israel's leading hawks, a stentorian spokesman for those Israelis who would absorb all of the "Administered Areas" occupied in the Six Day War — Gaza, Golan Heights, Sinai Peninsula, the West Bank of the Jordan (Judea and Samaria), and the old city of Jerusalem (and the adjoining areas to its east) and make all this comparatively vast territory and its occupants a permanent part of Israel. He and his colleagues argue that the million Arabs who live in these territories would welcome such absorption, even though they won't admit it. He sounds authoritative. He has had a lifetime of intimate acquaintance with Palestinian Arabs. He speaks good Arabic. It also must be recalled that Ben-Ami spent the greater part of his life in the narrow waist between Israel and Jordan. His beloved Netanya was at the very pinched center, only eight short miles separated the city from the Jordan border!

Retention of the present territories is only the beginning of the program the Committee for Greater Israel advocates. They want Israel to become one of the largest nations of the Middle East by acquiring additional territory — peacefully or by force of arms. Israel dominates the area militarily at the present time; of this there can be no question. Short of major direct intervention by a great power, specifically the U.S.S.R., there is for at least another generation no possibility of any combination or even all of the Arab nations together defeating the military machine that Israel has created. The Yom Kippur War of 1973 once more conclusively proved that, even as it proved the real vulnerability of Israel. Ben-Ami and his friends (not many in number, but extremely influential) unremittingly hammer their position home. Say they, either Israel seizes the present opportunity to maintain and expand its position to become the largest and most powerful nation in the Middle East or it will, by the very size and intense hatred of the horde of enemies surrounding it, be defeated and overrun, more likely exterminated. The only thing the Arab understands is force! Their arguments are harkened to by some friendly ears. Especially do the Israeli Afro-Asians and Sephardic Jews and the survivors of Hitler's Europe buy these exhortations with more than passive agreement.

The hawks don't care that their propaganda fuels the cries of "expansionism," "colonialism," even "fascism," that Israel's enemies hurl at her. They retort, "Survival means to strengthen and to grow — otherwise you die. We choose that Israel shall live!" Their rallying cry is that ancient shout, *"Am Yisrael Chai"* (The Nation of Israel Lives!). To some

Israelis this is heady liquor. The great majority of Israel's citizens, however, reject this jingoism out of hand, especially since the Yom Kippur War.

Ben-Ami and his friends would take over all of Jordan, by force of arms if necessary. They claim that Jordan is Palestine, the historical land of the Jews, all of which was intended for the Jewish Homeland by the League of Nations. Thus, say they, Jordan is a Bedouin Sheikdom, just another British colony dreamed up by Lawrence of Arabia and implemented by Winston Churchill in the Colonial Office after the Mandate was created; they say Jordan rightfully belongs to Israel. In truth the territory east of the Jordan in 1923 was broken off from the Mandate by the British — illegally and without League of Nations approval — and set up as a nation with Sheikh Abdullah as king; presumably this was as payment for the private and secret promises made by T.E. Lawence to the Arabs during World War I. But these arguments now sound like Hitler's rationale for invading the Sudetenland of Czechoslovakia! Ben-Ami's organization would also absorb substantial sections of southern Lebanon on the northern Israeli border. They point out that those lands were never truly part of Arabia, all of them were acquired by invasion and conquest in recent historical times. Now since the Yom Kippur War they would hold all of the Golan Plateau, even to the Gates of Damascus.

* * *

Places such as Ramle, Afula in the Lower Galilee, Herzylia, even Rishon and Petach Tikvah; and Kfar Saba and Ra'anana — towns of the Sharon Plain north and east of Tel-Aviv — and the now very big cities of Bat Yam and Holon south of Tel-Aviv and Jaffa and many others are fundamentally new cities built around an existing framework of little towns that were there before. For the most part these communities never had any particular individuality that made them very different. Most of them were pretty much similar in their drabness in the old days. Even if they did develop their own character from the people who settled there, the very numbers of immigrants who came after Independence pretty much erased their original ambiance.

A combination of bad taste, the need quickly to absorb large numbers of immigrants, obtuseness, venality, bureaucracy, and most of all, the automobile, the hamburger, movie-house, radio and television "civilization" of the United States are bringing aesthetic and moral pollution to lovely old cities. Safed in the Canaan Mountains of the Upper Galilee, Tiberias 16 kilometers down from Mount Canaan on the Sea of Galilee, Rehovet, just south of Rishow Le Zion and Tel-Aviv and others are experiencing the blight of badly planned growth. In Jerusalem there has been much care and thought and planning by the city administration and the Israeli government. International town planners, architects, artists, even philosophers and poets have been consulted and heeded. The religious establishments, the university, all the public bodies are concerned. Yet, the city is being bulldozed and scarred by new highways and streets cut into the ancient valleys, and by skyscraper hotels and office buildings; all these are inexorably changing the look and feel of ancient Jerusalem. Perhaps since the pace of immigration has slowed, some of the loveliness of the old places may be preserved.

Moledet and Ramat Zvi

Moledet B'nai Brith is an agricultural-industrial commune situated on some 3,000 acres of fertile prairie land in the center of the Jezreel valley in the lower Galilee. There 150 families live in pleasant one-story concrete block stucco houses built during the past thirty years. Almost all of the houses were enlarged and improved as time went on, and today, all of them have modern plumbing and kitchen facilities, tasteful furniture, carpets. Each of them is surrounded by shade and fruit trees and flower gardens. The obvious prosperity of the pleasant village testifies to the successful planning and hard work of the small band of pioneer founders who came to Palestine from Germany and Central Europe in the early 1930's to become tillers of the soil and hewers of wood in the land of their forebears.

Moledet was not always thus. The shadow of Hitler's fascism had loomed forebodingly over the settlers, but they did not come to Palestine as refugees. They came as dedicated Zionists, that first score of couples, prototypes of the first German Aliyah — it was a voluntary immigration of youthful idealists who had for years dreamed of going to Palestine to live a bucolic existence and to raise their offspring as children of the good earth.

The first settlement was on a section of land adjoining the present site. There the settlers labored for many months only to discover that the land was unsuitable for farming, and when typhoid fever, fear, and despair brought them to the point of giving up their dream, they were transferred to their present location by the Jewish National Fund. The site on which Moledet is now established was purchased by the JNF with a gift from the B'nai Brith of America. The struggling settlement acknowledged the gift by naming their venture "Moledet B'nai Brith" (homeland of the Sons of the Covenant). Adversity continued to plague them in the early years. No water could be found below the land, and shortly after they started anew, a fire destroyed most of their flimsy wooden buildings.

They carried on, their ranks increased by several new families. The earth was potentially good, rich and fertile, despite the lack of water. The annual rainfall permitted cultivation only of crops requiring little water, the supply of which was augmented by a district pipeline permitting some irrigation. Uncertainty about their survival from season to season did not deter them from drafting an elaborate, ambitious master plan that included streets, shops, store-rooms, barns for the cows, sheep, goats, chicken coops, the carpentry shop, an industrial area, a community center, a swimming pool (to serve as reservoir), kindergarten and school buildings, an infirmary, administrative offices, citrus groves, and, of course, a cemetery.

Significantly, these far-sighted *Yekke*, academicians and intellectuals all, decided that their community would be neither a straight *kibbutz* (commune) nor a straight *moshav* (freehold agricultural settlement) but an amalgam of the best features of both. From their newly-learned Hebrew, studied at home in Germany and on Palestine farms where some of them trained before coming to Moledet, they devised a descriptive term, *Moshav Shitufi* (partnership agricultural settlement). Like a kibbutz, all of the basic property, land, tools, machinery, houses, all of the buildings, the livestock, in fact, everything but their personal property, would be owned in common by the community. And all the production of their common labor, agricultural and industrial, would be shared equally by the members. The members likewise would, as in a kibbutz, do such work as they were assigned by the work committee. The entire operation and its administration would be conducted by committees democratically elected by the members, each member with one vote and everyone, man and woman, a member. However, the principle of private property and private ownership was not abandoned entirely as it has been (in theory) in the kibbutzim. (All of the production of a kibbutz, plus all the property, belongs to the kibbutz. A kibbutz member simply receives an allocation, the amount determined annually by its members.)

In the *moshav shitufi* the founders of Moledet decided that each member would receive his share of the net proceeds of the enterprise each year to do with as he pleased. Of course, the determination of the net proceeds involved the generous allocation of part of the production for the growth and development of the community and for the common cultural and amenity needs. These included public buildings, utilities, schools, community centers, library, landscaping, roads, transportation facilities and today, even automobiles for the use of members.

The most dramatic difference between a moshav and a kibbutz is the plan for family living. The Moledet pioners decided that traditional family structure would not be changed or abandoned as in the kibbutzim of the early days. Each family would live in its own house, and rear its own children. There would be no common nursery where children are brought up together, visiting their parents occasionally. There would be no common dining room for the entire village to take the same meals, prepared by members assigned to the kitchen and dining room brigade.

Perforce, for decades the distribution of the member's share of the common enterprise was only a paper credit in struggling Moledet. Today, however, the distribution is a bit of a reality, and in future generations the annual dividend may make the members wealthy. More important, the preservation of the family institution, pristine and untampered, has created a morale and sense of individual personality in Moledet that does not exist in many of the kibbutzim. The best testimony to the wisdom of the founding fathers and mothers of Moledet is that some 35 *moshavei shitufim* have been established based on the Moledet image.

Now it is all there in Moledet complete. In fact, several new enterprises have been added that were not even dreamed of originally — a metal pipe plant and a large complex of agricultural equipment that is rented to other settlements in the area, an important source of income for the settlement.

All of the members of the founders' group were well-educated from middle or upper middle class families. The men had been lawyers, business executives, bankers, educators, engineers, accountants, students. The wives, too, had been students, school teachers, librarians, secretaries in business firms. None of them had been farmers, but most of them had worked as farm hands at the Nahalal Training Center for their agricultural future.

Their leaders had carefully studied the history of communal and cooperative enterprises, not only in Palestine but in other parts of the world, and not only the modern prototypes, but 18th and 19th century communes in the Americas and Europe. Even before they started they knew something of the rudiments of scientific farming, crop rotation, irrigation, marketing, livestock breeding, and above all the economics of farm financing, capital allocation and loan credit. They determined to apply their knowledge carefully, and to continue to study and learn. Over the years, they sent members to the United States and other countries to study new methods, advances in machinery and methodology, the breeding of livestock. Members also had been sent abroad to study methods and processes in the industries started at Moledet.

Moledet's basic principle of cooperative enterprise has made it possible to invest capital and manpower in unusual and striking ways. Respect for manual labor — any and all kinds of labor — is basic. Everyone of the original settlers has served a stint in the chicken coops, with the cows, the sheep and the goats, has shoveled the manure, picked the fruit, slogged through the fields. Those who were mechanically adept drove tractors. The first member to go abroad as a representative of the organization of kibbutzim and moshavim in the late 1940's, Chanan Prinz, identified himself to me when I first met him in Chicago as a "tractorist." He also happened to have been a lawyer in Berlin. Upon his return, he became the village school-teacher. But respect for labor at Moledet does not mean the glorification of drudgery. Nor does it mean ignoring a member's specialized skills and knowledge if those skills can be used and the member is willing to make them available, as most surely he is.

Work on a farm can be peaceful, healthful, and rewarding. It also can be dull and boring, and back-breakingly hard. As Moledet has grown and prospered, the members have welcomed every chance to enhance their lives and to encourage the younger generation to study and acquire education and knowledge enriching for the individual and the community. Moledet bought a share in a bus cooperative in the Gilboa area where the settlement is located. The member driver enjoys his work and is proud that the substantial income he generates goes into the total income of his community. One of the younger members, Michael Gadri, has become an expert on preserving and canning farm produce. He is an executive of a nearby cannery and spends most of his time on that job. His salary goes to Moledet and he doesn't even think about it. A married man with a family, he was given a six month leave as a full member to take courses in food chemistry.

Shimon Regev is one of the original founders. In the early days he took great pleasure in organizing childrens' choirs in his spare time between regular chores as a farm worker in the fields. Later his fine voice was regularly heard in the tenor section of the national symphony chorus. In recent years, he has been on loan from Moledet as an executive of the Kibbutz and Moshav organization in Tel-Aviv, commuting home to Moledet several times a week.

Joseph and Tova Gadri joined Moledet in 1940, soon after the colony was established on its new site; they were one of the original half dozen families invited to augment the manpower of the original founders. Joseph is a Czechoslovakian Jew from the Sudetenland who was studying engineering in Vienna when Hitler "repatriated" that "German" province early in the machinations preceding World War II. He and his young Viennese bride came to Israel in 1938, recognizing as did almost all of the members of Moledet from Europe that they could fulfill themselves as complete human beings in Palestine, free from the oppressive anti-Semitism that was poisoning the lands of their birth. The handsome young couple were a welcome addition to the group. German speaking, filled with energy, spirit and good humor they set to with a will to help create the Moledet dream.

Their sons were all born in Moledet, the elder two now full members with their Moledet-born sabra wives. The youngest son has served three years in the army as his brothers did before him. They, like all the young men of Israel who were in the army fought in the Yom Kippur War. The married sons live in their own new homes, Michael and his wife in a larger one needed to accommodate their two third-generation sons. There are already some 40 of these third-generation grandchildren. Babies have become one of Moledet's most carefully cultivated and successful crops. Both Joseph and Tova have served on many of the committees that administer and plan the village. Such service is considered an honor and a privilege, though no compensation is involved. Each member who physically is able, continues to work at his job or skill regardless of the responsibilities of the committee assignments.

Tova is a clothes designer and dressmaker. Joseph is a lock and pipe smith. We became fast friends when Joseph spent six months in Chicago in the early 60's assembling an enterprise to manufacture architectural lettering. The factory was added to Moledet's small complex of industries on my recommendation. Though the business prospered, the colony was forced to sell it because of a lack of trained manpower.

Like all the oldtimers, the Gadris take modest pride in the part they have played and still play in the community that has been created. Their greatest pleasure is the fact that their sons chose as adults to become members of Moledet. Son Ilon will, like brothers Michael and Rami, probably return to live and work in Moledet, and more than likely will also find a bride among the daughters there.

Tova's mother and father also came to Israel in the late 1930's, and when father Pollak became ill they came to live in Moledet. Now the widowed grandmother spends more time at Moledet than she does in her flat in Tel-Aviv. She often drove up to Moledet with us when we lived in Israel. Many of the parents of the settlers spend their later years in the colony, welcome and honored residents. One of the original principles of the master plan was the creation of a haven for those of the older generation who were able to get to Israel before the doors slammed shut in Europe. A few survivors of the holocaust came to Moledet after the War.

Macabre windfalls in the form of German reparations were donated in part or *in toto* to the community to build a large, well-appointed swimming pool that also serves as a reservoir. It is a monument to victims of the holocaust who did not survive to swim in it.

Since most all of the members during the first decade of the community were from Germany or Austria, the Yekke stamp of planning and hard work, of respect for detail and punctuality, combined with a tinge of stuffiness and a touch of humorlessness and stubbornness, lingers. Today, there are members from Australia, South Africa, England, and the United States. Several of the second-generation sabra boys and girls have married Sephardi sabras who have become full members. This intermixture has proven to be a pleasant leavening, very welcome to the original *Yekke* founders.

One of the myths in Israel is the notion that all Yekke are without humor. A closer characterization would be that they have a kind of shyness and formality manifested by unease. Some of the Yekke do have a German inability to be casual, to unbend. Three generations in Israel, on the land and in contact with fellow Israelis from all over the world and with the Arab farmers in the neighborhood, have all but obliterated the Teutonic inheritance. If Moledet was ever a "Yekkishe" kind of place, it certainly isn't today. However, many positive attributes that have made Moledet the lovely oasis it is today surely can be traced to Yekke inheritance.

One man merits the title of *father of Moledet* — the late Meir Lanir. He died in September, 1969, only 58 years old. He fled Germany the day Hitler came to power, and found his way to Palestine and became a *chalutz.* It was Meir Wollner (Lanir) who went to the freeholders settlement (moshav) Nahalal to study farming while he worked as a farm laborer. And it was Meir who rounded up young Jews from Germany in Palestine to join in his plan to start an agricultural settlement based upon personal independence linked with cooperation and modern know-how. It was he who put together the little group of recent immigrant Zionists in 1936.

In 1936, his childhood sweetheart, Dora, arrived from Nuremberg and a few months afterward they were married and the young couple went back to Germany to recruit young Jews to come to Israel and go on the land. They did not have too much success because they were proselytizing for a middle class, private property settlement, and young idealistic Jews in Germany were interested in communal settlements, kibbutzim. The Wollners (Lanirs) returned in a few months and in 1937, the group left Nahalal for the Jezreel to found Moledet. Meir was the secretary and spent most of his time traveling Palestine to raise money and find new members for the struggling little settlement isolated among Arab farms and villages. It was Meir Lanir who had thrown off the incongruous Jewish religious orthodoxy of his strict upbringing within weeks after his arrival in Palestine and who suggested the amalgam between the freeholders moshav of Nahalal and the commune kibbutz, then dominant among the pioneer settlers.

Meir Lanir never found enough time to be in his beloved Moledet. He moved into many positions of authority and importance — as chairman of all the settlements and villages in the Gilboa District, as representative of the agricultural ministry (to teach the farmers of Ghana how to organize cooperative farm settlements), and in the Israeli youth hostel movement.

Three children, two girls and then a son, were born to the Lanirs. In his too short but complete life, Meir saw his settlement mature to substantial success, his daughters marry stalwart Israelis. He lived to enjoy grandchildren. His never-ceasing efforts to knit together the disparate settlements in the district, the Arab villages, the moshavim, the kibbutzim, cooperative relationships with the larger towns, Afula and even Nazareth, bore visible fruit. Meir played a leading role in the establishment of the many Biblical and historical sites in the area, as part of the national park system — the waters of Harod ("Mayan Harod"), Mount Gilboa, the great crusader fort of Belvoir, overlooking the Jordan valley, the Sachneh springs.

Dora had undertaken the job of looking after the cemetery of Moledet. Each morning she arose at four to tend the graves and with loving hands nurture the flowers and shrubs and trees where lay the fathers and sons, the daughters and mothers, the grandparents who had found peace in Israel for a few years after the hell of Hitler's Europe. There lay the young Moledet soldiers, a score of them who had been cut down in their prime in the Israeli wars. She volunteered to do this work because to most of the members it was a hard and disagreeable job. One autumn morning Dora returned from these chores to find Meir dead in his bed; he had had too much work left unfinished to heed the advice of the doctors that his weakened heart could not survive the strain he put upon it.

The pioneer days of Moledet have long since been over. More than 500 people live there now in relative comfort and complete security. During the four years we lived in Israel Moledet was our favorite place. We delighted in driving up there for the holidays and festivals, to attend a wedding or just to visit friends. Once it was a remote, lonely outpost virtually on the border of Jordan. The members took turns at night on the watchtower, rifle in hand, guarding against marauders and raiders. Today, Moledet exists in the center of Israel. Buses travel frequently to the village from nearby Afula seven miles away on well-paved asphalt roads. One can drive to Haifa in less than an hour, to Tiberias in half an hour, to Tel-Aviv in two hours, to the seashore in less than an hour, to Nazareth in 15 minutes. Many outside day workers, mostly Arabs from the neighboring villages, are needed to supplement the members and the youngsters in handling the sizable agricultural-industrial enterprise

Moledet has become. The direction and administration is rapidly passing into the hands of the second generation born in Moledet. Some of the third generation are already teen-agers.

The pioneers are members of a generation the likes of which will not again be seen in Israel. This fact of life, of course, also applies to all newcomers who came to the land before statehood and in the early years of Israel, whether as chalutzim or as refugees. But the first people of the settlements are a unique one-time breed. Their singleness of purpose, their idealism, and their diverse backgrounds will never be duplicated. On the other hand, their children are sabras, native Israelis, products of the new independent nation. They, too, in their way are idealistic. But their idealism is national, not moral. They are parochial, non-intellectual. They are not as well educated as their parents. They don't read books. They watch television. They have little awareness and less interest in the international scene. They are more involved with the fortunes of the national football team.

The second and third generations in successful settlements like Moledet generally remain in their birthplace and carry on the work of the parents. But they have much in common with, and are not much different in attitudes and values from, their sabra counterparts in the urban areas. All of them, too, are products of their army service and the Israeli educational system. Their children, too, will be very much like them, just as all the sabra children of today are very much like their sabra parents. In the case of Moledet and many other settlements it can be predicted that succeeding generations may wind up as wealthy brahmins, heirs of an enterprise the creation of which was hardly envisioned or intended by its founders for material aggrandizement.

Ramat Zvi

Ramat Zvi, a freeholder settlement (*moshav*) is a few kilometers from Moledet. It, too, was founded on land donated by the B'nai Brith. Its name, Hill of Henry, commemorates Henry Monsky. Its history is vastly different from its neighboring village. Settlers came to Ramat Zvi in 1945 and 1946 just after World War II. The majority of them were refugees from Europe who had escaped to Palestine before the Hitler massacres started.

Most of them were from Poland, others from Hungary and other Eastern European and Balkan countries. They had been in Palestine for a few years working as day laborers at odd jobs in Haifa and other cities around the country. Not an organized group, they were all married couples, none of them farmers, although several had worked as farm hands and knew something about farming in existing freehold settlements, including Nahalal, where the Moledet settlers had trained. The Jewish National Fund maintained a bureau through which newcomers applied for a piece of land to farm and when the B'nai Brith provided the funds for a piece of land the JNF quite haphazardly picked the future settlers of Ramat Zvi from their lists of applicants.

The early years had been very grim, unalleviated by the kind of camaraderie and idealistic planning that enspirited the Moledet settlers. The Ramat Zvi farmers persevered, however, and eventually were able to maintain themselves and eke out a decent living from the land. Through generous loans for equipment and seed and livestock, they succeeded in establishing themselves and even improving and enlarging their small two-room houses. Some of them became superb farmers and dairymen. (Alexander (Sasha) Shalev is the best farmer there, and the most public spirited. Since my first visit to the area, I have maintained a close relationship with him and his family (and not only because his wife, Miriam, is the best cook of Hungarian delicacies in all of Israel.)

As children were born and grew old enough to help around the *meshek* (farm), the settlers began to interest themselves in creating a community life with help and encouragement from our B'nai Brith Israel committee. They built a pleasant primary school for kindergarten to grade three and arranged an interchange system with Moledet so that all the youngsters in both communities could attend eight grades of school. In 1961, they built a handsome community center. I cherish a photograph of my daughter Sharon cutting the ribbon to inaugurate the building. She was in Israel after her graduation from Brandeis University and worked on a kibbutz in the Negev. Ramat Zvi also participates in the B'nai Brith summer youth program, delighted to welcome American youngsters whose visits as guests for a week or two in their homes provide a welcome break in the farming routine.

The middle 1960's witnessed the beginning of a psychological deterioration. Paradoxically, the success of the farms was at its height. The general prosperity in Israel and the knowledgeability of the settlers in running their farms brought them substantial returns. They were able to acquire more sophisticated labor-saving machinery. A new water tower and reservoir, a gift from the B'nai Brith Youth organization, alleviated the water and irrigation problem. At the same time, internal rivalry, bickering and ill feeling among the neighbors caused several of the more talented and community-minded families to leave. Newcomers could not be found to take over their farms. The children had grown up and left for army service. Arab labor was costly and day workers were hired only as a last resort. The old timers carried on, tired and worn and dispirited. Most of the young men did not return after their army service. Many of the young girls married or found employment in the cities. Today some of the farms and houses are deserted and the entire atmosphere of the community is drab and lackluster. It is questionable if the community will survive in its present form.

The fate of Ramat Zvi is not untypical of the moshavim of Israel. Those that were located near urban centers have fared better. Their land has in many cases become valuable as suburban housing estate sites. In some cases their favorable location near large cities has influenced the second generation to come back to work the farms because city life was nearby, and they could expect their inheritance to prove valuable in the future. But *moshavim* in remote areas like Ramat Zvi are steadily deteriorating. It may well be that the farmland will be taken over by neighboring cooperative settlements and kibbutzim. Perhaps large agrobusiness enterprises will be developed similar to those in the United States to farm the lands on a technological, impersonal business basis. Ramat Zvi is only a few kilometers from Moledet as space is measured. In many other ways it is eons distant.

7. Tel-Aviv and Tel-Avivians

Despite the physical fact of its inner city crampedness and its undistinguished birth as a sort of Jewish seaside suburb of Jaffa, Tel-Aviv, with a little luck and a lot of peace, may become one of the great cities of the world. It will never achieve the ancient and impressive solemnity of Jerusalem, nor match its beauty, shimmering in the clear air of the high Judean hills. It isn't likely either that its sometimes awful weather will improve. Tel-Aviv is oppressively hot and humid in the summer months and even in the evenings it doesn't cool off until late at night. But it is a very special place. It represents the Israel of today and tomorrow. Much of whatever Israel will be in the future will come out of Tel-Aviv, not out of Jerusalem. Hopefully, Jerusalem will deeply influence that future, that is to say, the best of the ancient tradition and culture, respect for learning, respect for leavened authority, respect for the verities, respect *stam* (just like that). But the modern Jewish inheritance is Tel-Aviv. Jerusalem represents a kind of living museum, a museum of what was, or what is believed and discerned to have been. Tel-Aviv represents what is and what will be. Its very strength and vitality is based on its lack of tradition. Tel-Aviv cannot be controlled by the past. For so many Tel-Avivians, the past is immediate, abhorrent, a nightmare. Thus, the thrust of Tel-Aviv is to build, not to rebuild. To construct, not to reconstruct.

Many observers are certain that the choked center of Tel-Aviv is well on its way to becoming a slum; this has been the fate of many of the inner cities of the world. Though founded hardly more than half a century ago, it was planned as a small city of no more than 50,000 people and its winding, tortuous streets were never intended for the thousands of motor vehicles, the bumper-to-bumper traffic gassing its people. The no-man's land between Tel-Aviv and Jaffa (now technically a part of Tel-Aviv) which lay in ruins for a whole generation after the War of Independence affords some limited area for development on the south side of the inner city. But the main expansion of the metropolis proper is heading north along the seacoast, and northeast into the countryside.

The northside of the city along the sea on both sides of the shore expressway contains attractive sites for expensive high-rise apartment buildings as the vacant spaces adjoining the Tel-Aviv University campus and the nearby suburban villages fill up. Only a few years ago, these areas were far out of the vortex of the city. Today, they are very much in the city, as the population center inexorably moves north. The most fashionable of these north side areas are Ramat-Aviv where the university is located and Bavli immediately southeast of Ramat Aviv. While spacious and comfortable apartments in the inner city can be rented or bought for still reasonable sums, the new apartments in the north of the city command figures approaching prices in London, Paris, or New York.

Today, these northside areas are in the deep center of Tel-Aviv, and in another generation they may become walk-up tenements. Hopefully, this gloomy prediction will be confounded by decent planning, and by Jewish-Israeli talent for intelligent improvisation. At least there does not exist in Tel-Aviv and other cities of Israel the hysteric human ugliness of escape from an invasion of "undesirables," a rush to avoid Black neighbors that is the tragic disgrace of American cities. If the politicos of the city government have the guts to ban private automobile traffic from the streets of the inner city, Tel-Aviv could develop a patina of charm still visible in the ancient cities of Europe and England, and even in sections of New York and Chicago.

In all events, the heart of Tel-Aviv is very much in the center of the town; that is where the Israelis live and the pulsebeat is quick and staccato and alive. Hayarkon Street is the Collins Avenue of Tel-Aviv. Starting at the old abandoned port on the north end of the city where the Yarkon River runs into the sea, it wends its way south along the seashore for several miles, ending in the old Yemenite quarter next to Jaffa. Two blocks beyond its humble beginnings in a workshop, garage, and bus-stop area (where our apartment overlooks the former customs-house), Hayarkon metamorphoses into a street of posh modern tourist hotels and the splendid Independence Park on a cliff above the sea. There the Sheraton and Hilton have now been joined by a dozen more hotels on the seashore where only a decade ago squatters' huts sitting haphazardly on the beaches exemplified the contrast between the old and the new that is Tel-Aviv.

The Dan Hotel is a mile south of the park on Hayarkon Street and several blocks farther on cheap bars, prostitute pads, and clip joint night clubs thrive. In the very center of this demi-mondaine section of Hayarkon stands the severe American Embassy building imperviously overlooking the Mediterranean. The Embassy was built in the 1950's to emphasize U.S. refusal to recognize Jerusalem as the capital of Israel.

Ben Yehuda and Dizengoff Streets start together with Hayarkon near the port. Many good restaurants have sprung up around this old harbor enclave. There, too, are a sprinkling of small sidewalk cafes, shops and new apartment houses. These two main arteries diverge and run south parallel to each other for about two miles into the heart of the city, separating at the main business area which is now old Tel-Aviv, as Dizengoff turns southeast. Dizengoff (named after the first mayor of Tel-Aviv) is the best known street in Israel. Day and night crowds of Israelis, the majority of them young, swirl up and down the wide, spacious, tumultuous mile of its center, sit endlessly in the sidewalk cafes over coffee and cakes or an aperitif and sandwich, shop in the smart stores, including several fine department stores, and create a kaleidoscope of liveliness that is a joy to behold.

The heart of Tel-Aviv, old and new, perhaps three square miles in all, contains myriads of little residential streets winding and twisting between the main arteries and the tree-shaded boulevards that bind the community together into an organic whole. Heavy vehicular traffic has required all of these to become one-way streets and a stranger driving on them can become hopelessly lost trying to get back to an address that he passed a block away.

Allenby Road into which all the streets seem to lead, directly or indirectly, traces a curve of the sea that flows southeast beyond the center of the town, and follows a chaotic, bustling route for several miles towards Jaffa. Allenby is the oldest main street of Tel-Aviv and remains the heart of the business and financial district. On or near Allenby can be found banks, office buildings, department stores, and hundreds of mercantile enterprises making and selling every kind of merchandise imaginable. The Shalom Tower, the tallest building in the Middle East, some 50 stories high, stands just off of the center of Allenby Road imposingly dominating the area.

Between Allenby Road and the Yemenite quarter a block away one finds Ha Shook Ha Carmel (The Carmel Market), a maze of twisting streets filled with vegetable and fruits stands, meat and fish stalls, dry goods carts and good natured merchants and their families lustily hawking their wares. Allenby Road with all the many streets it dominates in the daytime is the most alive part of Tel-Aviv, even more than Dizengoff. At night there are very few people to be found on Allenby. Quite like the financial and business districts of New York and Chicago, Allenby is a place of commerce, of occupation, of work.

At night the Tel-Avivians are to be found on Dizengoff, and in recent years in Jaffa in the port area, which the tourist ministry restored as an art and entertainment center. Designed primarily as a tourist attraction, this Jaffa playground has also become an attraction for Israelis with its art galleries, jewelry shops, boutiques, restaurants and night clubs. The original area has sprawled out into the old city center of Jaffa adjoining it as another rather honky-tonk night life spot. There, too, in the daytime is located the Shook ha Pishpishim (flea market) that is a favorite haunt of bargain hunters, rich and poor, tourists and Israelis.

Allenby Road ends up in Jaffa — another city — the oldest in Palestine, even older than Jerusalem. Although Jaffa now is a part of Tel-Aviv politically, completely under the administration of the Tel-Aviv municipality, it is and will continue to be itself. Though many of its majority of Arab inhabitants fled in 1948, many remained and many came back. Jaffa has an Arab flavor quite like Nazareth. The same Arabic stone block architecture dominates its physical appearance. Thousands of new immigrants, Ashkenazim and Sephardim have swelled its population since Independence. It was my observation that the Arabs and the new inhabitants of Jaffa seem to live and work together amicably enough.

"Big George"

Yehuda (George) Hameiri is a Tel-Avivian. Our children nicknamed him "Big George." We met him as the broker who sold us our apartment, and soon afterward he became a family friend and companion. He was brought to Palestine by his parents from Hungary at the age of five. (His parents on both sides came from a hassidic religious environment. His father and his mother, who also came from an educated hassidic family, had left the religious environment of their families, but were committed, non-proletarian Zionists. George's father became a successful realtor and businessman in the burgeoning city of Tel-Aviv, and his son was brought up in a cosmopolitan atmosphere of luxury and urbane comfort.

The family lived in a spacious apartment building on Rothschild Boulevard, where George still lives with his elderly mother. George attended good private schools, learned Hungarian, French, and English in addition to his native Hebrew. The family traveled frequently to Europe. In the forties George was a young ardent patriot and a British soldier during World War II, as were most of his peers. He was also a member of the Haganah underground. During the War of Independence and for many years afterward he was connected with Israeli intelligence activities, traveling in Europe, mostly in France but also in Italy, England, and the Balkans. He spent a good deal of time in Egypt posing as a prosperous French businessman where his serviceable Arabic and command of other languages were useful. In fact, he was a French businessman, having established a metal manufacturing company in the Paris suburbs. He married a non-Jewish Frenchwoman and was quite happy as a European cosmopolite, making frequent visits home to Israel.

His marriage fell apart, his business with it, and a serious heart attack forced him to return to Israel and re-establish himself in the family real estate business. A mountain of a man physically, he moves gracefully and lightly in the business and social circles of Tel-Aviv and Jerusalem. He is a gourmet, a master bridge player, and an amateur painter. Despite his years abroad, he is essentially an Israeli — by choice, more particularly, a Tel-Avivian. He is content to be once more living in the heart of his beloved city. To him, there is more excitement and vitality there than in the Paris he also knows and loves.

He frequently transacts business in Jerusalem through his connections with Arab Yerushalmis dating back to Mandate times, and the rapid development of the former Jordanian sections of Jerusalem provide opportunities for his real estate business. Hameiri, like most Israelis, is pleased with the expansion of Jerusalem and he predicts that the Arab sections of that city will become integrally Israeli, much like Jaffa in recent years. He does not believe, however, that the growth of Jerusalem presents a threat to the advance of Tel-Aviv, or that eventually Jerusalem will overtake Tel-Aviv in size and become the principal economic center of the the country. He compares the two cities to Washington and New York, one a political capital and the other the more vital financial and cultural capital. George tells you that Tel-Aviv is genuinely the cultural capital of Israel and that it will remain so.

The Salc's

Dr. Henko Salc is a rarity among Israeli dentists — he is both a medical doctor and an oral surgeon. He was our family dentist and I owe him an everlasting debt of gratitude for the bridges he made for me. Henko and his Mara are our dear friends. He came to Israel in his mature years after a long and successful career in his native Yugoslavia and has assiduously kept up with the new techniques and advances in his profession. In the Paris or New York of today he would be earning a fortune. He is contented enough to live in Tel-Aviv, his only concern being to slow down a bit in his practice now that he is in his 70's, yet still provide for his beloved wife and leave a bit of inheritance for their son.

He does not consider himself a Tel-Avivian, though his home has been there for a quarter of a century. But he is just that. He characterizes the cadre of skilled and talented European Jewish professionals who came to Israel from choice at the beginning of Independence because they discovered that the Europe they had known was gone, that there was no decently viable future there for them.

Mara, his young non-Jewish bride was an electrical engineer. They met at the beginning of the war when both were involved in the early partisan activities, he as a medical officer on Tito's underground army staff and Mara as a nurse and guerrilla fighter. When their situation became dangerous, they managed to escape to Switzerland with the help of Mara's family and shortly thereafter to Italy where they remained until the end of the war. They could have remained in Italy after the war very successfully, having developed close friendships with several wealthy Italian families. They also could have gone back to Switzerland where the doctor's talents were known. They chose rather, to go back to Belgrade, romantically convinced that they could reconstruct their lives in their native land.

In Belgrade they discovered how wrong they were. The rigid new hierarchy was no place for a non-communist Jew, no matter how sound his credentials or his military service. Tito Brosip and his Establishment boys, like most communist *aparatchiks* (political operators) had conveniently forgotten their war comrades. Even worse, the atmosphere was unattractive, the country was poverty-stricken, oppressive, sterile. Dr. Salc had never been an ardent Zionist, but he had come from a deeply committed Jewish family, and under the conditions that obtained in the almost *Judenrein* (clear of Jews) Yugoslavia of the post-war years, Israel seemed to offer opportunities to create a new life. When their young son was born in the same year Israel became a state, they joined the thousands of Jewish immigrants and refugees on the great Aliyah of the first years.

They arrived with practically nothing — a few personal possessions, keepsakes, clothing, a few dental tools, and a healthy little boy baby. They joined the thousands of others housed in the wretched *ma'abarot* on the sea north of Tel-Aviv and tried to find friends and relatives. Within a few months their original enthusiasm had worn thin by the primitivism and discomfort of the camp. In the worst days of the war in Yugoslavia they had not suffered as much physical discomfort. Even more disenchanting, they learned that they were merely numbers, as were all of the others. Their education, skills, professions counted for nothing. In those days the new nation, despite massive aid from overseas and the genuine dedicated organization of the Jewish Agency, simply could not cope with the hordes of immigrants. Israel was wholly unprepared to care for or integrate the newcomers except in the most sketchy fashion.

Within a few months,however, Dr. Salc was able to rent a little office as part of two tiny rooms that also served as living quarters. The location was most favorable, in the very center of old Tel-Aviv. With the benign strength of his Mara and the prospect of bringing up their son as a free Jew in a Jewish land, the doctor launched his practice as a dentist. They have made it both professionally and socially, still in those original quarters, now somewhat enlarged by an adjoining room. Many Yugoslavs who knew Dr. Salc from the old country (including the Embassy people during the years when Yugoslavia maintained diplomatic relations with Israel) became his patients. Mara abandoned her profession and became his skilled assistant, probably the most able dental technician in Tel-Aviv.

They are comfortably situated, not wealthy. Dr. Salc is recognized among his colleagues as a giant in the dental profession and has traveled abroad as a representative of the Israel Dental Society to lecture at universities and convocations in Europe and Australia. Life is easier for them now. Their son, Doron, is a grown man, has served his term in the armed forces, has studied years in the universities, has worked as an electronics technician, but as yet has not completely found himself. He is completely an Israeli — he has lived all his life in Israel. But he is not chauvinist nor nationalist, and his upbringing by his well bred, intellectual and urbane parents has given him a world, if not worldly, outlook on life that involves constant questioning about the quality of modern Israeli life. He has many friends with much the same background and exposure as his, who ask the same questions, and like Doron, do not find easy answers. They, too, are the Tel-Avivians of the present and the future. They, too, have a fierce, wry and disparaging love for their lively dirty city of concrete and asphalt and pulsing rhythm.

The Salc's are able to spend a few months each summer in Europe, visiting Mara's family in Yugoslavia (most of Dr. Salc's family were wiped out in the war) and friends in Italy, France, and Switzerland. These visits help them maintain their broad general perspective. If they ever doubted it, they now realize that theirs was no more an interbellum generation than any other period of the 20th Century, only more murderous. They experienced the deaths of their relatives and friends and many of the best of their contemporaries. However, they are able to find consolation in living in an Israel that offers at least as much prospect for the future as any other place their physical survival might have led them to. At least they are citizens of a nation to which they belong as a matter of right, not suffrance. In this sense, Mara is an Israelit if not a Jewess. This gives her infinite pleasure. And for this Dr. Salc is grateful, for himself and his beloved helpmate. Despite their sufferings, the years sit gracefully upon both of them. They have a light touch.

The Family Rasiel

Since I first met Ovadia Rasiel in Chicago in 1947 I have been accepted by the Rasiels almost as a member of the family. Ovadia and his wife Yaffa were born and raised in Tel-Aviv. The Rasiel family chronicle constitutes a segment of modern Israeli history. Ovadia's late father was the first secretary of the Histadrut Agriculture Department in the 1920's. Ben-Gurion was a close associate. Later, he broke away from his labor connections to become a founder of the philosophical wing of a centrist, more bourgeois and religious group from which the *Irgun Zvai Leumi* (Etzel — army organization of the nation) emerged in the late 1930's. Ovadia's cousin was the legendary David Rasiel, the founder of the military branch of the Irgun, who at the age of 24 was killed in an Arab ambush while scouting for the British army.

Esther Rasiel-Naor was a veteran Heirut member of the Knesset until 1973. She is Ovadia's cousin, sister of the late David. A fiery little black-eyed outspoken lady, she would be one of Israel's leading "women's libbers" if she had not retained a deep Orthodox Judaism that requires at least some superficial acknowledgement of male superiority. She has adroitly managed to stay within this formality, while asserting an awesome female egalitarianism. Esther Rasiel is a kind of conservative nationalistic Orthodox version of her Amerian Jewish liberal counterpart, Bella Abzug.

The Rasiel wives have always exerted a strong quiet influence. Ovadia's mother, a striking beauty, came to Palestine with her young husband in the 1920's. A daughter of a modern, not deeply religious family in her native Lithuania, she became an urbane educated wife and mother secure in the society of the early Tel-Aviv. She never completely forgave her son Amram, who had the temerity to go to the United States in the 1950's to complete his education as an electronics engineer, and who remained there, married an American girl, and carved out for himself a position as an electronics industrialist. Amram's frequent and dutiful visits to Israel, sometimes with his wife and children, were to his mother little recompense for what she regarded as desertion. The desertion in her view was much more personal than national.

Shoshana Rasiel is the widow of David. David and Shoshana were married for only three short years. They had been an inseparable team fighting for the liberation of their nation during the early war years in the fiercely idealistic and dynamic Irgun structure. When David Rasiel died, the great shining light of her life was extinguished. At his death she was still darkly beautiful, vivacious and strong. Born in the old city of Jerusalem into a family of learned Orthodox Jews, she was a third generation Palestinian Jewess. Her will to live, her burning Zionism, and her need to fulfill her martyred husband kept her going in those dark days.

Before the War of Independence, she journeyed to the United States for the Irgun and tried to find herself in another milieu. She even did a stint as an actress in *avant garde* theatre in Chicago. She remembers with affection a young fellow actor who was very kind to the unhappy Israelit widow. A few years later he was known to the world as Marlon Brando. I did not know her in the Chicago days. I met her in Jerusalem on my first visit in 1950 through a mutual friend and she located Ovadia for me in Tel-Aviv. I knew him then only as Ben David.

Shoshana never remarried. She has carried on with her school and her friends and her family, quietly unreconciled but not resigned and not bitter about an essentially dull fate that might have been otherwise. There is not an important figure in the Heirut or among the leaders of the government, especially the Ministry of Education, who do not know and respect her. Among all of the Rasiel clan she is most beloved. She is the essential Rasiel.

Yaffa, Ovadia's wife, is a placid homemaker who has carefully built her family life with her restless, stubborn, talented husband and his "Queen of Romania" mother and his myriad of family, colleagues, old friends, and *Etzel* comrades. Their sons, teen-aged Nimrod and young Asaf are so Israeli that they might be of the thirtieth instead of the third generation as they are. Yaffa's parents came to Israel between the wars in 1930 from urban Poland to urban Tel-Aviv and modestly established themselves in a neighborhood laundry business. Yaffa became a school teacher and met Ovadia when he too was a school teacher and later a grade school principal after the Independence War. They were married in 1954.

She has remained the self-same modest person that she was twenty-five years ago, except that as she came in contact with Americans and Europeans, her shyness and her monolingual Hebrew matured into social graces and good English plus a smattering of other languages. She has an acquaintanceship with people from all over the world that could be the envy of more ambitious Tel-Aviv society matrons. The Rasiels have a comfortable house in Ramat Chen, a northeast section of Tel-Aviv where they have lived since shortly after their marriage.

Ovadia was sent to Europe and the United States in 1947 as a trusted courier for the Irgun. He was a youth of 19, who covered his inexperience and fright with an imposing long British officer moustache and a very stern uncommunicative demeanor. This disguise also helped him get by with his very inadequate Palestine high school English. His earnestness and obvious sincerity were heightened by his shyness, and he returned to Palestine shortly before the outbreak of the hot war with a considerable fund collected from American and European friends of the cause. His pseudonym during this excursion was significantly, "Ben David," the name of his martyred cousin.

Several years later, he became the national president of the university students of Israel, the only political position he has ever held. He consistently resisted joining the Heirut political party that grew out of the Irgun, though his name and credentials and his considerable abilities would have assured him a brilliant political future. He chose rather to study law and is today a successful Tel-Aviv attorney. He is quietly gregarious, highly respected in the legal profession throughout the country. As a lawyer for tourist and airline interests he travels literally all over the world, an experience he enjoys very much.

Originally a very lily-white Ashkenazi who deplored the "Franks" whose immigration in great numbers seemed to him to be denigrating the "purity" of Israel, he has come full-scale around to recognize the quality of all Israelis — qua Israelis. Personally unambitious, he reveres rank, status, old family ties — he is a kind of an Israeli tory. A fighter against the British Mandatory power, he retains a lingering respect for the orderliness established during the British occupation of his youth. He was brought up by his religious father in a very observant atmosphere but is not at all observant himself. Yet he, like so many of his family and his Irgun friends, insists on the prime importance of the old established religion as the fundament of the state. Personally more than tolerant, essentially compassionate, he is like all vital human beings, a collection of contradictions, and being an Israeli and an old time Tel-Avivian, he is of course, a stiff-necked Jew — one of the finest examples of the breed.

Achia Rasiel

Achia Rasiel was a victim of the Israeli-Arab confrontation soon after Independence. If the complete story of his disappearance and murder is known, it is buried very deep, as deep as the real facts of the series of events variously known as "The Security Mishap", or "The Lavon Affair" that rocked the Israeli government in the middle 1950's; the repercussions still reverberate within the ruling parties.

Achia was in the vortex of the resistance activity in Jewish Palestine while still in short pants. He was only ten years old when his cousin Ben David was killed. Understandably this tragedy and the activity swirling around him made a deep impression on this keen, introspective lad. He was sixteen years old when the War of Independence started and already a veteran of daring missions for the Irgun. He had served a three-week stint in Damascus posing as a Syrian. His dark slim good looks and his near perfect Arabic and quiet, almost sullen self-assurance had seen him through.

The war over, he continued with his studies and received his degree as a geology major at the Technion University in Haifa. In 1951 he came to the University of Chicago to continue his studies. His ambition was to become an oil geologist to help find the oil he was certain existed in the Negev, in the Galilee, and along the Mediterranean shores. As a passionately dedicated Israeli, he aspired to help Israel avoid the economic pressure that would surely ensue unless the country possessed its own oil resources. He was very idealistic, very scholarly, and very young.

I never knew him in Israel. I met him in Chicago. Ovadia had asked me to help his shy kid brother adjust into the somewhat menacing atmosphere of a big American city. Except for his brief escapade in Syria, Achia had never been out of Israel. I found him delightful. Introspective, stubborn and opinionated, brilliant, with a fount of digested knowledge almost unbelievable at the age of 21, he was a welcome mealtime guest at our home. The meals were in connection with the Hebrew lessons he earnestly and unsuccessfully gave me each week. Twenty minutes of Hebrew and we would be deep into hours of discussion of Jewish history, recent Israeli events, religion, American politics, existentialism, geology. We learned from each other, I probably more than he, and in the few months I knew him we became fast friends.

One day in 1952 as the winter was ending he called to tell me that he was busy working on his thesis and apologized for not being able to continue our lessons for a few weeks. I was a bit surprised and chagrined, but gave the matter little thought. A month later he called my office and asked if he could come to see me that evening on a matter of some importance. He sounded very grave and serious, a bit worried.

He usually covered his shyness with wisecracks, so I took his opening question in stride.

"What would you say if I were to tell you that I have enlisted into the United States Army?" he asked.

I answered in the same vein, "I would say you were nuts."

"Well," he replied, "I have."

I soon found out that he was serious. At first he blandly explained that he had been called in by university authorities to ask if he would be interested in doing some work for the U.S. government involving a knowledge of Arabic. It seemed that the Defense Department, or the State Department, or some department of the American government (most likely the C.I.A., which was just then starting its global adventurism) was seeking an Israeli who could pass for an Arab and could speak the language, to perform a mission of importance both to the United States and Israel. Achia seemed to fit the bill perfectly. In retrospect, I have often wondered if he was not sent to Chicago specifically for the mission.

In any event, he told me that he had checked with the Israeli Embassy in Washington and had been urged to accept the assignment as a mission of great importance to his country; whereupon he enlisted in the United States Army. In a week he would leave for an army camp in the South for six weeks of boot training. The script sounded more and more weird to me. I told him straight out that I thought him the least likely Israeli to be interested in a military career in the United States Army. One of our primary areas of argument had centered on his harsh and unadulterated criticism of the United States, its culture, morals, pretensions, racism, materialism. He couldn't wait to leave the country. He then leveled with me. He had been told that he was permitted to make one trusted contact in the United States. He had chosen me because I was a friend of his family in Israel and, in connection with my B'nai Brith activities for Israel, would be traveling there frequently. I also seemed to be a logical choice because I held no official position, either with the United States government or with the Israeli government. He went on to tell me the nature of his assignment. He was to go to Egypt to perform certain intelligence surveillance for the U.S. and Israel and to carry out certain missions with other agents with whom he would be put in contact.

The six-week training period actually was a cover for briefing him on the details of the mission. He would then be given a medical discharge and thereafter make his way to New York where he would obtain a job as an ordinary seaman on a freighter plying between the United States and the Mediterranean. At an Egyptian port he would jump ship and disappear into the country to pose as a Syrian who had lived in the United States for several years. He had been told that he would be gone for a total of three years during which he would make no outside contacts with anyone — except me, if possible.

I was sworn to secrecy of course. Achia asked me to continue assuring his family that he was all right, whether I heard from him or not. Most likely, he added, he would simply walk in on me one day, or into his parent's home in Tel Aviv, without any previous warning. The whole story sounded like an elaborate hoax, a scenario outline for a bad B movie. Knowing Achia and the background of his short twenty years in an atmosphere of dangerous underground machinations, I was forced to accept his story at face value. He apologized for having chosen me to share his secret and in the same breath assured me that I would not personally be involved. We parted warmly, and he left in good spirits. I never saw him again.

He called me twice thereafter. A month after he left Chicago he telephoned me from the camp in the South. He was speaking from the hospital where he told me he was ill with stomach flu. "Nothing serious," he assured me. He expected to be up and around in a couple of days. As this information fitted in with the plan, I was not worried. A few days later I received a postcard telling me he was out of the infirmary and back in training. Two weeks later he called one early morning from a YMCA in Chicago. He was in town for a day or two to collect his belongings and take care of a few minor chores before leaving. He had been released from the army on a medical discharge, but he felt fine. He would call me later in the day and perhaps he could stop at my office for a chat before he left. I was not to call him.

I waited all day for his call and finally decided to go to the YMCA to find him. At the 'Y' I learned that he had registered the evening before and had checked out at three o'clock that afternoon. He left no forwarding address. I was miffed, but from his careful briefing and my knowledge of his professional cautiousness, I confidently assumed that his reasons for not seeing me before he left town were sound. "You are not to worry," he had said again and again. "I will be in touch with you when it is perfectly safe, and my associates approve. In fact you will most likely hear from me indirectly through strangers."

During the ensuing year, I received many letters from his older brother asking if I had heard from Achia. He had written the family about his enlistment in the U.S. Army, and also about his discharge in the summer of 1952. He had been very vague about his future plans. Achia had written his family that he was engaged in an oil geology project that would probably take him to Alaska, and that he wouldn't be able to write often. He mentioned to them that he planned to keep in touch with me and that I would in turn keep in touch with the family. I too wrote to his family, with vague assurances that all was well with our wandering Jew and I would explain more fully in person in the fall when I would be in Israel.

I have never faced a more distressing task than the effort to comfort and reassure Achia's parents in Tel-Aviv that he was safe, that he was in good health, and that they would be hearing from him in due course. When they pressed me for details, I could not furnish them. I could only repeat that I was sincere, knew whereof I spoke, and they were to believe me. My close friendship with Ovadia offered them some hope. But they were gently skeptical. My words sounded hollow and unconvincing, despite an effort to put on a good performance. It was apparent that they sensed my own grave doubts, which had grown with the months of silence. They were kind enough not to prod me too hard. These sensitive old people had grown wise from the tragedies they had witnessed and suffered during the nascent Israel years. I appreciated their sophisticated delicacy; in the end they seemed to be consoling me. I believe they intuitively even then knew the nature of Achia's mission. I had expected them to press me on the most inexplicable and absurd fact of all, his voluntary enlistment in the United States Army. To my great relief, they did not belabor the point.

A few years later, when hope that Achia was alive had almost run out, his mother and father solicited the help of the late David Ben-Gurion, an old friend from whom they had been estranged for many years. They never mentioned what he told them. Undoubtedly the old man knew something of Achia's fate and what his mission had been. Whether or not he disclosed what he knew to the parents, he did console and comfort them, and the reunion was cordial and friendly. They probably learned enough to deduce that Achia was one of the score of victims of the "security mishap" that precipitated the Lavon Affair in 1954 and brought Ben-Gurion back as Prime Minister of Israel in 1955.

Ovadia spent months in the United States in 1954 running down every lead and scrap of evidence to find out what had happened to his brother Achia. Every inquiry to the United States Army, the Pentagon, the immigration officials, the Israeli Embassy, the University of Chicago, was fruitless. Each path led into a *cul de sac.* Rumors that he had been seen on the University of Chicago campus, in Canada, in Alaska, turned out to be figments. One strange and disturbing story could never be verified except for one particular. He had been seen often while at the University in 1952 with a beautiful Egyptian girl, a student who had returned to Egypt at about the same time that Achia left Chicago. A fourth-hand bit of gossip had it that Achia was deeply in love with her and had said that he planned to marry the young lady and go to Egypt to live after he completed his studies. No corroboration of this romantic tale ever turned up.

There can be little doubt that the disappearance of Achia Rasiel is linked to the "security mishap." This strange tragic drama of futility will remain shrouded in contradiction and rumor for years to come. It is doubtful if the facts will ever become known. It is one of Israel's contributions to the growing list of Trojan Horse maneuvers — the games of espionage and counter-intelligence played in the practice of power politics and diplomacy in a technological age. The chief beneficiaries of these sinister activities are the writers of spy stories. The victims wind up on the gallows like Eli Cohen in Syria, or in a Soviet prison like Captain Powers of U-2 infamy or in a shallow grave on the beach of the Bay of Pigs in Cuba, in a pool of blood like General Diem in Saigon, in prison like the Watergate buggers, or shot out of the sky like the pilots of the naive plot to rescue American P.O.W.'s in North Vietnam in 1971, or God knows where — like Achia Rasiel.

The bare bones of the story have been guessed at. Israeli Army Intelligence developed a plan to emasculate the colonel's revolt in Egypt, which had overthrown King Farouk in 1952 and had taken control of the armed forces and the government. The front man in this plot was Colonel Naguib, but the real boss was Colonel Gamel Abdul Nasser, who shortly thereafter emerged as the dictator of Egypt. Whether the plan was worked out with the intelligence agencies of other countries — the United States, England, France — has been suggested but never substantiated. Although the plot was initiated while Ben-Gurion was prime minister, it is not likely that he himself knew about it.

The plan involved spiriting into Egypt several score of agents, mostly Israelis, to work with sympathetic Egyptian elements in establishing a new government favorable to the Western Powers and Israel. Most likely Naguib, Nasser, and others were marked for assassination. The denouement happened after Moshe Sharett became Prime Minister of Israel in 1953. His Defense Minister was Pinchas Lavon, the adroit veteran Mapai politician who for years had been powerful in labor party circles and in the Histadrut, the national labor union. Somehow, the Egyptians learned of the plot and those involved in it and as a result an unknown number of agents were fingered, captured, tortured, imprisoned, killed. Ben-Gurion blamed Lavon for the security mishap. Some victims had gotten to Egypt and were caught there. Others were disposed of in Europe and the United States. The best guess is that Achia Rasiel was killed in the United States by Egyptian agents.

Albert Halfon

Albert Halfon is a Greek Jew who came to Israel as a young man from Athens during the 1930's. His family had lived in Greece for generations, completely assimilated and not religious but proudly and quite naturally Jewish, as most Greek Jews are. Albert was neither a refugee nor a Zionist. He had signed on as deck hand on a Greek tramp steamer to see something of the world and had casually decided to stay in Palestine when his boat docked in Jaffa, a principal port for the British during the Mandate. He enjoyed his bachelor days working and carousing with fellow Greek Jewish sailors. Their meeting place was "Ariana," the oldest and most popular cafe and nightclub in Jaffa. Located in the center of the former port at the water's edge, its belly dancers gyrate to Bazouki Greek music played deafeningly on electronically amplified instruments, while swarthy good-humored patrons drink anise flavored ouzo and eat Greek, Turkish, Arabic food exactly like the patrons of any waterfront establishment in the ports of Greece. One hears as much Greek spoken at Ariana as Hebrew.

Albert joined the British Army in Palestine at the outbreak of World War II. By then he had become a passionate Jewish nationalist and looked forward to the day when Israel would be an independent Jewish nation with the help and consent of the British and their allies. He had already established a food shop in Jaffa, a business his family had been engaged in for generations in Greece and which he knew well. During the war he married a lovely young German Jewess who came to Palestine from Paris where she had lived since childhood, after leaving Germany with her parents to escape the Nazis. Jaffa after the war of 1948 was no longer a sensible place to operate a luxury food store, and Albert relocated his business in Tel-Aviv. During the ensuing years he and his wife opened other shops in Givatayim and Kfar Shmaryahu. Kitty and I were regular customers of the Kfar shop and came to know Albert and Vickie well. These shops today are meticulously operated by Albert, wife Vickie, and their two grown sons. They are perhaps the finest shops of their kind in all of Israel, non-kosher, of course. Albert sent his sons to France, Germany, and Greece after their army service was finished to learn about food delicacies and to acquire savoir-faire socially and in business. Their shops are strictly a family operation. The handsome wife of the oldest son also works in the stores in between looking after her two small children. Before she married an American stockbroker and went off to New York to live, the youngest Halfon daughter also worked as cashier in the stores. Though the Halfons now live in an apartment in the Kfar, their social life is centered in Tel-Aviv where most of their family and friends live. They are Tel-Avivians.

Albert is wise and worldly. In addition to unaccented Hebrew he speaks Greek, French, German, even some Yiddish and English. He is not ashamed of his Sephardic ancestry, but does not identify as an Oriental Israeli or even with the Greek community; no more than does wife Vickie identify with her *volk*, the *Yekke* of the German Jewish community.

Both of them regard themselves as Israelis of European background, which truly they are. Their children are typical sabras. The Halfon parents and children exemplify the generation gap between Israeli parents of European background and their adult sabra children. The parents are more cosmopolitan, more tolerant, more compassionate, and more flexible — in a word more Jewish. Both generations have similar values and attitudes towards their beloved country. They are all Israelis and their loyalties and ambitions for their own futures and that of their nation are identical. The parents look upon the parochialism of their children with tolerance and understanding, hoping that their outlooks and interests will broaden as they mature. Wiser and more affluent parents like the Halfons encourage their children to mix with immigrants and tourists from abroad and to travel and become acquainted with the world outside, although they are not happy to have them emigrate, as in the case of the Halfon daughter.

One difference between the generations is suggested in the way each relates to new immigrants and visitors from Europe and America. The older generation has much more in common with the Jews from the Diaspora. They know them better and can easily communicate with them. The young Israeli sabra is essentially monolingual, like his young American Jewish counterpart. The sabra has studied English for eight or more years, but unless he has had real opportunity to use the language, he finds it as difficult to speak English as Anglos do to speak Hebrew. The sabras don't like to talk English and often shun contacts that would require them to. They maneuver to keep their social life within a strictly Israeli and Hebrew context. Sabras or Israelis who have lived in Israel since early childhood mingle with their own peers and most of them avoid other contacts. Many resent new immigrants more than they are willing to admit even to themselves.

Their parents on the other hand, generally welcome new immigrant and enjoy meeting them and becoming acquainted with them. The Ha fon parental generation does not like to conjure with the existence of generation gap. They predict that the grandchildren will be broader a more worldly than their parents. I think they are mistaken. There not be a generation gap between the adult sabra generation of today their children. The turning inward progression of modern Israel t foreshadows a homogeneous population in the Israel of tomo v. Parents and children alike will be Israeli with the same ethnic k- ground, the same life experiences, and very likely the same pa of contact and exposure to other people and other places outsi their native habitat. The grandchildren will be like their parents, or more so.

The Yarons

"Bobbie" Yaron was a lieutenant in the British Mandatory Police for many years and after 1948 became one of the small body of elite professional Jewish police officers who accomplished the tough job of creating the Israeli police force. For several years he was chief of the Ramat Gan District police. Like so many able professional police officers, he is far from the policeman stereotype of the paperbacks. Though compactly built and smartly erect, reflecting the athletic activities of his youth and his British police training, he is mild, soft-spoken, shy, intellectual, and filled with droll humor. He was born and brought up in Vienna by his Hungarian father and Viennese mother in a non-religious assimilated Zionist family. In the early 1930's as a young man of twenty he traveled to Palestine as the secretary of the Austrian Maccabee athletes to participate in the sports contests initiated some years earlier as the international Jewish counterpart of the Olympic games. He was so intrigued by Jewish Palestine that he decided to remain as a *chalutz* and soon afterward joined the British police force in Jerusalem.

Several years later on a visit to his family in Vienna he met his Lili and remained long enough to bring her back to Palestine as his bride. The Yarons are of the generation of Israelis who did not suffer personally in the Holocaust. They settled in Israel voluntarily as Zionist Jews intrigued y the challenge of participating in the Zionist dream. They were epresentative of those thousands of pioneers who were not socialists, ot interested in going back to the soil. They were urban dwellers and d no desire to radically change their mode of life.

Bobbie's conspicuous position as a British police officer placed him in a y difficult and delicate position in the years when the Haganah and Irgun were consolidating the Jewish defense position after World II. Only a very few of the leaders of the Va'ad Leumi and the nah knew that he, like almost every Jew working for the British, double agent, and he was exposed for many years to vilification, he bore with outward equanimity.

contributions to the fight for independence were significantly ac vledged, together with his skills and urbanity, when he was appoi Consul-General in Chicago in the early 1950's. For the next fifteen rs, the Yaron family lived mainly abroad, while Bobbie pursued a dip atic career, as consul, minister and ambassador in the Americas and A a. His graceful attractive Lili was an invaluable companion and hostess ring the assignments overseas.

The ons were Israelis and they wanted their sabra children to be Israelis. hey returned to Israel after the Six-Day War to re-establish themselv in their beloved country. During our four years in Israel we renewed the friendship of the Chicago years. Their inestimable contributions to their nation had not brought material gain, but they managed to educate their children, see them married to fellow sabras, and readjust their lives back in the homeland. They live comfortably in the Givatyim suburb of Tel-Aviv. Bobbie has utilized his linguistic proficiency in English, Hebrew, German, Hungarian (with a smattering of Arabic learned during his police years) to become a prodigious translator. A few stints in domestic public service proved unrewarding. Lili, the children married and building their families, once more works as a part time secretary.

The Yarons are vaguely dissatisfied with their life in the Israel of today. Their many years abroad exposed them to a larger world and did not prepare them for the frenzied growth in Israel that occurred while they were away. The pace and tempo had accelerated. They were not prepared emotionally for the acquisitive "keeping up with the Cohens" of the Israel of the 1970's. Their idyllic memories clash with the harsh realities.

Nonetheless, there is no place else on earth where they would rather live than in Tel-Aviv. Their children and grandchildren are Israelis, and so are they. They had an integral part in creating the new fast-moving nation. And they are far from being on the shelf. Their memories of the fate of the members of their families who did not escape Hitler are eternally vivid. Having been involved in the defense of the country in the rough days of the trouble, they glory in the new strength and security of Israel rearmed. They want peace and security for their children and their children's children. They are convinced the path lies in military strength, economic strength, diplomatic accommodation.

Cultured folk that they are, the Yarons don't like what is happening in Israel as they see their values — elegance, manners, gentility — diminish. They have had good personal relationships with Arabs, like them and respect them. They don't enjoy the necessity to work diligently as they do to keep up with the rising cost of living and the inflation. But their complaints are low key, not bitter or plaintive. They are vexed. But they are home finally, and glad to be home. With their books, their friends, their children, their music, their work and their *Gemutlichkeit* they are happy enough. The Yarons are essential Israelis.

The Kadishsons

The Kadishsons, during our four years in Israel, were Kitty's closest friends. In the late 1950's when she visited Israel for the first time, she sought them out at the suggestion of Ava Brownlee, a fellow employee of

Kitty's at British Overseas Airlines in Chicago, and their kind hospitality made her trip memorable. Ava Kadishson and Ava Brownlee had been girlfriends in Yugoslavia before World War II. They both emigrated to Israel, but Ava Brownlee left for the U.S. after a year. By a quirk of fate I knew Ava's husband Itzchak casually, having met him at his club in Tel-Aviv through mutual friends. When we came to Israel in 1968 our friendship ripened. This fine Israeli family became lodestar not only for Kitty, Robert and Sara, but also for me.

The Kadishsons live in Tel-Aviv, with their children — Bennie, out of the army and trying to find himself, after being in the midst of the severest action during the Yom Kippur War — Raphie finishing his army service and knowing where he is going, and Shira, the beloved daughter of their mature years. Itzchak came to Palestine, a little boy of seven, with his father and mother from a small *shtetl* in Poland soon after the end of World War I. He was the eldest of the five children, the youngest an infant babe in arms. His father was a religious Zionist, his mother was not a Zionist at all, simply a passionately Orthodox woman, which she has remained to this day. Now in her 80's, she is an active member of *Neturei Karta* and a follower of the late Rabbi Amram Blau, the charismatic zealot who, with his fanatic disciples and his handsome convert Christian wife, awaited the coming of the Messiah and scorned the secular State of Israel.

In Tel-Aviv, Itzchak attended an Orthodox school not unlike his *cheder* in Poland. After his bar-mitzvah he was sent to a fundamentalist yeshiva seminary in Jerusalem to become a rabbi. During the two years he lasted there, he came to despise the crude, unthinking, medieval rote learning, the constant hunger, the poverty, the dirt, the stultification, and the hypocrisy. He was growing into a sturdy, handsome dark visaged young man, curly-haired, a twinkle in his eyes, and deep laugh lines forming at the corners of his generous mouth. The sedate religious air of Jerusalem and the Mea Shearim section where he lived and studied were not for him. He was enchanted by the feverish humanism of Tel-Aviv and Jaffa. He wanted to be a part of the new Jewish nationalism abuilding there. He became a city *chalutz* (pioneer).

Upon his return to Tel-Aviv, he did not go home to live in the little pension. He cut off his *payot* (side curls) and acquired secular clothes. He found odd jobs, an attic room to live in, and launched himself into a new life as a very young, very frightened, and very curious man of the world. His father, though not really deeply religious, was infuriated by his eldest son's defection from the religious heritage. Curiously enough, mother Kadishson accepted her son's new independence and resigned herself to it with grace and even good humor. She knew the steel of which he was made, and her mother love was too deep to permit any risk of estrangement from this stubborn colt of a son of hers. She insisted that he come home frequently to eat, which gratefully he did, and not only for the good food that sustained him in those hungry days. Mother Kadishson never asked him what he was doing. She respected his privacy.

Itzchak discovered the world of theater and entertainment while still in his teens and decided that was the world for him. He had no desire to be an actor or a performer. He realized that his capacities and his abilities lay in recognizing talent, managing performers and arranging presentations. He decided to become an impressario. He had come to the world of the stage as an errand boy in one of the theaters. There and in the cafes of Tel-Aviv and Jaffa he met and made friends with the people of the then very small theater world of Palestine; most of them Jews from eastern Europe. In those early days there were no homegrown talents. Occasionally, an entertainer would come to Palestine from England or America for a few weeks or a few months; even they were emigrants from East Europe performing in the teeming ghettos of New York and London.

By the time he was twenty years old, Itzchak was a small-time impressario, manager of actors and specialty performers, an indefatigable doer. He organized one-night stand performances in makeshift halls in and around Tel-Aviv. He hired performers, directors, musicians, stage hands. He printed posters and plastered them on any available wall or store window. He wrote advertisements, cajoled newspaper friends into giving him free notices. He peddled tickets to shops, and hotels. He manned the box office, collected tickets, ushered, and cleaned up the hall after the performance. He usually acted as master of ceremonies, introducing the performers, more often than not both in Hebrew and Yiddish. He was a natural comedian and could have been a successful stand-up comic had he wanted to, which he did not. His equanimity and straightforwardness made him popular among the theater fraternity and soon he found himself sought after by performers seeking engagements. Throughout his long career he never made a written contract.

Itzchak was the first impressario in Palestine to sense the hunger for divertissement in the lonely *kibbutzim* and villages of the hinterland, and for many years he led troupes of players around the land, transporting them in trucks, rickety buses, and an occasional foreign "star" in a taxi cab. Shortly before Israel became a state, a group of younger actors and directors and other members of the Habimah theater, the almost "regal" drama company that had originated in Russia in the years before World War I and became established in Israel in the 1920's, decided to break away to organize a more *avant garde* company. Itzchak was invited to become their general manager. The *Camerai* (Chamber Theater) has become a popular and famous theatrical company, second only to Habimah in prestige. When Itzchak left the company after fifteen years as manager, the new group had its own fine theater and to this day continues to be a major artistic institution in a country where the stage is second only to classical music in the cultural interests of the nation.

During the forties, Itzchak was active in the underground movements opposing the British occupation of Palestine. Though completely apolitical, he became a member of the Irgun, like many another young Jewish Palestinian of Polish descent. A younger brother was even more active in the movement as personal aide and later secretary to Menachem Begin, the Irgun leader who is now head of the Likud Party. Itzchak did not join Heirut though many of his friends and comrades did. He was busy with the theater and too immersed in his own interests for political activities.

One day in 1949, a young, intense blonde showed up at his office at the Chamber Theatre looking for a job as a set designer. She recited to Itzchak her background and qualifications in halting Hebrew and impeccable German, which Itzchak could understand with his Yiddish. She was a Yugoslav from Belgrade. Her late father was a Jew. He had been a prosperous businessman who was caught in the Nazi net and died in a concentration camp. Ava and her mother, a convert to Judaism, had escaped and were hidden by friends during the war years. Strong and resilient, Ava had fought with Tito's underground partisans until the war was over. She then returned to Belgrade where she found work in the theaters and motion picture studios. When Israel became a state, Ava and her mother decided to go there. She was not at all interested in Tito's communism, and though her family had been completely assimilated, her father and an older sister had been murdered simply because they were Jewish. Ava decided that she too was a Jewess, and that Yugoslavia was no place for a Jew after the war When she applied to Itzchak for a job, she and her mother were living in an immigrant *ma'abara* on the outskirts of Tel-Aviv.

Itzchak's experienced theatrical eye immediately recognized the talent of this spunky sprite and he hired her on the spot. He was intrigued by her fresh unpretentious beauty and her ingenuous direct intelligence and honesty. She told him straight out that she had checked on modern theater in Israel and was told who were the big guns in stage activities. All the answers she received pointed to the *Camerai* and to Itzchak Kadishson, so she had come directly to Itzchak with her credentials, a portfolio of stage sets designed in Yugoslavia. Itzchak found lodgings for her and her mother in the city near the theater, and within a few months

Ava became the principal set designer for Camerai. She also became Mrs. Itzchak Kadishson.

Itzchak had been a bachelor for years. Although he had had many casual romantic attachments, mostly with young actresses and entertainers, he had not contemplated marriage at all, despite the constant urgings of his Yiddische momma to settle down and raise a family. His brothers and sisters and his father were opposed to his marriage to a schikse, which Ava was to them, even though her mother had converted to Judaism in Yugoslavia. But Itzchak's mother, the only truly Jewish religious person in the family, welcomed Ava as a daughter. Mrs. Kadishson also became a close friend to Ava's mother, who found herself in a bewildering environment amongst strangers who spoke a language she could not understand, then and until her death. Ava loved her mother-in-law for the empathy she manifested towards her despite the disappointment that she was not a *rebbetzin* (a rabbi's wife). Itzchak's father died a few years after the marriage. Grandchildren were born and the relationship beween the mesdames Kadishson became even closer.

Ava and Itzhak became a team. Her artistic instinct and her intellectual bent fortified and supplemented his impressario talents. Ava was a born musician. Itzchak could judge the poise and grace of a singer on the stage and the reaction of an audience to a musician or performer. But he relied on Ava to judge the musicianship. In 1958, when Itzchak left the Camerai theatre, the Kadishson's purchased a spacious basement in the center of the city near the sea, and converted it into an intimate little theater club. Ava designed the whole place, simple and charming, with its wooden chairs, benches and tables, a small useful stage, sophisticated lighting, air-conditioning, tasteful decor. For the next ten years, the *Maadon Teatron* (theater club) became the most popular entertainment spot in Israel. Every tourist, whether he knew Hebrew or not, had the name of the club on his list of "musts" in Israel. Cabinet ministers and generals came incognito to the club to hear themselves lampooned by the clever young singers and satirists discovered by Itzchak and Ava. In its latter years, many big name singers and musicians from Europe and the United States played there.

After 1948, young Israeli sabras who had started as entertainers of the troops during the War of Independence and others who found opportunities in the Defense Forces during their army service came on the scene with Israeli songs and the then fresh nationalistic posture of the new nation. Almost without exception, the "stars" who have come out of Israel in recent years received their start with Kadishson or at the Theater Club. Likewise, many a song writer and script writer were seasoned at the Theater Club. Itzchak never had any ambitions to be the Sol Hurok of Israel; when the Kadishsons thought a young performer was growing stale within the format of the club, they urged him to move on. Haim Topol, who achieved world reknown in the movie "Fiddler on the Roof", was one of these.

The Kadishsons, after many years of hard work, decided to close the club and seek other interests. A disastrous experience with a similar club in Haifa soured them. They had been induced by the late mayor of Haifa, Abba Choushi, to bring their special brand of entertainment to that dull workers' city. There they encountered the kind of political maneuvering and bureaucracy they abhorred, and after several frustrating years and the loss of considerable money, they gave it up. The Theater Club was reopened in 1974 as a regular theater and also the original format of satirical presentations has successfully been revived.

Ava's mother lived with the Kadishsons in their apartment in the heart of Tel-Aviv. The old lady survived into her eighties, a sturdy gnarled oak. Till the end *Der Omee* refused to talk Hebrew. As a result the Kadishson children know German well and Itzchak's Yiddish has been successfully Germanized.

Ava busies herself with her drawing and painting, which she resumed after the club was closed. She has had several successful exhibits in Israel and abroad and has achieved a reputation as a serious and talented professional. Bennie, the oldest son is happily married and content as a member of one of Israel's most popular jazz combos. He is quiet and introspective. His parents worried about him. They needn't have. There has never been any question about Raphie, the younger son. At an early age he revealed an extraordinary gift for music, and music has been his all consuming interest.

Raphie and Bennie are completely Israeli, but in very different ways. Raphie through his musical interests has had contact with many European and American musicians and his horizons are cosmopolitan. He has an awareness of the world outside of Israel. He moves in a circle of companions with like interests whose families are involved with people beyond Israel's borders. In contrast, Bennie's circle of friends and companions are for the most part immersed in the Israeli scene. They are more concerned about security and peace with the Arabs, understandably, since they were stationed for three years either on the Golan Heights facing Syria or in bunkers on the Suez Canal. They faced danger and possible death every day of those long years. They cannot forget those experiences, nor the terrible weeks of October and November 1973.

Raphie is only four years younger than Bennie, but they are an Israeli generation apart. Raphie and his peers have been luckier than Bennie and his friends. Whether they are assigned to special services like Raphie or go into regular service, they were not, until the sudden Yom Kippur War, faced with the ominous threat of the hot war that Bennie had to look forward to every day when he went to the Suez in 1968.

Little Shira, now in her early teens, represents still another Israeli generation. She matures in the atmosphere of a nation now moving into adulthood. The history of her parents as pioneers and her strange old-country former Christian grandmother and her equally strange religious Jewish *Bobbe* on her father's side represent legends of remote people who might have lived hundreds of years ago. Their history is not real to her. It is storybook stuff. Bennie and even Raphie have some remote childhood memories of hardships and alarums, of a kind of unsettling state of affairs. She had none until the Yom Kippur War. Her recollection of the Six-Day War is of a day or two of concern followed by euphoric joyous celebration of victory. Since then, her life followed an even pattern of secure school and familial orderliness, not even deeply disrupted by the Yom Kippur War. She is the Israelit compleat.

Itzchak and Ava suffer from a dichotomy of concern for the security of their beloved country and their abhorrence of the hyper-nationalistic and materialistic parochialism that has developed in Israel. This dichotomy is characteristic of most of their social group, well-informed and thoughtful, intensely nationalistic, but not chauvinistic. They are all haunted by the physical threat of extermination from which Ava suffered in Europe as a child and Itzchak as a child in Palestine. They are, of course, proud of the achievements of their nation, but they are disturbed by the wave of the present. They observed committed Israeli leaders — who as friends in earlier years would remain after hours in their club to talk over a quiet drink about the future and the importance of character — become brahmin autocrats and are incensed by the heady power these high-placed men inhaled as members of the Establishment and their inadequacies revealed in the Yom Kippur tragedy. They see young men and women disaffected by their inability to marry because they cannot afford to buy or rent a decent home, to earn an adequate living in a maelstrom of dog-eat-dog civilian combat, as grim as the shooting war these young people faced in battle, but without the compensating motivation of defending their country. They see *protekzia* enthroned and mediocrity become fashionable. They are upset by the disappearance of Jewish involuted humor, the wariness of big shot posturing that helped sustain the Jew in his years of adversity. They cannot abide the bold new look — lower case phony. They bear bitter witness to a creeping parochialism among the Israelis.

At the height of his career as an impressario in the early 1960's, Itzchak traveled to Paris, Rome, New York. The acquaintances he had made in the theater assured for him a warm welcome wherever he went. He had heard and read about the entertainment and theater world outside of Israel. But he was not prepared for the quality and quantity of entertainment he was introduced to. In many ways, it was a searing trip for him. Thereafter, his honesty and scrupulous sense of judgment forced him to measure what was going on in Tel-Aviv against what he had witnessed abroad. From then on he somehow could not wholeheartedly continue in his profession. Whether from fatigue, boredom or disillusionment, he opted out for a time.

Itzchak sees what is accepted as entertainment in Israel, derivative music, blatantly heroic lyrics, graceless gyration — and knows how much better it all could be. He agonizes that in every poverty-stricken Oriental ghetto, in remote agricultural settlements and in out-of-the-way villages, everywhere, there exist talented young people aching for a chance to display their stuff. He deplores the fact that they are exposed to the kitch of radio, TV and pop records. There are few teachers and mentors to direct them away from bad imitations of the mediocre examples they parrot, even after they have become passé in the U.S. and Europe. They memorize English lyrics they don't understand and posture incongruous rhythms and phrasing.

Itzchak and Ava are not bitter about the current Israeli scene. Rather, theirs is a long and consistently tolerant view. Their motto is Biblical. "This too shall pass." They were saddened by the fact that we did not remain in Israel to accommodate to what Itzchak and Ava hope and believe is a period of transition. Ava knows only the Balkans of her childhood and the horrible war years, and the difficult but good years of her maturity in Israel. She knows the rest of the world vicariously through avid reading in English, which she mastered since coming to Israel. Her English is better than her Hebrew. Like so many untraveled Israelis, she half-believed the stories of the menace of big city life in America, until she visited the U.S. in 1974 and 1976. Itzchak is more nationalist than she, less secularly educated, but more realistic. He has seen Europe and America and paradoxically, he knows and is willing to say what Ava could not bring herself to admit — that Israel may be an oasis, the beloved land of the Kadishsons, but it is a very small oasis in a very big world — and finally, that an oasis is after all, by definition, a small green spot in a desert.

The Kadishsons and their circle of friends, more than most Israelis, are genuinely hospitable to immigrant Jews from the United States and the Western countries. They have always lived in a milieu of theater, music and the arts, a cosmopolitan world naturally interested in the current international scene. The world stage is bigger than the stage of the theater — they know this. Itzchak especially is concerned with what he considers a must for the future of Israel, the ingathering and intermix of American and European Jews with the present Israeli population. He is committed to the proposition that the Jewish population must grow to six or seven millions if the state is to remain viable and become a "Jewish" nation. He dreams up schemes and ideas, some of them most ingenious, for creating American Jewish communities in Israel, wherein the newcomers would continue their American Jewish way of life in comfort and yet join the cultural pluralism of the country. He is convinced of the positive effects that could result, especially to ameliorate the fearsome entrenched bureaucracy that now obtains.

Even Itzchak and Ava are somewhat ambivalent about Western immigration. They deeply sympathize with the young Israelis in their resentment of advantages given to the newcomers at what they consider their expense. They appreciate the desire of the Israeli, born and bred in the land they and their parents have molded into a new nation, to "do their own thing." They also know that substantial Western Jewish immigration has not and will not come. They have many American friends who visit Israel regularly and some who came as immigrants and have returned to their native land. Many Israelis of their acquaintance — actors, entertainers and musicians — have left to seek their fortunes in Europe and America. When friends leave, Americans and Israelis, the Kadishsons are saddened. They grieve about their personal loss, and they grieve for their country. They do not consider these friends as defectors, but they regard their departure as a kind of defect of Israel. They invariably say to them, "You will return." It is a prayer, not a prediction.

I once observed to Itzchak, "You always say to new immigrants *Baruchim ha ba'yim* (blessed is your coming), but most Israelis greet me with *Kol ha kavode* (all honor to you for your action). Do you agree on the subtlety of the difference?" "I agree," he answered ruefully.

Top: From left: the author, Israeli Consul General in Chicago, Assistant Consul Nachum Astar, and Israel Minister Gottheim at opening of the Israeli Consulate in Chicago, 1952.
Bottom: Dr. Joseph Schwartz, director of the Israel Bond Committee, far left, the author, third from left, Senator Hubert Humphrey, fifth from left, and Chicago leaders of Israel bonds.

8. Showcase of Sephardics

The Cohens of Katamon

Young Ezra Cohen was my driver in Jerusalem in November 1967 during meetings of the B'nai Brith Israel Commission. When we came to Israel the following year I looked him up and in the ensuing years we came to know his entire family. The Cohens lived in Katamon Gimmel. This is number three of five similar housing estates, *aleph, bet, gimmel, daled, heh,* built in a former Arab area by the municipality of Jerusalem and the housing division of the Ministry of Labor for new immigrants and for the Jews who spilled out of the Old City after the War of Independence.

Until 1948 the Cohens had lived in a one-room, ramshackle hut in a mixed Jewish-Arab neighborhood. For two years after the war they parceled themselves out to relatives, one child here, one child there, until they were allocated the new apartment in Katamon in 1950. Simcha, the mother, gathered her brood together once more and proudly moved into the new flat, two small rooms, a balcony and a bathroom and a separate W.C.

There were six of them then; the husband Shlomo, the two elder girls, daughters of her first husband, four-year-old Ezra and two-year-old Aryeh. During the next four years, three more babies were born, Yeshia, Yekira, Nissim. Shlomo, the father, was a handsome, dark-visaged gnome of a Yemenite Jew who had been brought to Palestine as a baby in 1912 and grew up a carefree illiterate vagabond in the Yemenite slums of the old city. He had made a haphazard living as an odd job laborer. The most concentrated effort of his life was to woo the handsome Iraqi girl Simcha, widowed at 26 with two little babies.

Simcha was born in the old city, one of ten children of religious parents who had emigrated to Jerusalem from Baghdad in 1910. Her father had been an educated prosperous middle-class merchant in Mesopotamia (Iraq). He came to Jewish Palestine to join relatives who had written of the opportunities for a good Jewish life in the burgeoning Old City. He did not prosper with his little carpet shop, and at seventeen, Simcha was happy to escape the huddled household to marry a handsome Russian who had come to Jerusalem as a child with his Orthodox family, escaping World War I and the Bolshevik revolution.

Simcha and her Russian lived a pleasant life in the little village amongst their Arab neighbors, her stalwart husband a good provider as a carpenter working on the buildings springing up in the new city. He was an ardent Zionist and a member of the Irgun Zvei Leumi. One night on a mission to scout the Jordanian forces near Bethlehem, he was caught by Jordanian soldiers and in the morning his disemboweled body was found in a ditch off a side road near his home. Simcha, left with two babies, gratefully accepted Shlomo's offer of marriage rather than return to her parents' overcrowded flat. She preferred to remain in the little hut outside the walls and work as a day maid in the new city, to try to make a life with shiftless Shlomo and her two baby daughters than to return to the confinement of the Iraqi ghetto in the twisted streets of the Jewish quarter.

Five new babies came, and two months after the youngest was born Shlomo left forever. The younger children never knew him. The family knows that he is living someplace in Israel but they don't know where; his name is never mentioned.

Simcha carried on in her flat in Katamon with her seven children, relieved from the burden of her little Yemenite husband and his babymaking. When Ezra was seven years old, she managed to send him to a kibbutz in the Judean Hills where he lived stalwart and self-sufficient for the next five years. During these years, she also placed Aryeh and Yeshia on kibbutzim and carried on with the remaining four children. She matured into a heavy-bodied, leathery-faced attractive woman, a matriarchal father and mother figure, determined and assured, not embittered, a bit of a *Yiddische momme* but not in the Portnoy sense. All of the children returned to Katamon in 1960. The older girls by this time were working, both of them having finished high school, and there was enough money for the boys to continue to go to school. Eventually all of them but Aryeh finished high school. All eight Cohens lived for many years in the tiny two-room flat in Katamon, the cramped space alleviated by the pleasant Jerusalem weather and the little yard in the back of the flat where they grew vegetables and flowers, and kept pets — dogs, kittens, white mice.

In 1962 the oldest daughter married a prosperous truck driver and moved out of the flat. Two years later her sister also married and left home. The two girls were beauties, burnished copper combinations of dark Iraqi and the rosy blond of the Russian steppes.

The marriage of the eldest daughter Mira and her fun-loving Circassian was a failure. Both of them were restless and ambitious, and domesticity did not become them. After two years they split amiably enough and Mira left for Argentina to live with an uncle in Buenos Aires. Two of her mother's many brothers had left the old Jerusalem ghetto in their teens to seek their fortune in the new world and had become wealthy hardware merchants. Mira stayed with them just long enough to pick up some Spanish and learn enough English to try New York. There she settled, working as a stenographer and secretary, utilizing her language skills to earn enough salary to live comfortably as a sophisticated bachelor girl, until she married an expatriate Israeli in N.Y. in 1975.

Sister Shula, two years younger and even more attractive than Mira is a *Yerushalmeet* (Jerusalem Ms.). Her husband was also a Jerusalem sabra of Sephardic parentage. They had a son and daughter now in their teens. Shula and Shmuel both worked for the government, he as a plumber in the municipal water department and she as a receptionist in the Ministry of Tourism.

Shortly after the Six-Day War the Housing Ministry appropriated a large tract of land in the hills of East Jerusalem northwest of the Old City between Jerusalem and the West Bank town of Ramallah and proceeded to develop it as a middle-class housing estate of individual villas. The area is known as Ramat Eshkol and is now a pleasant spacious suburb of winding streets and open spaces. All the houses are built of cut stone, the characteristic building material that gives all of Jerusalem its look of instant ancientness. To make the plots available to Jerusalem citizens of modest means and to persuade them to take the daring step of moving to what had been the Jordan and Arab side of the city, the authorities conducted a lottery for the original plots. The winners were leased the land for a renewable 49-year period at a nominal rental of a few pounds a year, an arrangement that enabled them to apply most of their capital to the building of their homes. The government required that they begin to build their houses within a year and to finish them, move into them, and not sell them for at least four years. Shmuel and Shula were among the "lucky" ones.

They found themselves squatting like itinerant gypsies in what one day would be a gracious upper middle-class home. The cost of the house if completed would be more than five years of their total combined net salaries. They were unhappy and harassed and would like nothing better (though they didn't admit it) than to be back with their Sephardic friends in the familiar Bukharin neighborhood where they had lived. Finally they sold the house and shortly afterward were divorced.

All of the seven Cohen children inherited the steel of their mother's character, her stubbornness and her fierce family loyalty. Most of all my friend, Ezra, her first-born son. After Shlomo took French leave, Simcha realized that her life's fulfillment lay in bringing up her children as a family unit with a sense of decency and respect for personal human values and pride in their inheritance as Jews and Israelis. She was bolstered by the rhythm of the times. Israel had just emerged as an independent state and she and her brood were in the vortex of the pioneer aristocratic status bestowed upon them as third-generation Jerusalem Sabras. Thousands of newcomers were arriving from the Arab and African nations and even though the Cohens were among the poorest of the poor, they easily held their heads high in the swirling maelstrom of the Jerusalem of the 50's and 60's. The martyrdom of the daughters' father also contributed to the special image of the family.

Ezra is small, wiry and very dark. He inherited his father's Yemenite looks and is self-conscious about it. He used to insist to me that his mother's family were Spanish (*Sephardi* in Hebrew) despite her reiteration that they were descended from many generations of Iraqi. Iraq was Mesopotamia, and Mesopotamia was Babylonia. Jews lived in Babylon long before there was any Spain to expel Jews. Simcha would say, "Some of my brothers speak Spanish because they went to Spain from Jerusalem and then emigrated to Argentina. And my father knew Ladino in Baghdad. I don't know where he learned it." Ezra had dropped the Spanish descent idea. He considers himself Sephardic, as the term is used in Israel to differentiate the non-Ashkenazi, and to avoid being taken for a Moroccan. It seems that the Moroccan Jews in Israel occupy the same low place among the Oriental and Afro-Asian Jews as the Galician Jews did among European Jews several generations ago.

Ezra is energetic, ambitious, self-confident, glib, though self-conscious and bantam roostery because of his size. He has his mother's sense of humor, if not yet her sense of the ridiculous. The years in the kibbutz widened his horizons and taught him to love the soil. It also deepened his Israeli nationalism and completed his rejection of Orthodox Judaism. Ezra returned to his home in Katamon, completed grade school and high school and then, like all Israeli eighteen-year-olds, entered the army. There he learned to drive half-tracks and tanks and acquired the training necessary to become an electrician and automobile mechanic. He had been out of the service two short months when the threat of the impending Six-Day War sent him back to his unit in the Negev. After the war, he became a taxi driver and a sometime tourist guide around the Jerusalem he knew so well. Of course, he couldn't remember the Old City of his infancy, but he quickly found himself at home there too.

Ezra was anxious to improve his skills but couldn't afford to enroll for additional scholastic training because his money was needed at home. His mother worked as she had for years as a cleaning woman in one of the government offices. Yakira operated a calculating machine in an accounting office. Aryeh was an occasional stonemason and odd job contractor. He was an erratic contributor, his chief contribution being his presence and the friends he brought home, mostly young women and generally at mealtimes. No one ever came to the Cohen home without a command to eat, whether he was hungry or not.

Ezra's relationship with Mother Simcha has always been the most complicated of all the children. He was at once child and adult. As the eldest son he had become surrogate husband and adult principal male image even as a very young boy. The only one of the boys who really suffered from the father's desertion, he tried to compensate for the betrayal. His uncanny physical resemblance to father Shlomo didn't help him in the jousts with his mother. The little owl of a boy returned from the spartan kibbutz atmosphere solemn and driven beyond his years.

Emancipation in the army for years had made the confinement of four adults living in a fish bowl of two tiny rooms completely intolerable for him. I offered him a job operating machinery in our labeling factory in Tel-Aviv. He did not want to leave Jerusalem. He realized, however, that as long as he remained in Jerusalem, unmarried and with insufficient money, he would be tied to the Cohen flat and to his mother's apron strings. Simcha hated to see him go, but in her maternal wisdom she realized that it was best for him and the family and she helped me to encourage him to take the new job. She wanted him to get married and settle down. He had never lacked for girl friends. As a taxi driver he met many personable tourists. One of Simcha's greatest fears was that one of them would entice him to leave Israel and try his wings in America or Europe.

Ezra left for the factory in Tel-Aviv. He rented a flat in a neighborhood not unlike Katamon in the northwest side of the city and in a few months everyone, Simcha included, realized that the third Cohen child had left the family nest. In fact, Ezra's flat, hardly smaller than the home in Katamon, became the second Cohen headquarters. Rarely a week-end that one or other of the brothers, and even Simcha and Yakira occasionally could be found there when they came to Petach Tikvah to visit relatives.

The years in Tel-Aviv were the greening of Ezra. As with most new industrial enterprises in Israel, the label affixing plant took more than a year to set up and run in. During this time, most of the day-to-day detail work of preparing the small factory and testing the American-made machinery became his responsibility. During this period Ezra became familiar with the industrial and technological community; with banks and government offices. His experience effectively sobered his heretofore belief in the superiority of Israeli resourcefulness and brough him an awareness of the limitations of improvisation.

Theater of the absurd bureaucracy is the usual scene at all government centers in Israel — post office; city hall; police station; Jewish Agency; licensing departments; tax office; Ministry of the Interior (where temporary residents must go to validate their sojourn and their right to work); land registration offices; customs; what have you. The same situation has spilled over into the private sector and is equally maddening. Some of the clerks and workers in airline and travel offices, banks, theater ticket agencies, auto repair shops, gas and electric services, hotels, telephone company, department stores, food markets, shops of all kinds, seem to take a sadistic delight in making life difficult. The Jewish talent for excellence through competition seems to have been lost in the Levantine atmosphere.

Ezra became dissatisfied with his job. When the plant started to run fairly smoothly, the work became routine. He had planned to accept his sister's offer to come to New York to learn the trade of automobile electrician. An Israeli trained in America in any phase of the automotive industry can pick and choose his job or find plenty of partners willing to back him in business. For Ezra the many American acquaintances made during his taxi hacking career offered an added inducement to visit the United States. However, he found his one true love and proposed. Ezra and his sabra Yemenite bride were married in the spring of 1973 to the delight of mother Simcha.

Nissim, the youngest son, is the most interesting of the other three brothers. Like Ezra, he, too, is short and dark, the most handsome of them all. His keen intelligence is revealed in his bright twinkling eyes and deprecating laugh lines at the corners of his mouth. As the baby, he had always been most favored by sisters, mother and brothers; but in the discipline of the Cohen menage there was no possibility for anyone to become spoiled. In his quiet way he is the most ambitious of all the children. Nissim attended night school for a short time to prepare himself for the *Bagroot* (matriculation) examinations that would enable him to enter university if he was able to swing it, but he soon dropped out. He and Ezra now operate a taxi which they have jointly bought.

The only one of Simcha's brood now living at home is Yeshia, taller and fairer than Ezra and Nissim, strongly built and ruggedly good-looking. Unimaginative and healthy, he moved through the army years easily, enjoyed himself and like all the others was glad to get out and get on with the business of living. He is adept with his hands and with tools but did not learn any particular trade or skill. He accepted some responsibility for supporting the household, but he was not eager to settle down to a steady job or a steady routine. His unimaginative restlessness is typical of many young men who get out of the defense forces and who have an undefined desire to have some fun and see something of the world before they settle down, as well they know they will. Yeshia's ambition was to save up money to take a trip to Europe. He hasn't made it yet.

Avraham

Avraham's mother, Victoria, worked for us in the Kfar for a few months when Sara Sa'adi had her baby. Victoria sent her son to me to help repair my car. Later he helped us fix up our apartment in Tel-Aviv. He wouldn't accept payment. We were friends, he explained simply. Avraham (Arturo) came to Israel with his family from Tripoli in Libya in 1966. He was then sixteen years old. His older brother was eighteen and his younger sisters, ten and thirteen. His family had lived in North Africa for many generations. Before Libya, they lived in Tunisia, and before that, Egypt, and before that, somewhere else in North Africa or Southern Europe.

The sojourn in Libya had started with his father's father who had emigrated from Tunis when Mussolini's brave Fascists took over that poverty-stricken Arab land in the middle twenties. It was easy enough for the grandfather to find a job with his adeptness at practical mechanics and his facility in Arabic and French, and sound enough in Italian amongst the skilled workers and middle-class merchants in the North African colony of the empire Mussolini was trying to create.

After World War II, Libya was lost to Italy and became an independent Arab nation in 1951. The position of the Italians and other non-Moslem, non-Arab residents at the beginning was not too seriously affected. They were needed to run the oil fields and businesses and government offices. They constituted the majority of the educated or at least literate population. The Arab politicians needed them to help run the show. But there were straws in the wind. The Moslem religious establishment began to assume importance in the national picture, and the Italians, Jews, Greeks, and others began to find their former easy accommodation not quite so easy. Avraham's father fell ill and the family experienced hard times. Like many of the Jews of Libya, they foresaw the *cul de sac* that would become the end of the road for the Jews and Italians in Libya.

The family left for Israel several years before Gadaffi and his military junta overthrew the ineffectual government of remnant colonial satraps. In modern times there were approximately forty thousand Jews living in Libya. Most of these had come from other Arab countries during the Mussolini period. Very few of them, unlike many Egyptian Jews and others in the Arab countries, had become wealthy or firmly established. It was easier for them to leave. The storm signals were visible. Between 1949 and 1951, 31,000 Libyan Jews emigrated to Israel.

Avraham is not completely happy in Israel, although he has adjusted well, has learned Hebrew, served only six months in the army, and now has a good job as an automobile mechanic, a civilian employee of the army. He and all of his family know that any possible good life for them in Libya ended well before they left. But pleasant memories linger on. When their father had been well and earning a good living, the life in Tripoli had been good. Though they lived in a Jewish section and consorted mainly with fellow Jews, the schools, shops, clubs and activities were quite as Italian as in any medium-sized city of Italy. Their friends and neighbors had not only been Jews, but Libyans and other Arabs and first and second generation Italians.

The father did not recover from his illness in Israel and after a two-year period of decline, both physically and mentally, died at the age of fifty. The boys had been excused from full regular military service because of the father's illness and with the mother's work as a housemaid, the family managed to survive decently enough. They had been allotted a two-bedroom flat by the Jewish Agency in an immigrant housing estate in Ra'annana, a village north of Tel-Aviv and a few miles east of the Mediterranean Sea. Many of their neighbors also are from Libya, and most of the others, almost all of them recent immigrants, are from other North African countries. In recent years immigrants from Soviet Russia also have been settled in Ra'annana. These new immigrants live in stuccoed concrete block apartment houses, typical of public housing the world over. The grounds outside the buildings are filled with litter and refuse. As yet, no tradition of neatness and care has been created. But the life of the neighborhood is good and the pulse is strong. The neighbors are disparate but not desperate. Even the occasional European family that finds itself in the midst of the squalor adjusts well, intrigued by the richness and the positiveness of the life.

Avraham's mother, Victoria, mixes socially only with other Libyan immigrants who speak Italian and Arabic among themselves, but Avraham and his friends speak only Hebrew. There are no ethnic barriers between them. Avraham organized a rock music group of which he became the leader. He had a new electric organ bought with his savings and with help from his older brother. There were five other members of his band, a sabra Yemenite, a Romanian boy who emigrated with his family in 1960, two brothers from the U.S.S.R. in Israel for only two years and another Russian, a pretty blond girl singer from the Soviet Union who joined the group only six months after leaving Odessa. Their group was the focal point of the social life of the neighborhood. They played in a teen-age clubroom provided in the center of the *shikun* (housing development) by the Jewish Agency. The meeting hall was filled every night with lively youngsters. The largest contingent were recent Soviet emigres, and most of the others were Orientals. There were no Anglos because the Agency and the Absorption Ministry settle most Anglo immigrants who apply for public housing into predominantly Anglo housing estates. There was always a large sprinkling of boys and girls in army uniform among the young people in the clubroom.

Arturo found it simple and desirable to change his name to Avraham in Israel, and made no effort or pretense to pass himself off as an Italian — not that he completely identifies himself as an Oriental or Arabian Jew. He is proud of his broader Europeanized background, and somewhat deplores the crudeness, primitiveness, and lack of education of Israeli Jews from other Eastern lands. He does not, however, identify with European Sephardi and he is not considered by them as European. He does not feel discriminated against because he and his family do not move in the more cosmopoltan society of the European Sephardi. Avraham and his friends in the close intimacy of public housing are quickly blending into their peer group to become homogeneous Israeli young adults.

The Romanos

The Romanos are also Israelis from Libya. They are a branch of a large Italian Sephardic family that emigrated from Italy to Libya at the turn of the century. The grandparents came to Libya as deeply committed Orthodox Jews and their close patriarchal family existence was quite naturally maintained in the Jewish community of Bengasi, where the men of the family carried on as sailors and fishermen as they had in Italy. Several of Grandfather Joseph's sons had gone to British Palestine in the 40's and had settled in the northern port city of Haifa. Joseph's son Isaac and his wife were among the first Libyan families to go to Israel in 1948 after Independence was declared, bringing with them their brood of six sons and two daughters, ranging in age from six months to fourteen years.

They did not come as refugees. They had not been driven out of Libya, but they were intense Jews and the prospect of living in the ancient homeland was exciting, even though father Isaac fully realized that life would be hard there.

The Romanos brought with them little more than their clothing and household effects and were settled in one of the many *ma'abara* camps established in the long stretch of Mediterranean shore between Tel-Aviv and Haifa. Though created as a temporary sheltering place housed in American Army surplus tents and makeshift huts, it remained as a permanent village. Many of the first "temporary" pre-fab houses still stand, occupied by the original tenants or their grown children and their families.

Father Isaac and his wife still live in the community, ensconced in a larger flat, one of the permanent housing units built during the twenty years in which the community casually grew into a permanent village. Their four younger children, the sabras born in Israel, live with the parents. Our friend, Amos, a babe-in-arms in 1948 has married and moved into one of the pre-fabs of the original *ma'abara.* His wife, Rita, is Amos' cousin, daughter of his mother's brother, who emigrated from Bengasi after the Six-Day War. Rita's family live in the Libyan community of Ra'anana, where many of the Romano clan have settled among relatives and friends. We had a merry time at their wedding — and met all the many Romanos.

The section in which the Romanos live is known as Sidni Ali, named for a picturesque 19th Century Moslem mosque perched on a steep cliff overlooking the sea. The mosque had been abandoned since 1948. In Mandate times it was in the center of a tiny Arab fishing community consisting of a dozen stone houses and a few wooden shacks. When the War of Independence started, all of the Arabs left and the buildings (not including the deserted mosque) were utilized as the nucleus of the refugee camp of immigrants to which the Romanos and several hundred Oriental Jews from Iraq, Syria, Yemen and Libya were brought in 1948 and 1949. It was inevitable that most of the settlers would insist on remaining there, despite the primitive and make-shift conditions. High on a cliff, the site commands an unimpeded view of Tel-Aviv 20 kilometers south and of the posh seashore section of Herzylia.

All of the Romano children completed grade school and thereafter went on to work to help support the family. The oldest brother rose from a Sidni Ali fisherman to become partner and captain of a large cooperative fishing vessel sailing out of the great new port of Ashdod. The older sons and daughters are married and have growing children. Most of them married relatives or Sephardi from Libya and other Oriental communities. They are a close-knit family, religious, and scrupulously observant. Their social life centers around the parents, the family and their hundreds of relatives and friends in Sidni Ali, Nof Yam, Herzylia, Ra'anana, Ashdod and Tel-Aviv. The two youngest sons have completed high school and have served in the armed forces, as did all their older six brothers.

The Isaac Romano family is one of the few large families of Israel that did not suffer casualties in the Israeli wars. The murder of the fourth brother, Yossi, by terrorist Arabs in Munich at the 1972 Olympic games, left the entire family stunned and shocked. The shadow that this tragedy has cast over them will continue to cloud this stalwart family for decades. Yossi was a short, powerfully built weightlifter, one of the outstanding athletes of Israel. He had won the middle-weight championship of Israel several years in a row and was a champion at the Asian games in 1970. Broad-faced and kinky-haired like all the Romanos, he was sunny tempered, a pixy, easy-going, but serious about his work, his children, his family, and his beloved nation. He was modest and mature and took his fame lightly, but delighted that all of his clan enjoyed his popularity and vicariously took pleasure in being identified with him. This was easy enough — all the Romanos look alike, short, powerfully built, grinning, krinkly faced. When Yossi qualified for the Olympic team, his family, including his wife and his employers, insisted that he take off six months from his job with a television sales company, to train. Two weeks before I left Israel in the summer of 1972 I saw Yossi for a moment as we drove alongside at a stop light on the highway. "All set for Munich?" I asked him. He flashed his irrepressible grin and raised his fingers in the victory sign. He never realized his moment of glory. He died with the wrestling coach, Moshe Weinberg, fighting off with bare hands the demented Arab terrorists, deterring them as long as possible in the hope that some of the other Israeli athletes and officials might escape.

The Romanos and their neighbors had come to the little abandoned Arab fishing village of Signi Ali in total poverty. They did not drive any Arabs from their homes. If the few Arab fishermen who had lived there had chosen to remain they would have thrived and prospered as all the Arabs who remained in Israel. The soldier sons of the Romano family have seen the refugee camps in Gaza, on the Golan Heights, and in Jericho where the Palestinian Arabs had been herded between 1948 and 1967 to vegetate in hopelessness. They could compare these places with the same primitive camp into which Isaac Romano and his kin had been ushered and had by the sweat of their brows built into a pleasant rural village.

The martyrdom of Yossi Romano will not be forgotten. Yossi Romano's brothers and their neighbors and their compatriots will not easily accept the assurances of the rulers of the earth that Israel can trust pious resolutions. They will remember that, as Yossi lay dying in his blood on the floor in Munich, the Olympic games went on. The chasm between the Israelis and the Arabs widens. Suspicion and distrust goes on and on. Someday, God willing, person to person, family to family, they may find peace through the essential personal respect that does develop with all peoples when they become neighbors without harassment and propaganda, when the pompous big shot chess players of the world stop moving them around like pawns on their oil slicked, gold encrusted boards.

The Yemenites

Sarah and Solomon Sa'adi are second generation Israeli Yemenites. They belong to a unique generation, the last with childhood ties and memories of Yemen. They and their contemporaries are the children who came with their parents in the famous exodus of 1948 and 1949 — "Operation Magic Carpet" — the meticulously organized transport of tens of thousands of Yemenite Jews to Israel. "On the wings of eagles thou shalt be flown to the land of thy fathers" was the prophecy in the Bible fulfilled in the 20th Century by the shining metal winged birds that brought these forgotten little people to the promised land.

For fifty years or more before 1948, a few Yemenite Jews had trickled into Palestine to settle with other pious Jews, mainly in Jerusalem. From them the early pioneers learned of the tens of thousands of Jews who lived in that obscure barren land deep in the Arabian desert. Their survival as Jews and as a community with their dignity and ethnic purity intact is probably the most striking example of Jewish will and the dynamics of survival in all of Jewish history. The basis of their survival indubitably was their practice of religious Judaism as a way of life. No other Jewish community was brought to Israel so swiftly, so completely, and so intact as the Yemenites.

Unfortunately, not all of the Jews of Yemen got to Israel. A group of Yemenite Jewish elders told me one evening in the Sa'adi home that more than 50,000 Jews are still living in Yemen. The figure is probably exaggerated. Some sporadic and clandestine contact is maintained with them. Occasionally a news sheet printed in Hebrew by daring Yemenites reaches their relatives in Israel. It tells of their continuing hard lot and their hopes to join their fellows in the Holy Land. But, by and large, they are a forgotten and tragic remnant. The establishment of Israel occasioned an upsurge of Moslem religious nationalism in Yemen. The overthrow of the monarchy and the division of the country into two nations has not ameliorated the status of the remnant Jewish community. Yemen has always been a poor, semi-nomadic pastoral Bedouin land, poor in natural resources and the most primitive and illiterate country of all Arabia. The Jews were always oppressed and denigrated. They were forbidden to engage in many trades and professions and severely restricted in the ownership of real property. They were even forbidden to ride on a donkey past a Yemenite on foot because they would thus be above their "superiors."

The sparse information and rumors about the Jews that filters out of Yemen today does not indicate that they are being treated in the unspeakable fashion suffered by the Jews in Egypt, Iraq, and particularly in Syria. They are not imprisoned. They are not constantly hounded, and their material belongings are not expropriated. The circumstance of their centuries of poverty and the endemic oppression and discrimination that was always the lot of the Yemenite Jew could not have become much worse than it always had been, unlike the degradation and near genocide the Syrian Jews now suffer in contrast to their once affluent and privileged middle-class status. The remnants may come out finally, if both Yemenite nations are offered sufficient bribes, paid for by the Jews of the world. The arrangements, of course, will be maneuvered through their good neighbors Saudi Arabia, which supports the monarchy and the old regime of South Yemen, while Egypt and Libya and the other new "socialist" Arab nations support North Yemen. Surprisingly, no organized effort to rescue the remaining Yemenite Jews has ever been made.

In any event, they will be a pitiful lot of elderly, sick, and discouraged people. There will not be many children among them. Many of those who remained in 1948 and 1949 were middle-aged and older and did so by their own choice, as did the Iraqis, Egyptians, and Syrians who remained in their native lands when Israel became an independent nation. The decision to stay in all these countries was based on the same reasons — prosperity, established business, status. Although the law forbade Yemenite Jews from owning property and from engaging in "aristocratic" business and professions — law, medicine and the like — or from occupying governmental and public offices, some of them had managed to evade these strictures with the skill and adroitness that has been the Jewish survival syndrome in every land in every age. Unlike many Jews in other lands, however, hardly any of them had forsaken their religion or their Jewish heritage and identity.

A substantial number managed over the generations to become prosperous and powerful through influence and talent. These are the Yemenite Jews who remained, only finally to be degraded and robbed as their fellows were in Syria, Iraq and Egypt, and to a lesser extent later on in the 50's and 60's in Morocco, Algeria, Tunis and Libya.

The remnant Jews being more affluent, were likewise more worldly, secularly educated, and less religiously committed — in short, more assimilated with the tiny privileged classes surrounding the monarchy and the ruling regimes. The establishment of Israel did not sound a clarion call to them to return to the homeland on "wings of eagles" or any other way. For many of them it will be too late. Those who may make aliyah to Israel, if they ever do, will not come with the spirit and freshness of the children like Sarah and Solomon or their parents.

Sarah and her family were settled in a little enclave of *ma'aborot* (temporary immigrant camps) in rural farm areas surrounding Petach Tikvah, Tel-Aviv, B'nai Brak, and the smaller towns and villages of the coastal plain north and south of Tel-Aviv. The plain is shown as *HaSharon*, the Plains of Sharon of the Bible. They were placed in little clusters of shacks and huts and partially destroyed stone Arab buildings even more decrepit, dilapidated, and make-shift than the chain of *Ma'aborot* farther north and west on the seashore. The Yemenites were the lowest on the totem pole of the new immigrants of the first years. Almost nothing was known about them even by the leaders of the Israeli government and the old time pioneers of the labor movement and kibbutzim. The Orthodox religious establishment, both Sephardic and Ashkenazi, had only vaguely been aware of their existence. Some even questioned the genuineness of their religious credentials as they did (and do still) those of the Karaites and the Jews from Cochin China who emigrated to Israel in the 1950's from Vietnam.

Israeli immigrants are different in appearance one from the other. Certainly all of the tens of thousands who came to Israel from Arab and North African lands at the beginning seemed strange to the Jews of Palestine and to their fellow immigrants from Europe. The Yemenites were the strangest of all. With few exceptions, they were tiny, skinny, dark brown. All of them had black curly hair, soulful black eyes, ready smiles. They were good-natured, quiet, polite, friendly, not obsequious, dignified, graceful, strange — altogether strange. They might have come from another planet. Some of the patriarchs came with two and three wives and many children. They were so pristinely and Biblically Orthodox Jews that they practiced legal polygamy, as did the Yemenite Moslems and Moslems in all the Arab countries, though the practice was discontinued by Jews in most Moslem countries hundreds of years ago.

Possibly the religious establishment in Israel was convinced of the validity of the Yemenite Judaism by the fact of their polygamy. In any event, it did pose a bit of a problem that was resolved quickly by the Solomonic decision of recognizing the legality of the existing marriages but prohibiting any future polygamy. There still remain in the Israel of the 1970's several Yemenite polygamous families carrying on their clan living in easy equanimity and unembarrassment. Unlike the Mormons of Utah, they made no effort to dispute the ban on continuing the practice. Their new life in Israel was too difficult for them at the beginning to permit the luxury of more than one wife.

Sarah's family was placed in a tent; Sarah, aged 11, her eight brothers and sisters, the oldest 15 and the youngest a babe in arms, and the parents. It was the winter of 1948-49, and bitterly cold. After a few days the immigration authorities collected all the children in the camp and brought them to a large concrete building where they would be warm. Sarah's mother would not let Sarah and her two sisters go with the other children. It was unseemly for girls to be with boys separated from parental watchfulness and authority. In the spring, the family was allotted a one-room wooden hut in the *ma'abara* and life was a little bit better for them, but only a bit.

Like all the Yemenite girls, Sarah had it tougher than the boys. She had to learn a new language from scratch, aided only by her native intelligence and the few Hebrew words she had heard in Yemen. She spoke Arabic fluently but could not read or write a word in any language. Yemenite girls were not expected to be educated or even to be literate. They were taught to cook, to sew, to garden, to clean house, to be good wives and mothers and to serve the males, their lords and masters. The boys were taught the Bible in little religious schools maintained by the Jews, and learned to read and write Hebrew and even some Arabic. It was comparatively easy for the males to apply their knowledge of the language to everyday uses. They had learned their Bible in oral recitative like the Ashkenazi in their ghetto *cheders* in Europe and America. But they, unlike the Europeans, had been taught the meaning of all the words and even some Hebrew grammar. All of the Yemenites, male and female, pronounce Hebrew naturally, in the Israeli Sephardic accent. In fact, the Yemenis are universally regarded as having the purest modern Israeli Hebrew accent.

Sarah's father objected strenuously to any schooling for the girls, but the law required all children to attend school until age 14. So Sarah did get three years of secular schooling and learned to read and write fluently. She was a good student and a quick learner and desperately wanted to continue her schooling. Her ambition was to be a nursery school or kindergarten teacher. Her mother was shocked at what then was an unheard of ambition, and her father flatly refused. She was sent to work in a little clothing factory in Petach Tikvah. True, the family was desperately poor and every able-bodied child had to contribute to the family upkeep. But even if Sarah's few lira a week were not needed, the traditions of Yemen were still too strong and fresh to be altered in the freer atmosphere of the new land. Girls didn't go to school and certainly they didn't go to school beyond the age required by the authorities.

Sarah's father was neither an unkindly man nor a dolt. In fact, by Yemenite Jewish standards he was an educated man, learned in the Torah, a part-time rabbi, cantor and ritual slaughterer. Sarah did not plead with him. She realized that it was useless and she loved him very much and did not want to offend him. She had hoped that the family's new life in Israel and the ardent enthusiastic nationalism of her father would influence him to adopt new ways and ideas. All too soon, at the tender age of 14, she realized that this could never be for her parents and their generation. They had survived through the centuries in Yemen because they had been born into and lived a way of life that was viable and meaningful, even pleasurable. In their wise ignorance of any other way, they serenely had transferred this way of life to their new abode and were willing to adopt only such of the opportunities and customs of the new land that would ameliorate, reinforce, and enrich the only way of living they knew or wanted to know.

For their children and especially their daughters this old country attitude was agony. Sarah saw other young girls her own age, not only from Ashkenazic, but even from Oriental families permitted to continue in school, to find occupations, and seek out companions with some freedom of choice. The other girls were not considered valuable chattels, inferior to the boys and men, ipso facto, regardless of their intelligence, talent, character, as the Yemenite girls were. In addition, Sarah was a plain girl, not as pretty as most of the Yemenite girls. Her parents were concerned that she would not find a husband, or at least one of a good family worthy of her better than average clan. She was well on the way to becoming an old maid by Yemenite standards, when she was married off to Solomon, at the ripe old age of 24.

Solomon was considered by her family to be something of a "catch." He was a second cousin who had come to Israel with his parents and his brothers and sisters on the same aliyah as Sarah's family. He was a handsome man, two years younger than Sarah, and had some considerable status as a *shochet* (ritual slaughterer), and *mohel* (circumciser) as well as an excellent gardener. His family likewise was delighted with the match because Sarah's father was greatly respected in the community, and her older brothers had done well as mechanics and skilled workers in the factories of the area. Sarah was liked and respected by all who knew her for her intelligence and serene temperament. Despite her plain face she was comely, with graceful figure and bearing.

Solomon had been able to buy a small truck and had a prosperous business transporting and selling vegetables and chickens to the famous Tel-Aviv market, HaShoukh HaCarmel. The newlyweds moved into a new one-room concrete block house in the center of a rural settlement established by the government and the Jewish Agency in the 1950's. The haphazard settlement was peopled almost entirely by Yemenites who could muster enough money from family and friends to build the little houses. The parcels of land, a dunam in size (¼ of an acre) were leased from the government land authority for 49 years at a rental of a few pounds a year. The area before 1948 had been owned and cultivated by Arab truck farmers. It was a logical location for settlement by Yemenites with their centuries of experience in growing vegetables on small plots of land.

The first three years of the marriage were good. Solomon was proud of his new adult position as husband and father. Children came, the first-born, a boy, was a source of great satisfaction to all. The little house was the scene of a great celebration. The Sa'adi clan and Sarah's family, the Mizrachis and their friends and relatives, several hundreds of them, came to feast and sing and dance in the traditional ceremony of the Pidyan HaBen — the ransoming with a gold coin of the exemption of the first-born male from priestly service to the Cohanim. All the women helped to make the great pots of meat and vegetable soup, and the piles of exotic highly spiced salads and tidbits for which the Yemenites are renowned. The women milled around the little kitchen space and the porch gossiping and giggling. The children shrieked and tumbled in the yards and dirt streets of the neighborhood, while the men sat in the main room drinking beer and Israeli brandy, respectfully attentive to the elders quoting from the *Tanach* (Bible) and the Talmud, and elucidating the explanations of how life should be conducted, liberally adding their personal observations on the applicability of the rules to the new life in the Homeland. Sarah's father with his grey forelocks (*payot*) and dignified sparse beard was especially in his element, openly pleased that his little cinderella was now a well-established matron.

A year later a baby girl was born. The little house became cramped and impossibly inadequate. Despite Sarah's forebodings, Solomon decided to build an addition, another large room and an inside bathroom and W.C. His brothers and Sarah's family would help to supplement their income. Solomon leased his little truck three nights a week to a neighbor. One night a few weeks later, the neighbor wrecked the truck completely and was himself seriously injured. Solomon had no insurance, nor did the neighbor. For a while Solomon was able to borrow a truck occasionally. He and Sarah tried to borrow money to buy another truck. They were unsuccessful. None of their family or friends had any spare cash. All of their contemporaries lived on what they and their children earned on a day-to-day and week-to-week basis. A Yemenite with a bank account was a rarity.

Solomon gave up the carting business and concentrated on the ritual slaughter of chickens and an occasional sheep and goat, and on odd jobs trimming shrubs and gardening for villa owners in the suburbs of Tel-Aviv. He earned an occasional few pounds circumcising a baby boy in the Yemenite communities.

Solomon was a flamboyant peacock sort of a man. The loss of his truck and the pressures of providing for his family were too much for him. Since boyhood he had had a touch of asthma. Soon this became virulent, and he had to give up the gardening and the chicken slaughtering. He was allergic to the feathers and the pollen. Though the baby girl was only three months old and the boy was only a year and a half, Sarah went to work as a housemaid and cleaner (*sponger* is the word for the occupation that the English Jews contributed to modern Hebrew). And sponger she remains after 12 years and three more babies. Solomon works from time to time slaughtering in the butcher shops in Tel-Aviv. When his asthma is not too extreme he does a bit of gardening and chicken slaughtering at home. He has worked less and less over the years, and Sarah has worked more and more.

Somehow the new room and bathroom got finished. The house has been painted and decorated on the inside in clean, excruciatingly bad taste, sort of Polack-Yemenite. The yard and garden are less unkempt. The older children have been trained since babyhood to assist in the chores of the household, including working in the vegetable garden which is an important source of food for the family. Solomon provides professional supervision as a knowledgeable farmer and Sarah has the traditional Yemenite green thumb. The oldest son, Uri, is a personable little dark-eyed rogue like his father. His younger sister fortunately is not only an assiduous worker like her mother, but pretty as well, and there is a solemn little brother of 12 who is already a man-child.

The years of hard work have not destroyed Sarah's spirit. She soon realized that Solomon's very real asthma combined with his very real malingering meant that she was committed to the permanent lot of chief provider for the family. She has made the best of it, determined that her children, particularly her daughters, would somehow have a chance to escape the chattel status of Yemenite girls. In some ways her position as chief provider has emboldened her to insist on a different future for her daughters.

Over the years, the Israeli way of life that includes a substantial degree of women's lib, has influenced all the Sephardic and Oriental communities, including the Yemenites. Most of the school teachers in the primary schools are women, and the majority of teachers in the general high schools are also women. Among the Ashkenazi in all secular activities and occupations, women are found in every profession and occupation, although their remuneration is still far from equal. It is only a matter of a generation before the egalitarian tradition of the socialist beginnings of the State reinforced by the insistence of equality in the kibbutzim will have created complete equal pay, if not equal job status, between men and women in Israel. Certainly there will be emancipation from the built-in chattel syndrome of the Old Testament. The Oriental women will catch up with their Ashkenazi sisters, but not without persistent rear guard opposition from their men. How comforting it has been for them to have the Word itself from the Fathers to back up their rationalizations that women were placed upon the earth to bear children and are ordained to serve man.

In practice, of course, the Yemenite Jewish women for centuries have learned how to mold for themselves a posture of dignity and importance in the family hierarchy within their males' miasmatic illusion of superiority and domination. This ancient female art has been universally practiced in all the tribes of man since the beginning of time. Portnoy's Yiddische momme did not spring full-grown as an earth figure from some Yiddische Zeus Kopf (head) in Newark, New Jersey. She is the prototype of all the Jewish mothers of the earth, and of the Goyische mothers as well, though gaining and maintaining power and authority through use of existing forms without outward change is not exclusively a woman's art. Sarah Sa'adi has achieved a measure of independence, d'esprit, by accepting the perimeter within which she lives and works, both the physical and the metaphysical boundaries. She has been more successful than the Israeli government in staking out and persuading her world to accept her "fixed and defensible" borders. Rather than a drag and a burden for her, Sarah's work as a "sponger" permits her a certain freedom of movement which she enjoys and uses to educate herself and broaden her horizons. She is not confined to the drudgery of cooking and looking after the house and children, plus gardening or piece work or factory work necesary to supplement the family income, as is the lot of so many Oriental women in Israel. She works in the homes of Anglo immigrants and has learned about the ways of the non-Yemenite world. She has picked up some English, French, and German. She has learned about hygiene, diet, clothing. She has been exposed to classical music, technological devices, plastic materials. In the course of her employment she has had short lessons in geography, ethnography, political science and modern child care. At the same time, she has taught her employers and their families about the Yemenite and Oriental Jewish way of life. She has been an expert teacher of Hebrew to immigrant children (including our daughter, Sara, who adored her), and has introduced their mothers to fragrant spices, the delights of pittah and sesame, and the curative properties of ancient desert herbs. The daily experiences of 12 years in the service of "westerners" have corroborated her intuition and her self-respect and have helped her to discard superstitions and old wives' tales.

The coming and going has been a two-way street, literally. On the two or three buses on which she has had to travel to get to her job, she has made many friends and acquaintances and has become familiar with Tel-Aviv and its environs. Her husband and children have been conned by her into believing that she is bored by her long rides on the stuffy, overcrowded buses, and are required to commiserate with her. *Hass v'chalilah* (God forbid) that they should know that these are hours of delicious relaxation, rest, and amusement. She looks forward to these moments as respite from the cares and chores at home and the hard labor of her job. During these moments she dreams and schemes for her children, especially for her daughters.

After the first four children were born during the first five years of her marriage, Sarah hoped that her family was complete. She dreaded the thought of more children to add to her already heavy burdens. When her youngest child was eight years old Sarah became pregnant. Solomon was delighted. He wanted another child as proof of his manhood despite his frequent illnesses. Sarah was appalled. My wife, Kitty, urged her to have an abortion. She offered to talk to Solomon or to have me talk to him about the importance of an abortion to Sarah's health and the well-being of the entire family. Sarah was amused at our naiveté. How little we understood the pride of the Jewish Yemenite male. Such a discussion with outsiders like us, however well-intentioned, would be an unforgivable insult.

Towards the end of the second month of her pregnancy, Sarah went to see a doctor whom she knew at the Kupat Holim (National Health Service) in Petach Tikvah. She was entitled to medical services, provided by us under legally required insurance. The doctor had delivered her last child, Gidon, who, unlike the first three was born in the hospital at Kfar Saba. She discussed with him the possibility of an abortion, and he agreed that he could recommend it on the grounds of her age — she was almost 40 — and the extraordinary circumstance that she was the principal support of the family; that her husband was ill and that she already had four young children. The doctor was not enthusiastic about talking to a Yemenite husband.

Sarah spent the next two weeks on her bus rides back and forth thinking it over, and finally decided to have the baby. No one in her family had ever had an abortion and her traditional upbringing was too strong for her to take this unheard-of step with all the censure it would bring. She decided, rather, to hope and pray that the child would be a girl. If it were a boy there would be the expense and preparation for another circumcision party that they could ill afford.

God was good and a girl baby was born, another black-eyed alert, perfectly formed infant. Sarah could look forward to four months at home, drawing an allowance from the health service, and assured of her position with the Alexanders when she was ready to go back to work. Solomon was disappointed and did not come to the hospital to bring his wife and new baby home. He pleaded illness, but he would not have been too sick to come to the hospital to bring another son home. Sarah insisted on naming the new baby Yael, a fashionable girl's name among the Ashkenazi Israeli, but not a traditional name for a Yemenite Jewess. Solomon protested a bit, "The family will be shocked," he said. Sarah was adamant. She didn't care what the family thought. It was her baby. She had given her a pretty name as well as a good Hebrew name. This small triumph of independence was her due. Solomon acknowledged her argument and protested no more. After all,his manhood had once more been proven. He had a good wife and five healthy children, and in a few weeks his eldest son, his first born, would be bar-mitzvahed. He was only 38 years old and despite his asthma, he could look forward to the years ahead with his children grown up, supporting him in style and providing him with grandchildren and building a clan, a "mispochah" (family) of which he would be the head. He would become a patriarch. In the meantime, he was enjoying the days as they came, the blessings and the problems, the good and the bad — all in the infinite wisdom of the Ineffable One — Blessed be His Name.

The Yemenite community in many ways is thrusting toward upper mobility, leading all the Oriental communities in Israel. Superficially, it would seem strange that the least educated, the most obscure physically deprived group of all the Jewish peoples of the Arab areas should have made the most progress in establishing themselves as integrated Israelis. On closer view, it is thoroughly understandable. They had remained a Jewish community during hundreds of years of isolation in the Arabian desert, and they had come to the Homeland uncomplicated, original and traditional Jews.

In 1972 the first non-Ashkenazi to be elected speaker of the Knesset (Parliament) was Yisrael Yesheyahu, a Yemenite — born in Yemen, no less. He is pleasant and affable, good-humored and gracefully at ease with his colleagues and with people generally. His chief credentials as far as the Establishment is concerned, are his unflagging and long-term faithfulness and service to the ruling labor party. He speaks only Hebrew (and Arabic); but the rather necessary attribute to communicate with the diplomatic community and VIP's from all over the world in some mutual language was considered a not insurmountable obstacle to his elevation to this highly visible position.

The significance of his election is that the Ashkenazi leaders of Israel, who have always been in firm control of the Establishment (they are, in a way, counterparts of the American WASPS) have acknowledged the importance of the Oriental communities, particularly the groups that came to Israel with the least attributes of power and influence, worldly goods, education, skills, sophistication, and without a base of influential groups of their fellows in Jewish communities in other lands. Many Sephardic Jews have achieved positions of power in government, finance, trade, science, and industry. They have been for the most part immigrants or Sabra descendants of Greeks, Turks, Egyptians, Italians, Iraqis, rarely Yemenites, Moroccans, Syrians, Bukharins or Kurds. The election of Yesheyahu as chief of the Knesset is much more than a token gesture. He is hardly to be compared to the symbolic "house nigger" or "House Jew" of the recent American administrations of Kennedy, Johnson, Nixon and Ford. The Sephardi and Afro-Asian Jews constitute a substantial majority of the Israeli population. They bear many more children than the Ashkenazi families and in a very few years their majority will increase greatly.

Sadly, perhaps cynically, the Ashkenazi leaders are aware that the Oriental Jews from the Arab countries are the most anti-Arab element in Israel for reasons that are obvious enough. The Hitler period in Europe is known to them only as a remote historical event in Jewish history — like the cruelty of the Pharaohs. They have no built-in race anger against Germans, as the Nazi camp surviors have. If some of them dislike Germans, their antipathy is personal toward German Jews in Israel, the *Yekke*, some of whom are condescending toward the *shvartzeh* (blacks) as the Oriental Israelis are sometimes privately referred to by the pale whites. But the Israeli Orientals generally dislike all Arabs, mainly because of their own mistreatment in Arab lands.

The strength in numbers of Oriental Israelis in the armed forces and as voters is a factor in the continuing Arab-Israel conflict. Immediately after the massacre of the Israeli Olympic athletes in Munich, Menachem Begin, the Heirut party leader, called for what amounted to a declaration of war against the Arab nations. This was sheer bombastic rabble-rousing for future vote-getting on the part of this wily Ashkenazi Israeli, originally from Poland; he wasn't serious. He knew it was a way of permitting the nation to blow-off steam and that it would be received with particular approbation by the Oriental Israelis. It was! His demand that Golda Meir resign as Prime Minister after the Yom Kippur War was the same kind of political ploy.

Left: The author and Senator Neuberger of Oregon, circa 1953.

Right: General Avrum Joffe, famous tank commander in the Sinai Campaign of 1956 and the Six Day War of June, 1967 and now chief of flora and fauna for the state of Israel, with the author, left, and unidentified man.

9. Israeli and Non-Israeli Arabs

The Arabs and the Jewish Israelis are different, culturally and religiously. The Arabs live pretty much the way their fathers and grandfathers did, as farmers and in the villages. The major difference in their life style now is technology. Tools, automobiles, and other amenities of modern life have greatly enhanced the quality of their daily existence and provided a degree of mobility. Their family, community, and religious organizations remain much the same as they have for generations.

The Arabs of the West Bank, Judea and Samaria, and Gaza — altogether some one million souls living in the "Administered Areas" — are exactly like their brethren, the Israeli Arabs. The merchants and town dwellers of Ramallah are no different than their counterparts in Abu Gosh. The jewellers and manufacturers of religious objects in Bethlehem are blood brethren of the merchants of Nazareth. The farmers in the rich Hebron hills and the farmers in the historical Wadi Ara area of the lower Galilee are much the same. No real differences have been created by the fact that the Bethlehemites, Ramallahans, and Hebronites lived in Jordan for twenty years, while the Nazarenes, the Abu Goshi, and the Arabs in Wadi Ara lived in Israel. The Israeli government would like to believe that the Arabs after twenty years of Jewish beneficence and equality that has made those living in Israel the wealthiest, healthiest and most literate in the entire Arab world, also are Israelis. They are not. They have become Israeli Arabs.

The Israeli Arabs do not hate Israel. But they do not love Israel either, and never will until it becomes their nation by virtue of genuine *de facto* as well as *de jure* first-class citizenship as members of an equal minority amongst other equal minorities. Their brethren of the West Bank who lived under the Jordanians during the same twenty years did not, for the most part, have the material advantages the Israeli Arabs enjoyed. Most Jewish Israelis believe, as do many supporters of Israel in the Western world, that the Palestinian Arabs of the "Areas" envy their Israeli brethren — their health, television sets, new houses, and furniture. Possibly they do, but I have spoken to Israeli Arabs who admit envying their Jordanian brothers because they belong to a tolerated minority while the Palestinians in Jordan before the Six-Day War were members of a respected majority from which came leading professionals, members of parliament, cabinet ministers, prime ministers, generals. The Palestinians in Jordan before the Six-Day War compared the status of their relatives in Israel to that of the Jews in Russia. The comparison was not entirely invalid.

The Israeli Arabs and the Arabs of the "Administered Areas," despite the shouting of the Arab propagandists who purport to speak for them, have a goal of equality, not national independence. They never were citizens of a geographical nation. That concept is a Western import. During all the years the Palestinian Arabs lived under the rule of Hussein's Hashemite Kingdom, they never agitated for independence. The only voices that were raised in those days were those of the Arab League, the U.A.R. and the other Arab nations who used the wretched Palestinians in the camps as an excuse to agitate against Israel. Few of the Palestinian Arabs in Jordan were in camps. Of course the camp dwellers cried for liberation because they wanted to go back to the homes they had fled. The Palestinians who remained at home, in Ramallah and Jericho and Bethlehem and Tulkarm and Jenin and Hebron and in all territories appropriated by Jordan in 1948 were quite satisfied to be a part of Jordan.

The Gazans for the most part did not run away, but their lives were made miserable by the influx of thousands of other Palestinians who had fled to Gaza in 1948. Both the Gazans and these refugees came under Egyptian rule. The Egyptians treated them like captive cattle. If the Arabs in Gaza had been accepted by the Egyptians as Egyptians, as the Jordanians had accepted the West Bank Palestinians, there would have been no refugees in Gaza. But the Egyptians did not regard these Palestinians as compatriots. They were considered and treated like peasant Bedouin, exploited to obtain funds from the U.N. and to show the world how the horrible Jews misused their fellow Moslems. In truth, the Egyptians enslaved them, filled them with hate. The territory became a convenient place to practice nepotism, a rather pleasant climate on the sea for Egyptian officers to live in comfortable military splendor. Privately, the

Gazans admit, but only privately, that the difference between Egyptian Gaza June 1967 and Israel Gaza 1976 is the difference between sunlight and darkness.

Most all the former Palestinian Arabs who live in the "Areas" and come into contact with Jewish Israelis believe that all Israelis are the same. They don't distinguish them by their country of origin or by their appearance, even if they speak Arabic, despite the evidence of their eyes and ears. The Afro-Asian Israelis who came from the Arab countries quite naturally foster the myth amongst Israeli Arabs that all Israelis are the same. They remember their treatment as a despised minority in the Arab lands, and their sabra children hearken to the stories told them by their parents. It's the same never-ending story of the oppressed becoming oppressors when they are emancipated. Always the poor innocents are the immediate and wrong targets. For Israeli Arab consumption, the Ashkenazi Israelis also foster the myth of Jewish-Israeli equality no matter how sharp the differences of education, wealth, position, social status, even values. There seems to exist an unspoken pact among all Jewish Israelis to present a united front to their immediate Arab neighbors.

Arab Profiles

Rustam Bustani now lives in the United States with his Jewish wife who had come to Israel with her German refugee family shortly before Independence. I met Rustam through Phillip Katz and spent some pleasant hours with him from time to time discussing Israel-Arab problems over delicious seafood dinners in our favorite restaurant in Acre. At my invitation he addressed the Israel Commission in Jerusalem in 1967. When we arrived in 1968, the Bustanis had left Israel. Bustani is famous in Israel not only because he is a member of an old line Arab family with roots in Palestine, Lebanon, and Syria, but because he was a prominent controversial figure in his native land before he left to become an expatriate in America.

He was born and brought up in Haifa when that city was Arab, not Jewish. Rustam was the first Arab Israeli architect to graduate from the Hebrew University. He became a darling of the left-wing Mapam party. He was a leader of the non-religious Arabs of Israel who sought to accommodate with the new democracy as equal citizens in an egalitarian socialist labor nation. He was one of the youngest persons ever to be elected to the Knesset. But his convictions voiced in impeccable Hebrew became too frank and impolitic for his fellow party members, and too pro-Israel (read Zionist) to please his fellow Arabs.

He decided to forego a political career and to devote himself to his profession. To his dismay, he discovered that being an Arab in the world of building construction, finance, and *protekzia* was hardly *open sesame*, especially if your name happened to be Rustam Bustani, and he became frustrated and angry. He could not abide the fact that the golden promise of viability for Arab and Jew alike in the new *Medinah* was not working out, was not even practiced by his liberal Jewish colleagues. A disastrous divorce from a daughter of an Arab family as distinguished as his own family gave both the Arab and the Jewish communities the opportunity to write him off.

His attachment to his Jewish wife occasioned stern disapproval and gleeful gossip. If he had been a Jewish Israeli it would have been considered a personal and private matter. Rustam worked as a town planner in the city of Haifa for a few years, but finally he and his brilliant and embittered wife decided that for them Israel would remain bleak indeed. There seemed to be no place in Israel for an Arab Israeli non-conformist, and less place for an Arab architect within the controlled Jewish Establishment.

Ovadia tended our garden for three years in the Kfar. He is a devout Moslem who lives in the small Arab village of his birth near Netanya. He was a young teen-ager when the war broke out in 1948, and he recalls gratefully that his family and all of the Arabs in their village accepted the assurances of the Jews that no harm would come to them. The family did not flee. His people had been working for years in Netanya and in the agricultural villages and *pardessim* (citrus orchards) of the neighborhood, and they knew their Jewish employers well. They trusted them.

After peace came Ovadia continued his work as a farmhand and gardener, married, and prospered. He saved enough money to buy a small truck and gardening tools. When Kfar Shmaryahu became a village of villas he developed a business of day gardening there. He owns his own home. He has five healthy children. His oldest son is now a teenager and helps his father on weekends and holidays. Ovadia is proud that his children will have at least eight years of schooling — that they are devout, obedient, well-mannered.

He has no strong feelings about Israel, neither as an Israeli citizen nor as an Arab nationalist. His material situation is much better, he knows, than if Israel had not come into being. His mode of living in his community is not much different than it was when he was a young boy during Mandate times. He is fully aware of the change in his status as a member of a conquered minority group, which at one time in his own memory had been the majority. However, neither he nor his family have suffered any personal indignities. He enjoys working for Anglos and new immigrants rather more than for old-line Israelis. Though most of the Israelis are polite and considerate, speak Hebrew with him and some even Arabic, which makes for easier communication, he is made to feel his place as a servitor, a hired hand, and as someone not quite to be trusted. He yearns for peace between Israel and the Arab nations, for himself, and even more, for the future dignity of his children who in many ways have been brought to realize that they are second class citizens.

The Yunises are an Arab family of many relatives, cousins, uncles, fathers, sons, and womenfolk. The main branch has lived in Jaffa for many generations, but the Yunises now live and work all over Israel — Tiberias, Jerusalem, Acre, Lydda. Their several restaurants are all separately owned, but reflects a family tradition and *esprit,* and the youngsters are placed in one or the other of the restaurants to train with the uncles and cousins. The tie of traditional Moslem orthodoxy also is strong among the older generation. They are all proud of the Yunis culinary tradition which means fish, always the best catch and superbly prepared, and exotic Arab salads and soups and sharply spiced appetizers and grilled lamb, beef, or liver on skewers. The original Yunis restaurant is situated in the very center of the Arab ghetto in Jaffa not far from the port. For years it was a favorite eating place of the British Mandatory officials and all the consular people, and before the British came, of the Turkish administrators. The restaurant was in Jaffa before Tel-Aviv existed and is still as popular as ever.

Over the generations of contact with foreigners, especially in Jaffa — the most polyglot center of Arab and Jewish mingling in all of Israel — the Yunis tribe acquired an ease and cheerful assurance quite different from most Israeli Arabs who meet the public. It is a truism that Arabs are naturally polite. But in their dealings with Jews they are cordial, distant, proper — no more. Often one can feel the mild disdain and dislike, even hatred, that vibrates from them. Not so with the Yunises. They have always moved freely in Jaffa and Tel-Aviv and Lod and in Tiberias where many of them live in a mixed Jewish-Arab urban milieu. They take delight in being recognized as a part of their famous restaurateur clan. At the pleasant outdoor garden restaurant on the Tel-Aviv-Lod road, they'll tell you that their food is better than at the Jaffa place — but with a broad grin and a quick addition that the cuisine there is also *metzooyan* (excellent).

A younger Yunis generation from Tiberias established one of the best eating places in Israel adjoining a service station on the shore highway in Herzylia, a three-minute drive from our house. There two bright young brothers, and their many cousins work hard to prove they have the best

Yunis food and service of all. Their claim to the widest variety of fish and seafood from the Sea of Galilee, the warm waters of the Red Sea, the Mediterranean, and in recent years, trout and other fish cultured in the kibbutz fish ponds in the Galilee — is authentic.

For a short period after the Six-Day War the Arab Israelis suffered occasional indignities, insults from swaggering soldiers, and more often young punks who never did serve in the armed forces. Little of this gangsterism ever happened in the establishments of the younger Yunises; their sense of being Israelis seems to come through even with the rudest of their fellow Israelis.

Sheik Abdullah is the Mukhtar of the village of Talbiyah, an Arab settlement in the Gilboa region (of which Moledet and Ein Harod are a part). I often met Abdullah in Moledet and occasionally at Ramat Zvi. We always had a drink together. He didn't obey the Moslem interdict against alcohol. Dora Lanir would kid me frequently, "Your friend, Abdullah is coming over tonight to see Meir. You'll be glad to see him." I was.

The tense days of 1948 when the Arab villagers and the isolated Jewish settlements waited to see who would win the war have long since passed. The ensuing quarter of a century has brought peace and cordiality to the region, and even a degree of friendship. Certainly the *modus vivendi* works well. Abdullah is convivial, outgoing, and moves easily and confidently in the *kibbutzim* and *moshavim*. He is welcome wherever he goes and in his person epitomizes the neighborly pride that the Jews and Arabs, Israelis all, take in the general prosperity of the Gilboa region. Abdullah is rich, he has several wives, many children, and many more cows, sheep, goats, chickens, and hundreds of dunams of fertile land. He shows up at all the public events of the region, resplendent in white robes and *kaffiyah* (Arab headdress). He speaks eloquently in Arabic and Hebrew, his broad gold-toothed smile emphasizing his good will. He rhapsodizes on good crops, the opportunities for the Arab villagers to work for good wages throughout the area, not only as farm hands, but as bricklayers, carpenters, plumbers, mechanics. He speaks of the mutual respect that enables the Arab Israelis to lead their traditional life enhanced but unchanged, and the Jews to live their lives alongside their Arab neighbors. He speaks of the health services, the veterinary services, the assistance given by the Ministry of Education for the schooling of the children. In recent years he has even cautiously dared to voice the hope that his relatives in the "Administered Areas" may soon be united with the Israeli Arabs under the Blue and White *degel* (flag). I believe he means it.

The Daughter-in-Law of the Kadi. One day my friend Yehuda Hameiri invited me to go with him to Jerusalem to visit an Arab friend in the old city. Yussef was waiting for us in front of his house in one of the narrow streets near the Western Wall close to the old Jewish quarter. He was a slight, dark, lithe man, with a toothbrush moustache and hazel eyes. Immaculately dressed in a dark business suit and necktie, despite the heat of summer, he greeted us with a cordial smile and exquisite manner. He apologized for not being able to invite us into the shuttered library in the corner building that, he explained in halting English and good Hebrew, was established by his family a century ago and contained books and manuscripts in Hebrew and Arabic on the history of Jerusalem, and of his own family, which has lived in Jerusalem for hundreds of years.

We ascended a narrow staircase to his apartment looking out on an open vista of gardens and terraces and a breathtaking panorama of the heart of the old city, gracious world that visitors to Jerusalem hardly know exists. His pretty little wife served us the inevitable Turkish coffee. She might have been the maid; Yussef did not introduce her to us. "Big George" asked him if we might meet his mother before we proceeded to our business. Yussef assented with pleasure, and we walked across a path leading to a higher level of steps that ascended to a still higher apartment situated on a terrace surrounded by lemon trees and a profusion of flowers and shrubs. As we approached, a little old lady came out of the apartment and descended the steps to greet us. She was small and stout, all toothless smile.

Yussef introduced us in Hebrew and she responded in Yiddish accented English. She then asked us in Yiddish if we could speak Momme loshen (mother tongue). I responded in Hebrew. "*Ktzat*" (a little bit), and continued in Yiddish, "How do you happen to know Yiddish?" In Yiddish she replied with absolute glee, "Why not, I'm a Jewish girl!" "Fahr voss nit ich bin a Yiddische maidel!" Yussuf grinned and Yehuda laughed out loud. I was flabbergasted. I turned to Yussuf and said in Hebrew, "Why, you're a Jew, after all. Your mother is a Jewess!" He answered grimly, "Yes, in a way, but I'm an Arab and a Moslem. My mother was born a Jewess, but when she married my father, she converted to the faith of Islam."

Then the whole story came out, which my rogue friend Yehuda knew well, but did not tell me because he wanted to enjoy the shock of my surprise. The lively little old lady was born in the heart of the old city, the daughter of a rabbinical family that had lived there since early in the 19th Century. Despite the strictures on intermingling she had met and fallen in love with her aristocratic Moslem beau and deserted her family to enter into the Arab world. Naturally when she married him, she was mourned by her family as if she were dead. But dead she was not.

Her father-in-law had been for years the Kadi, the chief Moslem religious official of Jerusalem. Her husband had been a prominent and respected merchant, and the mayor of Jerusalem for ten years under the

British Mandate. She bore seven children, three of them living in the United States where they had gone to become educated and remained to prosper with the help of her Jewish brothers, who had kept in touch with her despite her excommunication.

In her pleasant spare apartment she showed us photographs of her children and grandchildren. Hanging on the wall were formal photographs of her husband, the Mayor, and his distinguished father, the Kadi. The old lady was obviously delighted to talk to Jews and to speak the Yiddish which she remembered after almost a half century. She also spoke French and Spanish with Yehuda and slyly tested his Arabic. She explained to me that her English had become very rusty, and that the only language she had never mastered was Hebrew because in her pious Orthodox home as a child the Holy Language was forbidden, and anyway girls were inferior beings who were not required to learn anything that did not contribute to serving the menfolk. She was half-kidding, half-serious. I couldn't help contrast the respect and deference Yussuf showed towards his mother with the casual indifference he had manifested towards his wife.

Later we walked through the narrow streets and at almost every turn we stopped to meet merchants and others, all of whom seemed to be relatives of Yussuf. We completed the visit in an Arab restaurant near the Damascus Gate which was owned by the brother of a brother-in-law of Yussuf. The "small snack" turned out to be a ten-course meal lasting two hours. When I suggested to Yussuf that if his relative served such food at the prices I had noticed on the menu, he must lose money. Yussuf replied with a grin (we were sort of fellow Jews now), "Don't worry. He never serves food like this in the restaurant. This is what we eat in our homes." But he hastened to add, all Arab again, "But when you honor our family by coming again to eat here, my brother-in-law will be pleased to serve you always the food of our home." A few weeks later, I was grieved to learn from Yehuda that the old lady had died very suddenly.

Arab "Televisia"

Television for some years had been a subject of controversy in Israel. Opponents decried the "vast wasteland" of the American example. Proponents countered with the quality of BBC programming. The tremendous cost was a deterrent to indigenous Israeli TV. Priorities of public welfare, defense, immigration, and education could not easily be brushed aside. Precious foreign currency was required not only to set up broadcasting facilities but also to buy TV receivers. However, thousands of Israelis bought television sets during the middle sixties, erected high antennas on their roofs and watched programs from Jordan and Lebanon. "Progress" no longer could be denied. A few months before the Six-Day War, the dubious blessing of TV came to the Holy Land. The best that can be said for Israeli television thus far is that it isn't much worse than in the rest of the world. Programs from the British Broadcasting Company, the U.S. and from European countries are available a few years after their origination, at small cost. Above all, the inanity of commercials, American style, does not yet exist.

An attractive *plus* for Israeli TV are the Arabic programs. Somehow, despite the bureaucracy that instantly materialized when the television administration was created — a collage from the radio and newspaper world, official spokesmen for the government, and a heterogeneous collection of knowledgeables from the United States, England and Europe — and despite all the tugging and pulling by lily Jewish and Orthodox elements in the establishment, it was agreed that Arabs should have a voice in determining Israeli Arabic programming. As a result, the Arab programs are original, refreshing, and non-chauvinistic. A splendid cadre of talented Arabs, mostly from the Administered Areas and the old city of Jerusalem, has been recruited. The Israelis assigned to work with them also were well chosen. Two of these were friends and colleagues of mine, Rivka Friedman (Sneh) and Esther Soffer. I met them at Shoshana Rasiel's home in Jerusalem in 1967. Rivka is Shoshana's cousin. Both Esther and Rivka were born in the old city of Jerusalem and had been thrilled by the reunion of the two parts of the city after the war. They were then still on the staff of Kol Israel (the voice of Israel), the government radio station. Esther Soffer was known by a generation of Israeli children to whom she read children's stories each afternoon. Rivka was a drama director and program producer.

They invited me to help them produce a record of current life in the post war reunited Jerusalem. Our record "Jerusalem Calling" was issued simultaneously in Israel and the U.S. in early 1968, just before we emigrated to Israel. Pierre Van Paassen had graciously permitted me to use the title of his book "Jerusalem Calling" for our record and to quote a passage therefrom on the jacket — "Jerusalem, whose name is peace, becomes the heart and soul of humanity." I sent him the first copy of the record, but it reached his home in New York the day he died. He never heard it. One of my activities in Israel during the four years of our sojourn was a largely unsuccessful effort to distribute "Jerusalem Calling" in Israel, particularly to tourists. Esther, Rivka, and I were mollified, however, by the positive critical acclaim the record received in the Israel press.

From the start of the Arab programs there was no friction based upon "We Israelis — You Arabs." Quite the contrary: the Israeli Jews and the Arabs joined to present news, children's programs, educational programs for Arab women, music, art, vocational guidance. The Arabic programming might profitably have been emulated by the dreary, untalented Israeli side of the TV enterprise.

At the personal level, the Jewish and Arab colleagues worked well together, became comrades and friends. The bright young Arabs risked ostracism and worse. They were accused of being traitors, of selling out to the enemy — sort of Arab versions of Tokyo Rose. These canards have evaporated since the situation in Jerusalem and Bethlehem has settled down to a reasonably calm pleasant existence.

Victor, a handsome matinee idol type, is one of the news broadcasters. He courageously took his future and his life in his hands to become a news commentator for Israeli TV. His acquaintances and relatives in Bethlehem were aghast, then angry that he would work for the Jews in what many of them considered a pro-Jewish, anti-Arab job. Even some of his close friends felt this way at the beginning. But as months went by and they listened to his even-handed and fair reporting (which he did not prepare — the fairness came from the news staff, most of whom are Israeli Jews), handsome Victor became something of a star among the Arabs of Bethlehem, Jerusalem, the West Bank and Israeli Arabs. It pleased him that many people in his home town would stop to chat with him, even people he did not know began to greet him cordially.

I met Victor and most of the Arab TV staff through Rivka and Esther. Without exception they were bright and charming young people. A friend of mine in Chicago had an idea to sell sachets of Holy Land soil to American Catholics. Victor volunteered to introduce me to a priest friend of his at the Church of the Nativity in Bethlehem who furnished me with a hundred pounds of authenticated soil from the church gardens that I shipped to my friend. I learned later that the project bombed!

Gloria is a beautiful young Arab Christian who has had stage ambitions since she was a small child. Her father and brother own a goldsmith shop in Bethlehem, established by her great-grandfather; her brother is Victor's best friend, pals since childhood. The family is cultured and exquisitely hospitable. Bethlehem was least affected of all the cities taken over in 1948 by the Jordanians, and Gloria's family did not suffer under the Jordanian administration. Moslem King Hussein and his government were always were keenly aware of the special importance of Bethlehem to the Catholics of the world. Though they did little to improve the town, they did nothing to hinder it from continuing as a religious center for tourists from all the world. Gloria's family, even her young brother who was educated in France, remained strictly neutral after the Six-Day War, but a year after Israel occupied Bethlehem, Gloria persuaded her brother to ask Victor to help her obtain a position with the Arab programs of Israeli TV. That he did so gladly with the father's consent, was a mark of the real acceptance that the Arab TV programs had earned among the Arab population. She has become very popular with all the Israeli, this sprightly dark-eyed girl, with her perfect Arabic diction, her simplicity and poise.

Gloria and Victor belong now to a large group of Arab veterans of Israeli TV. One handsome young lady on the Arab staff fell in love with a Jewish colleague, converted to Judaism and married him. She is still the favorite Arab newscaster. All of them, those who are seen and those who work behind the scenes as technicians and writers, are part of a television authority in which everybody is accepted on their merits and for themselves. Some of the Arabs knew a bit of Hebrew. Now they speak Hebrew like Israeli sabras and have taught Arabic to some of their Jewish colleagues. Together they practice their English — an essential tool for communicating with the American and British experts who set up Israeli TV at the beginning. English continues to be important in the world of Israeli television.

Israeli television in general is indifferently bad, but the Arab programs stand out as a bright spot of the effort. These programs are contributing measurably to the understanding of Israel by the Arab population and to the evaporation of hostility through familiarity. The speed and completeness with which the Arabs and the Jews have learned to work together in the television establishment serves as a significant model for a future Israel. Neither the Israeli Jews nor the Arabs consider integration of peoples and cultures essential or even desirable. Privately, these earnest young people in the TV authority hope for the day when the jingoism and political chauvinism on both sides will end.

Murder on the Beach

Amram's family were citrus growers for a century or more and owners of large tracts of land on the Sharon plain near the Mediterranean Sea. Like most of the prosperous Arab families of Palestine they came originally from Lebanon, when that country was part of Ottoman Syria. The Arab community in Jaffa and the Sharon were a bit shocked when in 1920 young Amram wooed and married a daughter of one of the early Tel-Aviv Jewish merchants. The Jews, too, were a bit taken aback by this rare intermarriage. Amram's family accepted the union gracefully enough but when their children were born, Amram and his Jewish wife decided to bring them up as Jews and to cast their lot with the fast-growing community of Tel-Aviv.

There were few problems in those early fluid days, especially for educated and cultured Arabs and Jews who mingled freely in the same social and business milieu. Later, however, after World War II, tensions and exacerbations stemming from the Jewish fight to throw off the Mandate and gain independence, caused schisms and hardships. For many years, Amram had been involved with the Jewish National Fund and the *Vaad Leumi* in buying land from the Arabs. He had even arranged to sell some of the property of his own family to be used for agricultural settlements and other public purposes. Shortly after Independence, Amram was found on the beach north of Tel-Aviv, brutally murdered. His murderers were never discovered, but all the evidence indicated that he was a victim of an Arab terrorist vendetta. He had paid the supreme penalty for his allegiance to the Jewish cause and for his firm loyalty to the concept of an independent Israel.

His children are Jewish Israelis. Two daughters live in Tel-Aviv with their sabra husbands, close to Amram's widow who still mourns her handsome and gallant husband. A son found his bride in the very same Jewish community in New Jersey from which his mother had come many years ago. He is a sophisticated businessman, educated in Israel, Europe, and the United States. They live in Israel now in Kfar Shmaryahu. His handsome and easy-going wife teaches English in the American School. Their three children attended Rishpon-Kfar School. The whole family moves easily between the United States and Israel. They have strong attachments to both countries, but they essentially are Israelis, even the American wife. A few of their neighbors in their village still recall the family's Arab connection, which in some indefinable cruel way sets them a bit apart from the hyper-Jewish patriots.

* * *

Achmed was a young Arab from the Gaza Strip, fresh out of high school. His family operated a large garage and auto repair business in the city of Gaza, and by the standards of that poverty-stricken area, which the twenty years of Egyptian occupation had converted into a massive concentration camp, they were wealthy. Achmed, a classmate of mine at Ulpan Akiva, had enrolled at the Ulpan at his father's insistence but with a great deal of trepidation, to learn Hebrew. His quiet dignified father would drive up from the Gaza Strip to visit his son from time to time. The father sat silent and smiling. The only language Achmed's father knew was Arabic. Obviously, he believed that the connection between

Israel and Gaza was a long-term matter, possibly permanent, whatever political form would finally emerge. A Gazan who knew Hebrew, he reasoned, would have a great advantage. Achmed was happy that he was welcome at the Ulpan and that so many of his fellow students came from all over the world and were not Israeli. He was delighted that he could not distinguish them as Jew or non-Jew, just as Americans or Frenchmen or Englishmen or Scandinavians or Greeks.

Achmed learned Hebrew easily enough with his Arabic base, as easily as a lad from Rotterdam can learn German in Munich. Despite his dark good looks and his graceful politeness, he was not much liked by his fellow students, neither Jew nor Gentile, Shulamit, of course, doted on him. He was her exhibit "A" for the glorious rapprochement she predicted between the Arabs of the "Administered Areas" and the Israelis. The sensitive *Goyim* in the school found him rather obtuse and dumb. The Jews did too, with an added visceral sense of distrust. He came on like a sort of Arab Uriah Heep. Achmed found that the English he learned in the Ulpan was of more value to him than the Hebrew because it helped him later to get into the University of Cairo, which had been his real ambition.

The Druse

To be completely accurate, Achmed was not Shulamit's exhibit "A" — he was "A" minus. Her star pupil was *Sheikh Jabber Muadi*, member of the Knesset, a long-time political chieftain of the Druse in Israel. He had attended the Ulpan for a number of summers to improve his imperfect Hebrew. A resplendent figure dressed in immaculate flowing white caftan, his head engulfed in a linen *Kaffiyah* (Arab headdress), he was driven regularly to the school by his chauffeur in his American limousine, quite like a Mafia godfather in the United States. The comparison is not inapt. Muadi rose to power on the strength of the Druse loyalty to the new State at the beginning of Independence, and his ability to deliver soldiers, police recruits, and votes. During the years that followed, his tough guy reputation has grown to awesome frightening rumor, but not easily corroborated within the secrecy that has surrounded this strange Arab sect for hundreds of years. Muadi had been a convenient and faithful Mapai party hack, and the consolidated Labor Party certainly did not want to lift up the rocks in the Galilee villages to see what worms swarmed below the immaculate robes and the exaggerated good manners.

Muadi was appointed a deputy minister of communications to emphasize the political importance of the Druse and all the loyal Israeli Arab communities. For vote getting purposes it doesn't seem important that neither Druse nor Arab considers the Druse as Arabs. In all of the Middle East there exists a centuries old enmity between Druse and Arabs, whether Moslems or Christians. I went on a safari Shulamit and Muadi arranged for the Ulpan students to the tomb of Jethro, the Druse saint (father-in-law of Moses) in the Carmel mountains. We were cordially welcomed by the hearty, handsome red-bearded freckled-faced men and lavishly wined and dined. (The women, traditionally, were kept out of sight, though rumor has it that privately they rule the roost). Some anthropologists attribute the coloration and Nordic appearance of many Druse to the long occupation of the crusaders in Palestine during the eleventh and twelfth centuries.

There are 70,000 Druse in Israel, mostly in the central and upper Galilee. They are now closely in contact with their brethren in the Golan plateau, who, while the Syrians fled, remained on the Golan to welcome their liberation from Syria during the Six-Day War. Remnants of these interesting and attractive people can be found in the mountain fastnesses of all the northern Arab countries of Asia — Lebanon, Syria, Iraq. They were once Moslems and Arabs, and in many ways still are, though they themselves don't admit it. The sounds of revolt amongst the Israeli Druse against the strong arm rule of Muadi and the old line leaders have become louder and clearer. A kind of Druse women's lib is also developing in the villages. The Druse integration as Israelis, although by no means complete, is measurably more advanced than that of the Arab. Because of their long history of oppression by Arab Moslems, the Druses have a genuine attitude of loyalty to the state based on mutual antipathies — sort of "our enemy is your enemy". This attitude was enhanced in the Yom Kippur War by the brutal shelling of Druse villages in the Mount Hermon region of the Golan Heights by the Syrians.

More positively, the Druse enjoy being policemen and border guards, an aptitude-inheritance of their centuries as hunters and warriors in their mountain fastnesses. Since the early pioneer days the relationship between Jew and Druse has been cordial and warm. But there is little more social intercourse between them than between Jew and Arab. The Druse is content to lead his traditional family and clan life as his forebears did for generations, pleased to be respected as a citizen, to travel freely and work where and at what he pleases — equal, but separate (by choice).

The history of the Drusi since 1948 demonstrates that cultural pluralism can work in Israel when suspicion of differentness is replaced by respect for differentness. The Israeli Jews made no effort to homogenize the Drusi into the dominant culture but the not-so-subtle suspicion of the

Arab Israelis was never visited on them. The Druse has always been accepted as part of the Israeli scene. They belong to the landscape.

The rich Arab culture and Arab presence must also be accepted inside and outside of Israel. Hopefully, the Yom Kippur War may have stripped the blindfold from Israeli eyes. The Israelis are discovering at long last that the Arabs, too, belong to the landscape. After four years of living in Israel the adult members of the Alexander family decided that they did not.

The author and film star Joan Blondell at an Israel fund-raising affair in Chicago, 1954.

The author addressing audience at the dedication of the B'nai Brith Martyrs Forest in the Judean Hills near Jerusalem, 1959.

10. The Alexanders Go Home

For us, as for most of its residents, Kfar Shmaryahu is a suburb of Tel-Aviv, not a self-contained village, a place to come home to after working elsewhere. For Kitty and me this created a sense of impermanence and dissatisfaction. Although life in the Kfar was ideal for the children, we did not come to Israel to retire to suburbia. After three years there we came to realize that wherever we might reside in Israel we would be living in suburbia, outsiders on the outskirts of a life style that was not ours.

Had I found a niche for myself, in some Israeli enterprise — one for which I long searched — sometimes grabbed at, but never quite held on to — Israeli life for Kitty and me would surely have been different and certainly good for the children.

As the baby Sara grew older and all of us became adjusted to comfortable living in Kfar Shmaryahu, Kitty, too, became restive in her role as housewife. She had made several efforts to resume her profession as dress designer; these had not proved rewarding. Our friend, Ava Kadishson had introduced her to two sisters who operated a salon for facial care in Tel-Aviv. They practiced a European discipline, learned much earlier in Paris. For years the sisters had conducted a school in connection with their salon, but had long since given up training students. Kitty was intrigued by their methods and expertise and induced Nina and Bella to let her learn their disciplines. For two years, she assiduously studied and worked at the Ninabella Salon and by the time we returned to the States in 1972, she had become as expert as her teachers and was ready to establish her own salon in Ann Arbor. Nina and Bella were very proud of her. They told me she was the best colleague they ever had in their thirty years of practice.

By the middle of 1971 Kitty and I decided to divide our time between Israel and the United States, remaining in the States most of the time. We had come to realize that we were too American to live any place but in our native land. However, to assure that we would always have a place to come back to in Israel, we purchased a small apartment in Tel-Aviv. This gesture was especially pleasing to Robert who wanted to be certain that he would be coming back to Israel from time to time to see his chums and even to attend school in later years.

The apartment had been used as the office of a private secondary school and had never been lived in. Though fairly new it was filthy with grime. During the summer and fall months of 1971 we all spent many hours making the place habitable. We scrubbed and painted and polished the walls and the floors. The plumbing was renewed by our friend "Luxy" from Ramat Gan. Our friends Ezra Cohen and his brothers helped us with the heavier work and the electrical wiring. Avraham (Arturo) lent a willing and skillful hand. Mark came from the States to visit during the summer and he too pitched in for a couple of months. Even little Sara helped out. Kitty and I and Ava Kadishson shopped for furnishings in the Arab markets of Jaffa, Jerusalem, and Hebron. We bought some new things in department stores and in little shops in Tel-Aviv.

By the beginning of winter the apartment had been transformed into a cheerful and comfortable little home. My friends Solomon Levadi and his wife Hanna came to Israel in November and lived in the apartment for three months. When Dr. Levadi died in the spring of 1973 Kitty and I were comforted that he had graced our home in Israel on his last sojourn in the land that had been central to his life.

We moved into the apartment for a few weeks before we left, to get a taste of Tel-Aviv living in our own home, and corroborated our conviction that we were still city folk at heart. Friends arranged a number of parties and get-togethers to say farewell to us and we also entertained some of them in the apartment to repay the hospitality we had enjoyed over the years. It was important to us to assure our friends that we were not leaving Israel altogether and the fact of our apartment did provide some evidence that we would be coming back as often as possible. But the leave taking was sad. We had come to Israel as immigrants to live but were going back to our native land. When we returnd thereafter it would be as American visitors, not as Israelis, not even as former Israelis, because we had never become Israelis — except Robert perhaps who in a way will be an Israeli at heart all of his life. We left Israel in July to come back to an America that had changed more than we realized in the four years since we left. In retrospect, we also came to know that Israel, too, had changed very much during the four years we lived there. Little did we know that a year later a Yom Kippur War would once again irrevocably alter the destiny of that buffeted land.

The author and Dora Lanir of Moledet, planting olive trees at dedication of community center in 1959.

V

Epilogue

Since coming back to the U.S. in September 1972, I have reflected on my four-year sojourn in Israel, trying to put into perspective my reasons for going there to live and my reasons for returning to my native land. In the preceding pages I have written a factual though obviously subjective account of my relations with Israel and with Zionism — an account that spans the first twenty-five years of the State of Israel — as a pro-Israel activist in the U.S. and as an Israeli resident.

After several years back in the U.S. and visits to Israel before and after the Yom Kippur War in 1973, 1974 and 1975, some truths are coming into focus for this latter day Zionist and ex-Israeli. I now realize that the reality of a Jewish nation and the rush of world events have completely subverted the Zionist dream, even if many of the myths of Zionism still persist. Though it is not within the scope of this book or the competence of this writer to trace the history of the Zionist movement, some general observations are in order on the nature of the connection betwen the people of Israel and the Jews of the Diaspora during the past twenty-seven years and since the Yom Kippur War of 1973.

The Zionist Dream

The Zionist dream began to disintegrate when Israel became an independent nation in 1948, but the myth of Zionism persisted for twenty-five years. The dream was diminished by the Six-Day War of 1967 and ended forever on Yom Kippur Day, October 6, 1973. The explosive victory of June 1967 launched a process of enlargement, a binge of national grandiosity far from the Zionist dream. The nightmare of the Yom Kippur War wrenched Israelis and diaspora Jews alike into a gray dawn of reality — a sobriety even further from the Zionist dream.

Zionism was an idealistic concept of the diaspora. It could not survive the inexorable crunch of the history of the Jews in the 20th Century. Its finest hours occurred in the early years of the century when a trickle of romantic pioneers, from choice and conviction, came to Palestine to establish a homeland for Jews on the ancient soil and later on between World War I and World War II when their supporters created a political framework of Zionist organizations that culminated in the creation of the State of Israel in 1948.

The simple definition of modern Zionism as the effort to reestablish all Jews in their Biblical homeland applies to all the many organizations that made up the Zionist movement since its beginning in Europe in the latter half of the 19th Century. Above this basic foundation, however, the cause has been widely divergent in goals and methodology. It is these divergencies that explain to me the collection of disparities and contradictions that is Israel. Four major divisions of Zionism have existed since the beginning of the movement, each representing different points of view beyond the common goal.

The labor Zionists had as their goal the creation in Palestine of a Marxist socialist nation of farmers and workers. These proletariat zealots constituted the majority of the early pioneers and because they got there first and in the greatest numbers their successors and descendants dominated the governments of Israel from the beginning and still do, more or less. But the egalitarian dream of the first pioneers and the dictum that all Jews should emigrate to the workers' paradise abuilding have been watered down and unrecognizably altered by the sweet incense of power. When the state came into being the labor Zionist movement (whose principal founder was David Ben-Gurion) merged into the political parties of Mapam, Mapai, Achdut Avodah, and later Rafi. In 1968 they all united to become the Ma'arach — the alignment labor party of Golda Meir, Moshe Dayan, Pinchas Sapir, Itzak Rabin and Yigal Alon.

The middle of the road Zionists sought to create a traditional capitalist democratic nation, patterned after the United States and the Western European countries. From the beginning they were anti-Marxist and after the U.S.S.R. came into being, consistently anti-Soviet. In America they were the Zionist Organization of America (ZOA) and in Europe they were the general Zionists in England of Chaim Weitzmann, the revisionists of Vladimir Jabotinsky and the Zionist organizations of Nordau, Ruppin, Nachum Goldmann and others in the Central and Eastern European countries. When Israel became a nation they organized as the

Heirut Party of Menachem Begin, and the Liberal and Progressive Parties of the German and Polish immigrants who came to Israel before and after the rise of Hitler. Today most all of these parties are consolidated into the main opposition party — the Likud.

The third major Zionist movement was made up of the religious Zionists. In varying degrees of fundamentalism, their goal was the recreation of the ancient theocratic state, a literal restoration of the priest kingdom, a rebuilding of the temple of Solomon. As it was said in the prayers from the early days of the dispersion, *Ha shana ha ba'a b'Yerushalayim* (next year in Jerusalem). Today their incessant political clericalism is expressed in Israel by the National Religious Party (NRP) and the Agudat Israel Party. They sought, and still do, immigration from the diaspora, but true believers only, if you please. Theirs is the only consistent Zionism that has survived the vicissitudes of the past twenty-five years. Their reckless rectitude is exhibited by their refusal to join a coalition government after the elections of December 1973 unless conversion to Judaism was controlled as a matter of law by the Orthodox rabbinate.

The fourth major movement of Zionism was never organized, never a defined entity, and only in the light of present history can it be recognized as a powerful force that contributed greatly to the creation of Israel. This Zionism consisted of the majority of the Jews in the free nations of the world who supported the idea of the creation of a Jewish state and who were very helpful in bringing Israel into being. This amorphous body of non-Zionist Zionists remain supporters of Israel although many of them are disaffected and critical of the Israel of today, especially of the antics of the Orthodoxy.

Many forces brought the Zionist dream into being in the 19th Century — the preservation of the Jewish ethos through the maintenance of the orthodox religion as a way of life, the oppression and ghettoization of the Jews in Eastern Europe, later the opportunity for Jews to emigrate from Russia and Poland to Central Europe and the Americas — but, all of these forces were superseded by world events after World War I. It is altogether valid to observe that in the end Hitler created Israel. During the four years of World War I almost as many Jews left Palestine as had come there in the previous 20 years. During the 1920's Zionism was a peripheral interest to most Jews who were making a good life for themselves in the nations of the world, even in Poland and Eastern Europe. And in the Soviet Union most of the almost 3 million Jews were (and still are) ardent adherents of the U.S.S.R., as in the United States the Jews were (and are) among the most ardent American patriots. In pre-Hitler Germany the Jews were the most patriotic Kultur vultures.

Although the contribution of the Zionist zealots to the creation of Israel cannot be minimized, I believe that Israel exists today mainly because the dislocations caused by World War II required a place to transport Hitler's surviving Jewish victims; and when they were brought to Palestine in large numbers, a voluntary and forced exodus of Jews from the Arab lands, North Africa and Southeastern Europe resulted. In other words, Israel came into being by historical happenstance and not as the culmination of the Zionist dream. The growing awareness of Hitler's contribution to the Zionist achievement has, during the past 25 years, created an ambivalent attitude toward Israel among Jews. The accidentalness of the creation of Israel has also created confused attitudes about Israel in the non-Jewish world.

The measure of the Zionist contribution in creating Israel is of little importance to the Israelis today. The history of the Zionist movement is to them an historical explanation of the beginnings of some of Israel's political, economic and cultural institutions. And this history is almost as remote as the Bible stories. Zionism did remain a force in Israel after 1948, but only among those pioneers who came to Palestine well before 1948, and long before Hitler had impelled Jews in Europe to seek escape from his "final solution". The Jews who came after World War II and those who came from Africa and the Arabian countries before the state was established were not Zionists. They were DP's, refugees, as were the hundreds of thousands who immigrated in the early years after 1948. They and their children and grandchildren now constitute the majority of the Israelis.

Though Zionism was finally peripheral to bringing Israel into being, Zionist precepts and history have certainly influenced the tone of Israel's political style and to some degree its cultural and economic history. This historical basis, however, is only a foundation at most, and in the Israel of the 1970's is as anachronistic as the influence of the founding fathers on the United States in these days. The Holocaust, the resurgence of Western Europe after World War II, the rise of Arab nationalism, the burgeoning interest of the U.S.S.R. in the Middle East, the cold war, and the fact that the majority of the Israelis today are Sephardic and Oriental Jews and their children, all of these factors are more significant for an understanding of the strange little land. None of these had anything to do with the Zionist movement.

The End of the Zionist Dream

The evaporation of the Zionist dream into the reality of Israel did not occur overnight, nor in the diaspora nor in Israel. Not until the Six-Day

War of 1967 did awareness that Zionism had effectively ended in 1948 impinge upon the consciousness of the Jews of the world. And it took the watershed of the Yom Kippur War to bring the picture completely into focus. Now some of the Jews outside of Israel and some of the Israelis, too, know that the Zionist movement did not establish the nation — that it was created by forces and events neither directed or controlled by Jews. This awareness — made acute by the wrench of the Yom Kippur War — underscores the realization that the continued existence of Israel and the course of its future will depend largely on world political forces and historical happenstance much more than on what the Jews inside or outside of Israel do or do not do. It is a bitter pill for the Jews of the world to swallow, even more bitter for the embattled Israelis.

During the rush of activities after the end of World War I all the Jews in and out of Palestine, the Zionists and the non-Zionist Zionists, were too occupied to give much thought to the kind of a Jewish nation they were trying to bring into being. Even the religious Zionists put aside their political clericalism to join in the effort to bring the displaced survivors of the war to Israel and help get them established. It took two decades for the Jews in the diaspora to become aware that hundreds of thousands of Jews from Arabia, North Africa and other lands outside of Europe and the Americas had emigrated to Israel and constituted the majority of the people of Israel. Concommittantly it also dawned on us that these swarthy, black-eyed gentle folk were not Jews as we traditionally conceived of Jews.

That many Oriental Jews worship the God of Israel like our fathers and grandfathers did has served only to accentuate the alienation. Our fathers and grandfathers in the diaspora were aliens in lands that were not theirs — but they were ours. Their ways, and dress and language were an embarrassment to us, but their differentness we had to live with because they were our fathers. The differentness, however, of the Oriental Israelis — in appearance, language and culture — is not ameliorated by familial ties. Though we know they are relatives, we viscerally react to them as cousins almost as we accept the Arabs as fellow descendants of Shem.

During the years after 1948, a donor-client sort of mystique developed in the diaspora to displace the Zionism that had previously motivated Jewish interest in Palestine. The great and immediate needs persuaded the Israeli leadership to accept this unflattering relationship in lieu of the more egalitarian co-partnership that had obtained during the golden years of the Zionist movement. We Jews in the diaspora thought we were practicing pragmatic Zionism, but we weren't. We were playing Rothschild. We were carrying on for the Israelis the Jewish federation and welfare activity established in the 19th century by prosperous German Jews in the U.S. for their immigrant brethren from Poland and Russia. Understandably, the Israelis were uncomfortable and resentful about this, as all beneficiaries of charity always are. They were, of course, mollified in a measure by the exaggerated respect for their military prowess, their courage and resourcefulness that developed in the diaspora as a result of the victories of 1948, 1956 and especially 1967.

The myth of continuing Zionist activity as the basis for the connection between the Jews of the diaspora and the Israelis came unstuck after the Six-Day War. The diaspora began to realize that Israel was an organic nation of very different Jews, and these very different Jews were a new breed that had never existed before. Now, finally it is clear to some of us that the existence of a new Jewish nation in its own land has spawned a new race of Jewish descendants, a race of brave self-determined Jews, to be sure, but in many ways an alien race, that is to say, alien to us, the Anglos and Western European Jews.

This was but dimly realized, however, by me and most Anglos even after the Six-Day War. The euphoria of that victory and the notion that Israel was now master of its own fate and had set out on a path of enlargement — geographically, economically and numerically, blurred the process of alienation from differentness that started in 1948. I confess that it took four years of living in Israel and several years thereafter back in the States for me to learn that the Israelis were not Jews as I knew Jews, that they were an interesting heterogeneous grouping of people all different from each other, and certainly different from the Western Jew I was and knew. I have also become convinced that the fulfillment of the aspirations yet unformed is the job of the Israelis — especially the young Israelis. To have become an "essential" Israeli I should have emigrated there as a young man. I will never know if I missed the boat two generations ago.

* * *

Arab nationalism was never a factor in the Zionist dream. My own blindness to the reality of Arab nationalism was characteristic of the myopia of all Jews — before the establishment of Israel and during most of the years that have since elapsed. There were early Zionist leaders who foresaw inexorable tragedy if the Jews of the world and the Israelis continued to ignore Arab aspirations, no matter how successful Israel might be with force of arms. Yehudah Magnes, an early chancellor of Hebrew University, Moshe Sneh, a thoughtful Mapam leader, Nachum Goldmann and even to some extent Moshe Sharett and Ben-Gurion, early on spoke of the impending problems and seriously suggested Israeli-Arab bi-nationalism for Palestine. But their forebodings were voices in the wilderness. After the Six-Day War almost all Jews, in and out of Israel, and most of the world for that matter, were persuaded that the Israelis were invincible and that the military and economic safety of the nation was assured. The Yom Kippur War has exploded that myth forever. If that sad tragedy will have swept away the chauvinism and the impossible dreams that have too long characterized the connection between the diaspora and Israel, that war will not have been fought entirely in vain.

After Yom Kippur

The need for agonizing reappraisal of the basic for the connection between the Jews of the world and the Israelis does not mean a diminution of the attachment that exists and that I am convinced will always exist between Israelis and their diaspora relatives. I belive I speak as a representative American Jew in affirming that my personal interest in Israel and its people has not been watered down by recent events. I am now convinced that Israel and the Jews of the world have not made a decent and sustained effort to establish viable relationships with the Arab citizens of Israel and the Arab nations; that the military-industrial establishment in Israel is a burgeoning golem; that the quality of life in Israel is becoming a *pastiche*; that the old, worn out and uninspired political establishment must be swept away; that substantial Western immigration is impossible and undesirable; that the obtrusive dead hand of fundamentalist religious orthodoxy must be lifted off the Israeli body politic; that the supra government of the Jewish Agency in and out of Israel must be dismantled or at least completely reorganized and democratized; that class and racial discrimination in Israel must be eradicated. None of these observations connote denigration. Quite the contrary, I seek to suggest a new ordering of things that should be the challenge to the new generations of Israelis who, hopefully, will take over control and chart directions for their nation.

The generation of the desert has had its day in Israel. This was confirmed to me during several visits to Israel in 1974. Possibly the end might have been postponed for some years had not the Yom Kippur War intervened. But no one who had visited Israel after that war can doubt that an orderly revolution — but a revolution nonetheless — is brewing there. The Israelis, all of them, are a bit sad, somewhat frightened, and very angry. They do not feel they lost the Yom Kippur War. They did not. In fact, at the end they had a brilliant military victory, in some ways more complete than the Six-Day War. But they feel that they lost the fruits of the victory.

The peace they longed for has not been achieved and this failure they lay squarely at the doorstep of the incumbent government and their military leaders. They keenly feel they had been betrayed. They are convinced their military and political leadership, through ineptness, laziness, slothfulness, overconfidence, arrant disregard for the safety of the population, corruption, amateurism, led the nation down a primrose path to the edge of total extermination. The Israelis are convinced that only the valor and guts will to live, the loving nationalism of the young people who fought, bled and died in the struggle, saved the day. They are angry because their children and their husbands and lovers were sent into battle unprepared and inadequately armed, that the Bar Lev Line on the Sinai turned out to be a farcical Maginot Line. After the smoke cleared, they were angry because of the high cost of living, the inflation and the almost unbearable taxation that have combined to double the cost of basic foods and put simple amenities of life beyond the reach of most of the population. All of this I heard from scores of friends, acquaintances and strangers with whom I talked a few months after the cease fire. They also told me that the only reason the government was not swept out in the election of December 1973 was that the alternative of Likud headed by Menachem Bigin was Tweedledee to Golda's Tweedledum — with the added disadvantages of non-experience and demagoguery.

The Yom Kippur War I found also created an awareness among the Israelis of Arab strength, military and political. Gone, probably forever, is the bombast and braggadocio, the contempt for the Arab as soldier and as person that I witnessed when I lived in Israel. Sadat, and even King Hussein and Assad of Syria are now respected and feared by the Israelis as Nasser never was.

The future of Israel is in the hands of the young people. It was altogether amazing that the Israeli youth were quiescent, almost placid, until the Yom Kippur War. Perhaps they were wise beyond their years and understood that they must await the demise of the generation of the desert. All that is over now. The Yom Kippur War served as a catalyst to precipitate Israeli youth into a posture of deep, unmitigated, unforgiving anger. The bumbling of the Defense Ministry and the military command almost caused their extermination and resulted in the death and wounding of thousands of their comrades. Say they, it must not happen again! And they will not allow it to happen again, if they can prevent it. They are sick unto death of war — hot and cold — and of constant military service. They will reject this routine for themselves, and they will strive to create a climate that will not require it for their children — the toddlers and the yet unborn. They are beginning to insist on taking over their destiny now. I think they will.

The newly developed respect for the Arab is especially evident among Israeli youth. It was tempered on the anvil of battle against a worthy foe.

All my young soldier friends, Ashkenazi and Sephardi, spoke of it. This changed attitude augurs well for the difficult accommodation with the neighbors that lies ahead.

The Israeli young people are a new breed of Jew, a special and splendid breed in many ways — certainly altogether different from their predecessors. They have blurred the ethnic lines between Ashkenazi and Sephardi by intermarriage, common sabra background and the comradeship of shared risks in the armed forces during the uneasy truce years and in three shooting wars within a single decade. If their parents are old fashioned Jews filled with ghetto mentality or European prejudice, they are not. They do not seek Jewish homogeneity — the goal for most of them is Israeli egalitarian cultural pluralism. They, all of them, no matter where their parents or grandparents came from, are Israelis. Their race memory encompasses only the land of their birth — Israel. They have guarded their little country, they have fought and have seen their comrades die for it; they love their land and it is theirs. Time is on their side.

The obscene nonsense of "Who is a Jew?" that the Orthodoxy persists in inflicting on the stricken nation is peripheral to these young Israelis, especially since the blood-letting of the Yom Kippur War. Somehow, though, their Jewish umbilical cords, though frayed, have not been completely severed. When asked what it means to be a Jew in Israel today and what an Israeli Jew has in common with Jews in the diaspora, a young soldier is likely to answer that he feels himself a Jew because he is a Jew — but first of all he's an Israeli, that Judaism has become a matter of nationality and that he feels more Israeli than Jewish — that the gap is growing and the differences intensifying.

If it is pointed out that the time is not far off when the Jews of Israel and the Jews of the diaspora will be two distinct nations, he will agree and add, "As a matter of fact that is what is happening". Many of the young people will tell you that they don't have anything in common with the Jews of the diaspora. When it is suggested to them that if they feel that way, why should other Jews have any special feelings towards Israelis, some will reply they don't think they should.

These youngsters would probably be surprised to learn that many of their young cousins across the seas are wrestling with similar questions and coming up with similar answers about their own Jewish identities. Their umbilical cords, too, are frayed, and so is their Israeli connection (even though they may continue to "play Rothschild" as their parents did). In all events, the ultimate intramural future of Israel lies in the hands of these young Israelis who have never known the diaspora — and who don't much care if they never do.

Glossary

ACHDOT AVODAH (Heb.) — United Labor Party
ADON (Heb.) — Sir, mister
AIN BRERAH (Heb.) — No choice
ALIYAH (Heb.) — Immigration (literally, an ascent)
AM (Heb.) — Nation
AM YISROEL CHAI (Heb.) — The Nation of Israel lives.
AMERIKANEET (Heb., fem. singular) — An American
ARETZ (Heb.) — Land; Ha Aretz — The Land (of Israel)

BAGROOT (Heb.) — Matriculation exams
BAR MITZVAH (Heb.) — Religious confirmation at age 13
BARUCH HA BA'A (Heb.) — Welcome; Bless your coming; (plu.) Baruchim ha ba'im
BARUCH HA SHEM (Heb.) — Blessed be the Name (of the Lord)
BET AM (Heb.) Community house
BILU (Heb.; acronym, from the Bible phrase, "House of Jacob, let us go" — Isaiah) — The first immigrants from Eastern Europe in modern times, 1880-1890.

BOBBE (Yid.) — Grandmother
B'RECHOV (Heb.) — In the street (as language "from the street")

CH (Heb. letter — pronounced as guttural H)
CHACHAM (Heb.) — Wise man; sage
CHALUTZ (Heb.) — Pioneer; (plu.) Chalutzim
CHAS V'CHALILAH (Heb.) — May God forbid!
CHASSID (Hassid) (Heb.) — Member of an Orthodox Jewish sect. Also, a holy person.
CHAVER (Heb.) — Comrade, friend; (plu.) Chaverim; (fem.) Chavera
CHEDER (Heb.) — Room; (Yid.) Small Hebrew school
CHEVREH (Yid.) — Friends, pals, "the bunch"
CHUMMIS (Arab & Heb.) Sweet paste made from chick peas
CHUTZ L'ARETZ (Heb.) — Outside of the country
CHUTZPAH (Heb. and Yid.) — Nerve, gall, crust
COHEN (Heb.) — Priest; (plu.) Cohanim

DEGEL (Heb.) — Flag
DIKKDUK (Heb.) — Grammar
DRUSI (Heb., plu.) — Druse
DUNAM (Heb.) — Land measurement — one quarter of an acre
DYBBUK (Yid. folklore) — Evil spirit of a dead person inhabiting the body of a living person

EPPES (Yid.) — A something; "Something special"
ERETZ (Heb.) — Land
ERETZ YISROEL (Heb.) — Land of Israel
ETZEL (Heb.; acronym, Irgun Zvei Leumi, "Organization of the Nation") — An underground illegal guerrilla organization of the 1940's
ETZELNIK (Heb.) — Member of adherant of Etzel

FELAFEL (Arab. and Heb.) — Popular sandwich made with chick peas and spices

GAN (Heb.) — Garden
GANENIT (Heb., fem.) — Kindergarten teacher
GALEI T'CHELET (Heb.) — Blue waves
GALUT (Heb.) — Exile; Diaspora
GOLDENEH MEDINAH (Yid.-Amer. slang) — The golden land, i.e., the U.S. (from the sacred Moslem city in Saudi Arabia)
GOLEM (Yid. folklore) — Artificial human (or robot) endowed with supernatural powers

GOY (Heb.) — Stranger, gentile; (plu.) Goyim
GROOZIA (Heb.) — Georgia (U.S.S.R.)
GROOZEET (Heb.) — Language of Georgia

HA (Heb.) — The
HACHAM — See Chacham
HASSID — See Chassid
HATIKVAH (Heb.) — The hope; title of Israel and Jewish national anthem
HEIRUT (Heb.) — Freedom; a major Israel political party
HISTADRUT (Heb.) — Labor union

IVRIT (Heb.) — Hebrew language

JEZREEL (Heb.) — A large valley area in southeast Galilee
JIHAD (Arab) — Holy war

KADI (Arab.) — Religious administrator
KAFFIYAH (Arab.) — Cloth scarf headdress
KASHER (Heb.) — Conforming to religious dietary rules; (Yid.) Kosher
KASHRUT (Heb.) — Kosher rules
KAVODE (Heb.) — Honor
KIBBUTZ (Heb.) Communal agricultural settlement
KIBBITZER (Yid.) — A kidder; prankster
KINDERSHPIEL (Ger.-Yid.) — Child's play
KIPAH (Heb.) — Skull cap worn by religious Jews
KIRYA (Heb.) — Small town
KITAH (Heb.) — Class (of school)
KLITAH (Heb.) — Absorption
KNESSET (Heb.) — Israel parliament
KNIPPEL (Yid.) — Knot in handkerchief (to hold money)
KOL HA KAVODE (Heb.) — All honor; bravo
KOVAH (Heb.) — Hat
KOVAH TEMBEL (Heb. slang) — Peaked hat worn by kibbutznicks (Possibly from "dumbbell")
KOVET (Yid.) — honor (from Heb. "kavode")
K'TZAT (Heb.) — a little bit sick
KUPAT HOLIM (Heb.) — Sick fund; infirmary
KVISH (Heb.) — Highway

LAMA LO (Heb.) — Why not?
LANDSMENSCHAFTEN (Germ.-Yid.) — countrymen's societies

MA'ABARA (Heb.) — Temporary dwelling for immigrants; (plu.) Ma'abarot
MA'ADON TEATRON (Heb.) — Theater club
MACHER (Yid.) — Big shot; VIP
MAGEN (Heb.) — Shield
MAGEN DAVID (Heb.) — Shield of David
MAGEN DAVID ADOM (Heb.) — Israel counterpart of the Red Cross
MALKA (Heb.) — Queen
MATREEK (Heb. slang from English) — Matriculation
MENSCHE (Yid.) — Nice person; (plu.) Menschen
MESHEK (Heb.) — Farm
MESHIACH (Heb.) — Messiah
MESHIACH TZEITEN (Yid.) — The times of the Messiah
METZOOYAN (Heb.) — Excellent
MIKVAH (Heb.) — Ritual bath
MILOOEEM (Heb.) — Army reserve service
MISNAGID (Yid.) — (from Hebrew word neged "against") — Non-Hassidic Orthodox Jew
MISHPOCHAH (Heb. and Yid.) — family
MITOON (Heb.) — Economic depression
MITZVAH (Heb. and Yid.) — Good deed; Religious rule of conduct; (plu.) Mitzvot
MOHEL (Heb.) — Circumciser
MOLEDET (Heb.) — Homeland
MOMME LOSHEN (Yid.) — Mother tongue (referring to Yiddish)
MOSHAV (Heb.) — Freeholders' agricultural settlement
MOSHE (Heb.) — Moses

NETUREI KARTA (Heb.) — Extremist fundamentalist Orthodox religious sect, mainly in Jerusalem, awaiting the coming of the Messiah. The sect does not recognize the existence of the State of Israel

OLEH (Heb.) — Immigrant
OLEH HADASH (Heb.) — New immigrant
OLIM (Heb. plu.) — New immigrants

PARDESS (Heb.) — Citrus grove
PAYOT (Heb.) — Side curls worn by religious Jews
PIDYAN HA BEN (Heb.) — Ceremony of ransoming first born child, if a son, from serving the priests (Cohanim) in the temple
PIASTRE (Turk-Arab) — Smallest coin denomination in Israel and Arab countries

PITTAH (Arab.) — Round flat bread
PITUACH (Heb.) — Development
PROTEKZIA (Heb. slang) — Influence, pull

RAMAH (Heb.) — Hill, plateau
RAV (Heb.) — Rabbi
REBBETZIN (Yid.) — Rabbi's wife
ROSH HA KVUTZAH (Heb.) — Head of (town) council

SANHEDRIN (Heb.) — Highest ruling council of ancient Israel
SCHIKSE (Yid.) — Gentile girl
SEPHARDI (Heb.) — literally "Spanish," now applied broadly to southern European and north African Jews
SHALIYACH (Heb.) — Messenger, contact man to Jewish communities outside of Israel; (plu.) Shleechim
SHABBAT (Heb.) — Sabbath
SHADCHAN (Heb.) — Matchmaker
SHAMIS (Yid.) — Sexton; (Yid.-Amer. slang) police officer, cop
SHEM MISHPOCHAH (Heb.) — Family name
SHIKUN (Heb.) — Housing estate, (plu.) Shikunim
SHIMSHON (Heb.) — Samson
SHLOMO (Heb.) — Solomon
SHLUMP (Yid. slang) — Lump; Slattern
SHOCHET (Heb.) — Ritual slaughterer
SHOMER (Heb.) — Guard; (plu.) Shomrim
SHTETL (Yid.) — Small town, village (in eastern Europe)
SHTREMELE (Yid.) — Round fur trimmed hat worn by religious Jews
SHULE (Yid.) — Synagogue
SHVARTZEH (Yid. slang) — Black, Negro
SHVESTER (Yid.) — Sister
SMICHUT (Heb.) — Ordination of a Rabbi
SOUK (Arab.-Heb., also, or schouk or shook) — Market
STAM (Heb.) — Because, just so, no reason, just like that
TALLIT (Heb.) — Tallis; (Yid.) — Prayer shawl
TANACH (Heb.) — Bible
TELEVISIA (New Heb.) — Television
TIKVAH (Heb.) — Hope
TVILLIM (Heb.) — Phylacteries

ULPAN (Heb.) — Studio; school for intensive teaching of Hebrew

VA'AD (Heb.) — Committee
VA'AD LEMAN HACHAYIL (Heb.) — Soldiers' welfare committee

VA'AD LEUMI (Heb.) — Committee for the nation
VATIK (Heb.) — Old timer, veteran; (plu.) Vatikim

YAD (Heb.) — Hand, arm
YAR (Heb.) Forest
YAR HA'KDOSHIM (Heb.) — Forest of the Martyrs
YEKKE (Heb. slang) — German Jew
YERUSHALMI (Heb.) — Native of Jerusalem; (fem.) Yerushalmeet
YENNIM'S (Yid.) — The other guy's (property)
YESHIVA (Heb. and Yid.) — Religious seminary
YESHIVA BACHER (Heb.) — Seminary student
YIDDISCHE MOMME (Yid.) — Jewish mother
YIDDISCHKEIT (Yid.) — Jewishness
YIDDISCHEIS (Yid.) — A protagonist of Yiddish literature and culture
YISHUV (Heb.) — Jewish community of Palestine
YOFFEE (Heb. slang, from Heb. jaffeh "pretty, nice") — Beautiful, great, lovely
YOM (Heb.) — Day
YOM KIPPUR (Heb.) — Day of Atonement, the holiest day of the Jewish religion, observed by all denominations of Jews

ZAHAL (Heb. acronym, Zavah Haganah Leumi, "Army for the Defense of the Nation") — Israel Defense Forces — (IDF)
ZAYDEH (Yid.) — Grandfather